Contemporary Cases in Tourism

Volume 1

Also available online!

All the cases within *Contemporary Cases in Tourism Volume 1* are available for individual download from the Contemporary Cases Online website at:

www.goodfellowpublishers.com

Ideal for student and seminar use, the online cases are packed with hyperlinks to original sources, further readings and websites. Readers can immediately follow these links to obtain further information about the specific concepts, terms, issues and organisations identified in each case.

Cases can also be purchased in a 'pick-and-mix' fashion to suit course content or research requirements.

Contemporary Cases in

Tourism Heritage Hospitality Leisure Retail Events Sport

Series editors: Brian Garrod (Aberystwyth University) and Alan Fyall (Bournemouth University)

Contemporary Cases in Tourism

Volume 1

Edited by
Brian Garrod
Alan Fyall

 Goodfellow Publishers Ltd

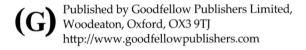 Published by Goodfellow Publishers Limited,
Woodeaton, Oxford, OX3 9TJ
http://www.goodfellowpublishers.com

British Library Cataloguing in Publication Data: a catalogue record for
this title is available from the British Library.

Library of Congress Catalog Card Number: on file.

ISBN: 978-1-906884-53-6

 Design and typesetting by P.K. McBride, www.macbride.org.uk

Printed by Marston Book Services, www.marston.co.uk/

Cover design by Cylinder, www.cylindermedia.com

About the Editors

Dr Brian Garrod is Senior Lecturer in Tourism Management at Aberystwyth University. His interests span all aspects of tourism and recreation but his particular areas of specialism are in sustainable tourism, ecotourism and heritage tourism. He is also fascinated by the role of photography in tourism. He has published widely, including several text books with Alan Fyall. He has worked as a consultant to the United Nations World Tourism Organization (UNWTO), the Organisation for Economic Cooperation and Development (OECD) and the Welsh Assembly Government (WAG). He is currently Books Reviews Editor of the Journal of Heritage Tourism and a member of the editorial boards of the Journal of Ecotourism, the International Journal of Tourism Research and Tourism in Marine Environments. He lives deep in the Welsh countryside with his wife and three children, and in his spare time enjoys rocking out on his bass guitar.

Dr Alan Fyall is Professor in Tourism and Deputy Dean Research and Enterprise in the School of Tourism, Bournemouth University. Alan has published widely in his fields of expertise and is the author of over 100 articles, book chapters and conference papers as well as 11 books including Tourism Principles & Practice, one of the leading international textbooks on the subject published by Pearson, which is also published in Spanish, Portuguese and Mandarin. He also serves on the editorial boards of Annals of Tourism Research, the International Journal of Tourism Research and Journal of Heritage Tourism, while he is Book Reviews Editor for Anatolia. Alan's current research interests lie in destination management and emerging destination management structures, and the impact of generational change on patterns of buying behaviour in the context of attractions and destinations. Alan is a former Member of the Bournemouth Tourism Management Board and has conducted numerous consulting and applied research projects for clients across the UK and overseas for the likes of the European Union, Commonwealth Secretariat, Grant Thornton, Government of Saudi Arabia and Malaysian Ministry of Tourism. Alan lives in Bournemouth with his wife and two children and spends as much time as possible with his family enjoying the outdoor advantages of living on the South Coast.

Acknowledgements

The editors would like to thank the students who have been the 'guinea pigs' for pilot versions of these case studies in the various institutions in which the chapter authors are based.

Thanks are also due to Tim Goodfellow and Sally North of Goodfellow Publishers Limited, for backing this new and innovative form of publication and for bearing with us through the development process.

The Case Study Approach:

Wrongly Maligned?

Brian Garrod and Alan Fyall

The case study approach has often been marked out as an academic pariah, depicted at best as a highly inferior method of advancing human knowledge about a subject (Xiao and Smith, 2006), at worse as a refuge of academic charlatans "whose disciplinary origins do not include the tools necessary to analyze and theorize the complex cultural and social processes" associated with tourism (Franklin and Crang, 2001, p.5). Xiao and Smith (2006) further note that case studies have been described as atheoretical, ungeneralisable, fundamentally intuitive, primitive and unmanageable. Much of this denigration of the case study approach has actually come from within the social sciences, with those hailing from disciplines with a quantitative tradition tending to be among its most vociferous critics.

Such arguments, which can probably be attributed as much to academic snobbery as they can to a clear understanding of the principles of research methodology, have tended to suppress the use of the case study approach in tourism research. Many academics have avoided case study research because they fear that it will not be accepted by peers, let alone published in the learned journals. Even so, Xiao and Smith (2006) identified a total of 78 articles based on case studies published between 2000 and 2004 in the *Journal of Travel Research, Annals of Tourism Research, Tourism Analysis* and *Tourism Management*, representing nearly 10% of the total number of articles published in those four journals over that time period. This represents not an insubstantial proportion of the research that tourism academics have been publishing.

Setting aside for the moment arguments concerning the value of the case study approach in the context of research, it will be evident to readers who regularly work in the classroom that students, at all levels of ability and from all backgrounds, appreciate the opportunity to learn through case studies. When asked why they like case studies, students often reply that they help them to consolidate what they are learning and to apply it to the 'real world' they see around them. Are we then to believe that our students must be misguided in their desire to learn through case studies? Perhaps they have failed to appreciate that case studies really have no intellectual value and hence deserve no place in the classroom? Their craving for case studies must simply be a phase they are going through; all we really need to do is to wait patiently for them to grow out of it?

We believe otherwise. The intention of this series of books is to demonstrate that not only do case studies merit a place in the classroom but that they can be extremely effective pedagogical tools. Indeed, no scheme of work should be without one or more in-depth case studies to help students to appreciate more fully the conceptual and theoretical material we are delivering to them. We believe that students are not fundamentally mistaken in their liking of the case study approach. When students are continually fed a diet of dry theory, it is only natural that they will show cravings for the occasional juicy case study to help them to swallow down their meals. Rather than being something to avoid at all costs, case studies can be a positive asset in our teaching.

The major problem faced by potential users of case studies in the classroom is, however, that case studies can take an inordinate amount of time and effort to write. The purpose of a case study should be to communicate facts, not broad concepts or general principles, so that students can situate their learning in a particular context, thereby developing their understanding of how concepts and theories can be applied to the world outside their classroom window. But the facts specific to a particular case are often hard to track down. Writing an effective case study also requires that the author appreciates not only what the readers are supposed to learn from the case but how they are supposed to learn it. Writers of cases will need to anticipate the learning process in order that by reading the text of the case, examining the accompanying material, discussing issues raised in the case with each other, answering the questions at the end and reflecting on what it all means, readers will be able to develop a deeper understanding of what the case is all about. If writing good case studies was easy, then presumably there would be a lot more of them freely available for educators to introduce directly into their courses.

Sadly this is not the case. Until the publication of this book, there have been very few sets of ready-made case studies for the educator to call upon that are relevant to the needs of students, instructive and contemporary. Part of the problem is that much material that is labelled as a case study turns out not to be especially useful in the classroom. Many of the so-called case studies included in textbooks simply take the form of extended examples: perhaps a few hundred words to illustrate a particular point the author wishes to emphasise. This kind of case study tends not to be sufficiently extensive or in-depth for students to get a very good grasp of the background to the subject, the forces coming to bear on a particular problem, the actors involved, the potential range of solutions, the constraints presently faced or the implications of any of this. Students therefore tend to struggle to use such case studies to develop their understanding of the subject they relate to. They are, to be blunt, often of strictly limited value as pedagogical tools.

Case studies can also quickly go out of date: economic conditions alter, government policy contexts change, new actors enter while others exit, existing problems are overcome (or accommodated) while new problems emerge to take their place. Young people do not have long memories; nor do they relate well to case studies set in the context of the world they lived in when they were children, maybe even before they were born. As such, there is always room for new cases to be developed for use in the classroom: contemporary cases that relate to the problems of today in the context of today. It is often possible for existing cases that have become outdated to be modernised. Cases that consider very recent issues and subjects will usually, however, have to be written from scratch. Keeping one's case studies fresh is always going to be a problem for the instructor wishing to use them in his or her schemes of work.

The purpose of the *Contemporary Cases* series is to rehabilitate the case study approach and instate it on the educational map by establishing a ready resource of in-depth, high-quality, up-to-date case studies for instructors to use in their teaching. Each volume will focus on one of the subject areas covered by the series as a whole – events, heritage, hospitality, leisure, tourism, retail and sport – and provide a number of detailed, in-depth case studies that can be inserted, more or less directly, in the scheme of work of a module covering these subjects. At the end of each chapter will be a number of self-test questions for students to consider. These are designed to encourage students to reflect on the case, mentally wrestle with the issues it covers, apply their prior learning to the case and draw appropriate lessons from it. Each case study chapter will also include some suggestions for further reading and websites related to the material presented in the case study. All of the case study chapters will have a Quick Response (QR) code printed at the end. These can be scanned with a camera phone to enable to reader to follow the various web links on an Internet-enabled smart phone.

Each case study will also be made available electronically via the *Contemporary Cases Online* (CCO) website. Cases can be purchased this way individually or as a bundle. The major benefit of purchasing the electronic version of the chapters is that readers with a web browser will be able to follow the various hyperlinks included in the chapters to obtain further information about the specific concepts, terms, issues and organisations identified in each case. The CCO website will also include an instructor's pack for each case study for separate purchase. These will include a number of essay questions based on the case, ideas for specific themes that can be developed from the case material, links to further teaching resources and a number of questions that can be used in an examination, along with guideline answers. The instructor's pack will also include a slideshow presentation that can be used in the class to remind students of the themes considered in the case and look at any of the photographs or diagrams accompanying the case in full colour.

It is the intention of the series editors that, wherever possible, the material published on the web will be regularly updated. This will help to ensure that the cases remain contemporary, relevant, vibrant and easy for students to relate to.

What is a case study?

Stake (1995, p.xi) provides a basic definition of the case study approach, that being:

> "the study of the complexity and particularity of a single case, coming to understand its activity within important circumstances".

The purpose of a case study, then, is to attempt to develop a nuanced understanding of what is happening at a specific point of time in a specific context and why it is happening. As such, a case study will attempt to answer questions such as what are the processes of change, what are the external and internal factors that influence those processes, and what the changes might imply for those implicated in them, be it directly or indirectly, actively or passively.

Stake goes on to identify three types of case study: **intrinsic, instrumental** and **collective**. The first type, the intrinsic case study, is intended simply to study a particular case, with no attempt to learn about other cases or draw wider lessons. Second is the instrumental case study, the purpose of which is to learn wider lessons for the study of the subject, issue, organisation or problem at hand. The intention is that by studying one case in depth we will get a clearer picture of what is going on in the broader context. In view of this aim, it is sometimes better to choose to study an atypical case rather than a typical one. Indeed, an atypical case study may allow us to draw more relevant lessons than a typical one. For example, holiday companies expect, or at least hope, that their holidays will usually be delivered success-fully from the holidaymaker's point of view. Sometimes, however, things will go wrong. Arguably there are more valuable lessons to be learned from the minority of cases where the holiday has been unsatisfactory than from the majority of cases where it has proceeded successfully. The third type of case study according to Stake is the collective case study. This is part of a set of case studies related to a particular context or problem, the cases being selected in such as way as to enable comparisons and contrasts to be drawn across them. In this way a broader and more detailed picture can be built up of the subject as a whole.

Perhaps the best-know definition of the case study approach, however, is that of Yin (1994, p.13), who defines a case study as the:

> "investigation of a contemporary phenomenon within its real-life con-text, especially when the boundaries between phenomenon and con-text are not clearly evident, and that relies on multiple sources of evi-dence, with data needing to converge in a triangulating fashion"

For Yin, then, the emphasis is on investigating a phenomenon that is so deep-ly embedded in its context that it is hard to distinguish one from the other. To divorce the problem from its context would be to risk, almost guarantee, that the problem will be misunderstood. In order to learn about the problem, and hopefully develop solutions to it, we need to study it in the specific con-text in which it is situated. Abstracted study of the problem that is divorced from its context will not yield meaningful or effective answers.

The definition suggested by Yin also emphasises the need to draw upon multiple sources of information, bringing them together in the context of the case study through a process of triangulation (Decrop, 1999; Oppermann, 2000). This enables the researcher to examine the issue or problem at hand from a number of different perspectives, yielding insights that they would not be possible to gain by examining the situation from a single viewpoint. In this way, case studies paint a rich picture of the subject, enabling readers to appreciate more fully what is going on and why.

Yin (2003) then goes on to identify six different kinds of case study that fit within his definition. First, any case can be a **single case study** or a **multiple case study**, depending on whether it focuses on just one instance of the phenomenon or on several instances. Either way, the purpose is to draw out wider lessons about the subject. Secondly, any case, whether single or multiple, can be an **exploratory, descriptive** or **explanatory case study**. The first of these, exploratory case studies, are intended to help to define questions and hypothesis about the phenomenon being studied. These questions can then be effectively addressed by other kinds of case study (descriptive or explanatory) or through alternative research methods if they are deemed better suited to the task. The purpose of the second type, the descriptive case study, is to describe the phenomenon at hand, perhaps in greater detail than has been achieved before or perhaps focusing on some aspect of the phenomenon that has hitherto been overlooked. The third type, the explanatory case study, attempts to identify cause-and-effect relationships, explaining how and perhaps why things happened in the way that they did.

The purpose of single case studies will often be **deductive**: to see how well a concept or theory can be applied to a real-world situation, or to investigate how a concept or theory might be modified to a particular context. The purpose of multiple case studies, meanwhile, will often be **inductive**: to compare, contrast and identify patterns and regularities within and between cases, thereby enabling a broader understanding of the subject to be achieved (Xiao and Smith, 2006).

While single case studies are often criticised on methodological grounds, Yin (2003) provides a number of styles of single case study which he considers to be potentially useful: the **critical case study**, which tries to bring out the pros and cons of a particular case (for example, to consider the critical incidents in a process); the **extreme/unique case study**, which attempts to bring out lessons by considering what happens at the extremes of the phenomenon; the **representative/typical case study**, which attempts to explain what 'normally' happens in a particular context; the **revelatory case study**, which attempts to challenge and reshape the reader's preconceptions; and the **longitudinal case study**, which provides a series of snapshots of the case over a period of time, often encouraging readers to decide what they would do to solve a problem and to discover whether that solution would indeed have worked. This latter kind of case study is actually very similar to a simulation exercise, which may be based around some form of decision tree so that users can go back and explore the implications of alternative decisions they could have made.

What are the benefits of using case studies in the classroom?

While the case study approach is often maligned by academics, it also has a number of fierce proponents. The latter tend to advocate the use of case studies in the classroom for the following reasons:

◆ Case studies can help students to see for themselves how theory links to practice, encourage them to think more deeply about the subject at hand and persuade them to consider more carefully the implications of what they have learned.

◆ The multi-source nature of case studies enables alternative viewpoints of various stakeholders to be illustrated, as well as demonstrating the interaction among and between the different actors and variables concerned.

◆ The open-ended character of case studies helps to show students that there is very often no 'right' or 'wrong' answer to a problem. As such, case studies reflect the true nature of knowledge-building, which is frequently contextual, situated, complex and ambiguous.

◆ Case studies can stimulate students' interest and get them thinking seriously about the issues concerned. This promotes active rather than passive learning. It also emphasises free-thinking and exploration as opposed to prescription or prediction.

◆ It is possible to simulate the passage of time through longitudinal case studies, which allows students to see the consequences of decisions made by actors in the case or by themselves (a form of simulation game).

♦ Working with case studies helps students to develop and apply various transferable skills, including problem-solving, critical thinking, inter-personal communication and team-working.

♦ The 'real-world' nature of case studies helps students to link their learning to their personal goals, helping them to see the relevance of what they are learning and thus harnessing their enthusiasm to learn.

♦ Using case studies can encourage greater, two-way interaction among students, and between the students and the instructor.

The chapters that follow in this book embody the various authors' attempts to capture such benefits. The editors sincerely hope that readers will adopt some of these cases for use in their classrooms and would be very interested to receive users' feedback. Whether you have had positive or negative experiences of using these cases, please do let us know.

Brian Garrod (bgg@aber.ac.uk)

Alan Fyall (afyall@bournemouth.ac.uk)

June 2011

References

Decrop A. 1999. Triangulation in qualitative tourism research. *Tourism Management* **20** (1): 157-161.

Franklin A, Crang M. 2001. The trouble with tourism and travel theory. *Tourist Studies* **1** (1): 5-22.

Oppermann M. 2000. Triangulation: A methodological discussion. *International Journal of Tourism Research* **2** (2): 141-145.

Stake R.E. 1995. *The Art of Case Study Research*, Thousand Oaks, London and New Delhi: Sage.

Xiao H, Smith S.L.J. 2006. Case studies in tourism research: A state-of-the-art analysis, *Tourism Management* **27** (5): 738-749.

Yin R.K. 1994. *Case Study Research: Design and Methods*, 2nd Edition, Thousand Oaks: Sage.

SECTION ONE

MARKETING

TOURISM

1

'This Other Eden':

Marketing the National Botanic Garden of Wales

Ian Keirle

Introduction

The National Botanic Garden of Wales (NBGW) was opened in the year 2000 as one of the many 'Millennium'-funded projects[1] established around the United Kingdom at that time. The NBGW has often been compared to other gardens in terms of its design, product offering, horticultural acclaim, media profile and financial stability. Comparisons have sometimes been made with the other national botanic gardens in Great Britain, namely the Royal Botanic Garden, Kew, in England, and the Royal Botanic Garden, Edinburgh, in Scotland. Sometimes the NBGW has been compared with other major gardens, such as the Royal Horticultural Society Garden at Wisley. The comparison most often made, however, is between the NBGW and the Eden Project in Cornwall, another garden attraction that received Millennium funding and was opened at the same time as the NBGW. The NBGW has tended to fare unfavourably in such a comparison. Indeed, while the Eden Project has generally been acclaimed as a shining example of success on almost every front, the NBGW has faced a number of setbacks over the years and been received by what can best be described as a lukewarm reception by the public. Indeed, while initial visitor numbers to the NBGW exceeded expectations, these quickly subsided and by 2003 the Garden was nearing a state of financial collapse. It was only rescued by a major injection of public finance, which has had to be repeated at intervals since that time. Various improvements have, however, since been made to the development of the product and to its promotion. As a result, the Garden is now slowly increasing its visitor numbers and is putting itself on a sounder financial footing.

---

1   Millennium projects were funded by the National Lottery and were projects that were designed to be lasting monuments to the achievements and aspirations of people of the United Kingdom.

This case study examines why and how the Garden was established, the factors that led to its near collapse in the early 2000s, and the measures that have been undertaken since that time to increase visitor numbers and try to ensure a more financially secure future. In particular, the case illustrates how considering, understanding and applying the marketing mix (Keirle, 2002) can have significant impacts on the success or otherwise of a visitor attraction. The study concludes by drawing a number of comparisons between the Eden Project and the NBGW. The most important lesson to be drawn from this exercise is that while the public often find it convenient to think of the Eden Project in Cornwall and 'this other Eden' in Wales, direct comparisons between the two can be unfair and potentially very misleading. The two attractions were established for very different purposes and with different measures of performance, leading to different decisions being taken about the design of each garden, their day-to-day operation, the nature of the visitor experience and the way in each was marketed. This case study contends that one of the mistakes made with the NBGW was that it was expected to be too much like Eden.

Gardens as visitor attractions

Gardens represent a significant attraction to visitors. VisitBritain[2] (2006) considered that gardens in the early years of the 21st century represent 7% of the attractions sector and 5% of all visits. Indeed, Connell (2005) found that there were an estimated 1,000 gardens in the UK open to the public. Many have very high visitor numbers. For example the Royal Botanic Garden at Kew had 1.3 million visitors in 2009, while the Royal Horticultural Society Garden at Wisley had 964,212 (VisitEngland[3], 2009). Gardens come in a variety of shapes and sizes, and have an array of different functions. Many are attached to historic properties and parks, some sit alongside garden centres, while a few operate as true botanic gardens, whose origins and primary purposes originate in the collection, classification and conservation of botanical biodiversity. Botanic gardens have been defined as "institutions holding documented collections of living plants for the purposes of scientific research, conservation, display and education" (BGCI, 2010, n.p.). In recent years, the emphasis of botanic gardens has broadened out and many are actively trying to increase visitor numbers by developing themselves as visitor attrac-

---

2   VisitBritain is the National Tourism Authority of Britain and functions to market tourism in Britain to the rest of the world.

3   VisitEngland is the National Tourism Authority for England and its function is to promote and develop tourism within England.

tions, complete with increasingly sophisticated visitor infrastructure and product offerings. While there is a financial motivation in doing this, there is also a newer and some would say more urgent driver to encouraging visits to gardens. With global warming, population explosion and food shortages becoming more prevalent, gardens have a vital role in terms of conservation, education and encouraging sustainable development.

Gardens attract a wide variety of people. Connell (2004) found that middle-aged or older people have a greater propensity to visit gardens than young people and that there was also significant bias in favour of higher occupation groups. Other studies, such as that by Berry and Shepard (2001), indicate that gardens particularly attract females. Connell (2004) found that 70% of visitors to gardens stated that they had a general interest in gardening, 10% had a special horticultural interest and 20% wanted a pleasant day out. As such, gardens appeal primarily to older visitors who have some interest in plants and gardening.

Issues that make gardens different from other attractions

Botanic gardens are different from most visitor attractions in that the core product is living plants. Plants from particular geographic localities require specialist conditions to grow in and so gardens frequently have to recreate climatic conditions in greenhouses such as tropical or alpine houses. Plants also have a variety of life-spans, ranging from annual plants that only live for a year, to trees that sometimes live for hundreds of years. This means that gardens as products can take a long time to develop into maturity, and that there is a need for continuous planting and maintenance. Once started, a garden is never finished. For many people, the highlights of a garden are the flowers, which provide colour, texture and smell. This can create seasonality problems in gardens, as plants often only flower for a short season, usually from spring to summer.

The National Botanic Garden of Wales

The concept of a national botanic garden for Wales developed in the 1990s, based upon the increasing popularity of gardens across the UK and the feeling that Wales did not have its own 'national' garden. However, it was not until the introduction of National Lottery funding in the mid-1990s that the idea became a potential reality. In 1995, a feasibility study was carried out by consultants Eres (funded by the Welsh Office[4]), to consider a range of issues including location, market, management costs, funding opportunities, contribution to science and learning, and economic benefits. The study suggested that the role of such a garden should be:

♦   Conservation

♦   Scientific research

♦   Commercialisation of knowledge

♦   Development of tourism

♦   Education – both formal and informal (Eres, 1995).

It can be seen that only the final two bullet points related to visitors and tourism. This reflects the traditional role of botanic gardens, which have historically developed out of plant collections and research centres, and have diversified over time to become tourist attractions.

Four potential sites were considered and evaluated. These were the Clyne Valley in Swansea, Bute Park in Central Cardiff, Penhein on the Gwent Levels, and Middleton Hall near Carmarthen (the site eventually chosen). The sites were compared according to a range of attributes, including their catchment area, local population, topography, climate, soil and accessibility. In addition, a full economic appraisal was carried out considering potential visitor numbers, construction costs, operating costs and job creation. Projected visitor numbers for the planned opening date of 2000/2001 were estimated as:

Middleton:	110,000 - 125,000
Clyne Valley:	130,000 - 160,000
Bute Park:	210,000 - 250,000
Penhein:	380,000 - 390,000

Building costs were fairly similar across the sites but the projected financial viability of the sites was very different. Based upon calculations of income compared with operating expenditure, the operating deficits shown in Table 1 were calculated from the tenth year of operation.

It can be seen that all of the sites were predicted to run at a deficit but that the eventual site for the NBGW at Middleton was estimated as having the largest operating deficit. This was largely due to the smaller predicted income from admission fees based on the lower predicted number of visitors.

---

4   The Welsh Office was a department of the UK Government that had responsibility for executing Government policy in Wales. It was disbanded in 1999 when its responsibilities were taken over by the Welsh Assembly Government.

Table 1: Predicted operating deficits for the four proposed sites for the National Botanic Garden of Wales after 10 years

		Middleton £000's	Clyne Valley £000's	Bute Park £000's	Penhein £000's
Income	Admission fees	705	825	1,188	**2,118**
	Other	316	385	495	**678**
Expenditure	Wages and salaries	1,328	1,397	1,683	**1,397**
	Other	1,328	1,058	1,157	**1,293**
Operating deficit		1,309	1,245	620	**106**

Source: Eres (1995)

Of these four sites, Middleton had the most developed organisation behind it in the form of the Welsh Historic Gardens Trust[5] (which had been created to restore the Middleton Estate), the Welsh Development Agency (WDA)[6] and Dyfed County Council. As such, it was the only one of the four sites to apply for the first round of Millennium funding in 1995. In February 1996, the Millennium Commission[7] announced that it would grant about half of the £43.6 million of capital funding needed to establish the Garden. This funding was match-funded by the European Regional Development Fund (ERDF)[8] (£6.3 million), the WDA (£2.1 million) and the Wales Tourist Board (WTB)[9] (£1.2 million).

A business plan was finalised in May 1996 that assumed an opening date of May 2000. In this plan, an initial three-year operating deficit was predicted (to be financed by an overdraft agreement with its bank), followed by annual income exceeding expenditure and the Garden being financially self-sustaining, with no further requirement for public-sector financing. With the benefit of hindsight, this business plan was over-optimistic, with most national botanic gardens receiving substantial continuing financial support from pub-

---

5   The Welsh Historic Gardens Trust is a charitable trust concerned with the conservation and protection of gardens and parks in Wales.

6   The Welsh Development Agency was a Welsh Assembly sponsored public body set up in 1976 to encourage business development and investment in Wales. It was abolished in 2006 and its functions taken into the Welsh Assembly Government.

7   The Millennium Commission was a non-departmental public body set up to distribute lottery money to Millennium Projects. It was disbanded in 2006.

8   The European Regional Development Fund (ERDF) is a fund allocated by the European Union to promote regional development.

9   The Wales Tourist Board was established in 1969 to promote and develop tourism in Wales. It ceased operating in 2005 when its functions were transferred into the Welsh Assembly Government.

lic-sector sources. For example, in 2009/10 the Royal Botanic Gardens, Kew, received grant aid from the Department for Environment, Food and Rural Affairs (DEFRA)[10] of £17.6 million (Royal Botanic Gardens, Kew, 2010).

In April 2000, prior to opening, the Garden announced that it still had a £1.4 million shortfall in the funding needed to match-fund its Millennium Commission grant. The Welsh Assembly Government (WAG)[11] was approached and it provided £500,000 to be routed through the WTB. In May 2000, funding was also secured by a leaseback agreement for the Garden with a commercial bank (Welsh Audit Office, 2005). In May 2000 the Garden opened.

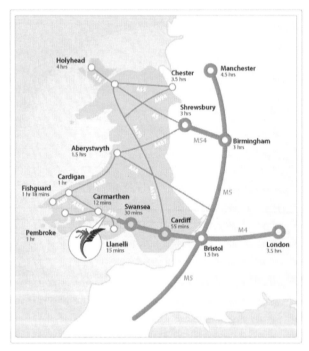

Figure 1: The location of the National Botanic Garden of Wales. Reproduced by kind permission of the NBGW

About Middleton

Middleton was the estate of the Middleton family, who built a mansion there in the early 17th century. In the 18th century the estate was developed by William Caxton into a picturesque-style landscape, including the creation

---

10   The Department for Environment, Food and Rural Affairs (DEFRA) is the UK government department responsible for environmental protection, food production and standards, agriculture, fisheries and rural communities.

11   The Welsh Assembly Government is the devolved government for Wales that makes policy and laws for the people of Wales.

of a water park with lakes, ponds and streams, and an impressive walled garden. The mansion burned down in 1931, after which the estate went into decline. By the end of the century, the estate and the grounds were derelict and in need of restoration.

Middleton is located in South Wales, 10 miles east of Carmarthen. It is set in a remote rural setting, with the nearest large conurbations being Swansea (30 minutes drive away), Cardiff (55 minutes away) and Bristol (1½ hours away). It is located on the A48 close to the western end of the M4 motorway. However, its location is not within one of the popular tourism areas of Wales, such as the Pembrokeshire Coast or Snowdonia. This is the reason why the initial projected figures for visitor numbers were the lowest for the Middleton site. The location of the site can be seen in Figure 1.

The National Botanic Garden of Wales as a product

Between the decision to go ahead with the development of the Garden in 1996 and the opening in 2000, considerable work went into developing the Middleton site into a botanic garden. Capital improvement works reflected the initial aims for the Garden, which were conservation, scientific research, commercialisation of knowledge, development of tourism and education – both formal and informal. As such, areas were needed to grow a wide variety of plants and provide opportunities to conserve and study them. The focus of this was a large glasshouse built to house plants of the Mediterranean flora, as well as outdoor planting areas to display and conserve plants from Wales. A science centre (completed August 2002 at a cost of £3.24 million) was built to provide state-of-the-art research facilities for botanical research and to provide a location for businesses to commercialise knowledge linked to plants. Development also occurred to make the site attractive for visitors and to provide interpretation about the plants displayed. Linked in with this was the development of an education centre to provide a base for educational activities particularly focussing on schools. A map of the site can be seen in Figure 2.

The Gatehouse (1 on map)

Designed as the entrance for the site, where visitors pay for entry and gain access to information about the site. As such, it is the starting point for all visitor activities on the site. It also establishes the visitor's first impression of the site. As well as providing information, the gatehouse has toilets and is the station for electric vehicles that provide access to the site for people with disabilities.

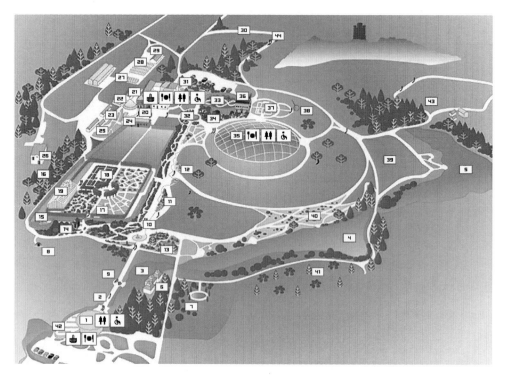

Figure 2: Visitor map of the National Botanic Garden of Wales. Reproduced by kind permission of the NBGW

The Great Glasshouse (35 on map)

Designed by Lord Norman Foster, this is the largest single-span greenhouse in the world, with a roof measuring 110 by 60 metres (see Figure 3). The Great Glasshouse has been designed to exhibit plants of the Mediterranean flora from California, Australia, the Canary Islands, Chile, South Africa and the Mediterranean Basin, in a geographically zoned display. Heated by a biomass boiler and solar radiation, the glasshouse reproduces the hot, dry climate of Mediterranean regions. The building was designed to complement the landscape around it and not to dominate the views. In the summer, tea and coffee is available from the 'Mediterranean Café'.

Tropical Greenhouse (19 on map)

Opened in 2007, this greenhouse houses plants from tropical regions including orchids, gingers, aroids, palms and bromeliads. With its hot and humid atmosphere, it provides a very different experience from the Great Glasshouse.

Figure 3: The inside of the Great Glasshouse. Photo credit: Ian Keirle

The Double-Walled Garden (18 on map)

At over 30 acres, this garden was developed alongside the mansion to provide fruit and vegetable produce for a household of 30 people and employed 12 gardeners. These formal gardens (see Figure 4) have now been developed to tell the story of the evolution of flowering plants from primitive plants to the latest cultivars. One section of this garden is given over to demonstrate growing practices for a modern kitchen garden.

Other gardens (13, 14, 15, 23, 34 and 39 on map)

There is a range of other planted areas located around the site, including Japanese, boulder, bog, bee, Welsh rare plants and wild gardens.

Figure 4: The Double-Walled Garden with the Great Glasshouse in the background. Photo credit: Ian Keirle

Theatr Botanica (22 on map)

This circular cinema was built to show a 360-degree film about the 'Planet of Plants'.

Plants for Health Exhibition (Apothecary Hall) (24 on map)

In this stone barn is a reconstruction of a late 19th century pharmacy, at which time most medicines were made from plant extracts. There is also an interpretive exhibition on how plants have been used to cure illness and disease across the world.

Welsh Water Discovery Centre (6 on map)

Packed full of microscopes and study aids this building provides the focus for education activities on the site.

The Science Centre

Built in 2002, this building overlooks the site and was not designed for visitors but to be the centre for botanical research for the Garden, as well as providing a home to private-sector companies to commercialise knowledge based upon plants. The initial business plan for the site envisaged that funding for the Science Centre would come from visitor revenues. Due to the financial difficulties experienced by the Garden, this facility has not been used and remains an empty shell. As such much of the research and commercialisation aspirations of the Garden are yet to be met.

Garden centre (42 on map)

Located at the exit to the Garden is a small garden centre and coffee shop.

Art gallery (21 on map)

The 'Stables' art gallery is situated in a renovated stable block adjacent to the Seasons Café and shop and provides space for art exhibitions on a rolling programme.

Visitor services

There is a range of visitor services supplied within the site including:

- Toilets
- A shop, selling merchandise relating to plants, gardening and wildlife
- A café selling a variety of food and drink
- A small children's play area
- Sculpture and hard landscaping.

Throughout the site are located a range of sculptures, water features and interesting hard landscape features such as paths and rockeries.

Pricing and entry

In 2011, the price of admission was as follows:

Adults	£8.00
Concessions	£6.50
Children (5 – 16)	£4.00
Family (2 adults and up to 4 children)	£19.50
Under 5s	Free

The Garden is open every day except Christmas Day.

Who visits the Garden?

To manage any visitor attraction, it is essential to have detailed knowledge of who the visitors are and what their views are on the attraction. The most recent detailed survey carried out at the Garden was carried out by Beaufort

Research in 2007. They talked to 1,000 non-visitors in their homes and carried out 1,000 exit surveys. Some of the results from this survey can be found in Figures 5 and 6.

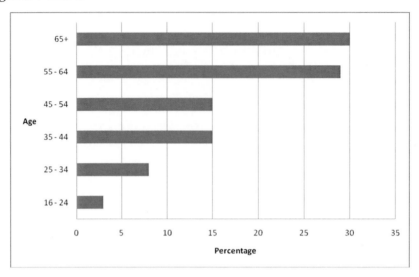

Figure 5: Age profile of visitors to the Garden. *Source*: Beaufort Research (2007)

It can be seen in Figure 5 that the age profile is very skewed towards older visitors with low numbers visiting in the age groups 16 to 34.

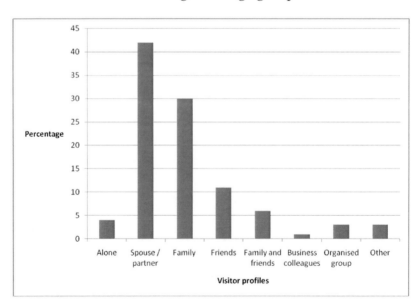

Figure 6: Profile of visitors to the Garden. *Source*: Beaufort Research (2007)

Furthermore:

♦ Visitors most frequently visit the Garden with their spouse/partner or with friends.

♦ 59% of visitors to the Garden are female and 41% male.

♦ When prompted, over 70% of Welsh adults had heard of the Garden, with awareness highest in those living locally and in the ABC1 social classes.

♦ Just over a quarter of Welsh adults had visited the Garden.

♦ 61% agreed the Garden was 'a good place for a family visit', 64% felt 'it was not for my age group' and 59% thought that it 'was only for keen gardeners'.

♦ Visitors are predominantly 55 years and over in age and from the ABC1 social classes. Only 16% had children at home.

♦ 60% of people questioned were on their first visit, but nearly 10% had visited more than 11 times before.

♦ The main reason given for visiting was for an outing or day trip, or being on holiday in the area.

♦ The most-visited sections of the Garden were the Great Glasshouse, the Double-Walled Garden and the shop.

♦ Visitors were very happy with most aspects of the Garden, with 93% being very satisfied with their visit overall.

♦ 60% of visitors found that the experience was better than expected.

♦ 98% of visitors recommended a visit to the Garden and 83% said they would revisit.

Initial success and then decline

In the first year of operation, the number of visitors to the site exceeded expectations, with 234,000 visitors entering through the gates. However, initial optimism quickly evaporated, as visitor numbers steadily declined. By 2003/4, visitor numbers were down to 133,000 (see Figure 7).

By 2003/4, the Garden was facing impending financial disaster. Revenue from visitors was not matching the costs of staffing, maintenance and running costs. In addition, operating costs were higher than anticipated. The Garden had already approached the Millennium Commission and WAG in January 2002 with a revised business plan, seeking £5 million for capital works and £750,000 in revenue support. WAG provided a total of £1.57 million in revenue funding to last from July 2002 to October 2003 in order to offset cash-flow problems and keep the Garden open. In March 2003, the name of the Garden was changed to 'Middleton' as part of a re-branding exercise designed to increase visitor numbers. This name change did not, however, last very long and the name soon returned to being the National Botanic Garden of Wales. In October 2003, WAG provided the Garden with a further £150,000, with a similar amount coming from Carmarthenshire County Council and £50,000 from the Millennium Commission. By this time, the financial situation of the Garden had reached a critical stage, with accumulated debts of £2.8 million. To avoid calling in the receivers, 76 staff were made redundant, leaving the Garden to be run be a skeleton staff of just 18. The Garden only remained operational at this time through extensive use of volunteers. In November 2003, the Garden submitted a recovery strategy plan to WAG.

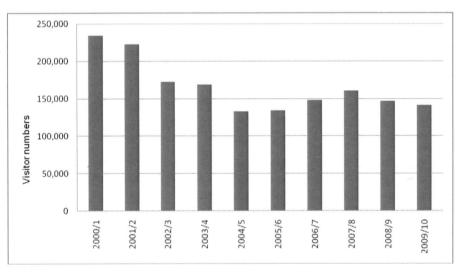

Figure 7: Visitor numbers at the Garden. *Source*: Beaufort Research (2007)

At the same time, WTB published a report on the outcome of a two-day think tank comprising a panel of five leading international tourism experts, brought together to examine the future of the Garden (BBC, 2003). Those attending had expertise and experience in visitor attraction management, financial and organisational management, science and healthcare. The findings were compiled by tourism expert Professor Terry Stevens.

Those involved in the report said they were saddened by what they called the Garden trustees' low aspirations. They said "[t]he group is concerned that public confidence in the product as an attraction is now at such a nadir it is likely to be irrecoverable with the garden in its current format" (BBC, 2003, n.p.). The report concluded that, as a visitor attraction, the product on offer was extremely weak. As such, the Garden was unlikely to break even and a different approach was needed if public access to the site was to be maintained.

In March 2004, WAG, the Millennium Commission and Carmarthenshire County Council agreed to support a five-year recovery plan and provided £300,000 each as part of an agreed strategy. This funding was provided in the clear understanding that the way the Garden was managed had to change. In addition, WAG agreed to provide a further £150,000 in each of the four subsequent years, with the first instalment paid in 2005. In May 2004, some of the staff who had been laid-off were re-employed. In November 2005, a £1.35 million capital grant from the Lottery Fund was secured to build the new Tropical House. In 2008, the Garden was given a further £1.9 million by WAG, as well as having its annual funding increased to £500,000 for the following three years. Carmarthenshire County Council also agreed to convert an existing £1.35 million loan into a grant. In November 2010, WAG gave the Garden a further £250,000 as a short-term package of financial support to offset cash-flow difficulties. In February 2011, following a 'value-for-money review', WAG committed to a three-year financial package linked to the Garden's contribution to delivering some of WAG's core performance targets, notably in terms of biodiversity and sustainability. This settlement heralded a major change in funding for the Garden, with WAG now providing core funding in a long-term and secure manner. This move from 'bail-out money' to the 'normalisation' of funding marks a significant turning point for the Garden and it can now plan ahead with a greater degree of financial certainty and the knowledge that the Garden and its aspirations are supported both in principle and financially by WAG. However, while this is welcome news, the WAG funding only represents approximately 29% of the operating costs, a much smaller level of public support either than the Royal Botanic Garden, Kew, or the Royal Botanic Garden in Edinburgh.

What went wrong?

The financial difficulties that the Garden has faced throughout its short history have a number of causes that collectively have made operating the Garden as a profitable visitor attraction a challenging proposition.

The initial aims of the site were too complex and overambitious

The role of the Garden, as established in the feasibility study undertaken by Eres (1995), shaped the development of the site, with the science components of conservation along with scientific research and the commercialisation of knowledge being given the highest profiles. This reflected the functions of established botanic gardens around the world and, in particular, at Kew in London. The emphasis on the science element is illustrated by the initial staffing of the site, with key management personnel being primarily plant scientists who had a limited understanding and experience of visitor attraction management or marketing. This may inadvertently have led at an early stage in development to poor decisions being made with regard to the development of the site product and the production of a business plan that was too optimistic in terms of potential visitor numbers or financial viability.

Soon after opening, it became apparent that conservation and scientific research could only exist on the back of a financially secure visitor attraction. Indeed, the Science Centre, built at a cost of £3.2 million, never opened, as the money needed to equip and run it was diverted into securing the financial viability of the Garden as a visitor attraction. Following the near collapse of the Garden in 2003, the management focus of the Garden was turned primarily to the development and running of the Garden as a visitor attraction, with any scientific work being small in scale and undertaken primarily in partnership with third parties, such as universities. However, with improvements in the management of the site, a focus on research and conservation work is reasserting itself and has been re-established as a central function of the Garden. As an example, over the last couple of years the NBGW has produced a DNA bar-code for the entire flora of Wales (1,143 species), making Wales the first country in the world to have done so. In addition, the Garden has been involved with various partners in a wide variety of other projects, such as assessing the importance of tea in treating C Difficile and the Welsh Rare Plants Project.

Poor location of the site

At the beginning of this case study it was highlighted that initially four sites were considered for the development of a Welsh botanic garden. The feasibility study (Eres, 1995) compared the merits of these sites based upon 11 criteria. Of these, six criteria were related to the potential of the site as a garden (size, variable topography, micro-climate, water, topography and established planting) and five to the potential as a site as a visitor attraction (catchment area, local population, public transport, access and providing 'something special' in the area). In all of the six criteria associated with the potential of the site as a visitor attraction, Middleton scored the lowest and overall across all criteria shared the lowest score with Penhein. The potential site at Bute, Cardiff, had the highest aggregate score, while the Clyne Valley site, Swansea, scored second highest.

In particular, as highlighted earlier in this case study, Middleton was predicted to have the lowest potential for visitor numbers due to it being located away from areas of high population density and busy tourist areas. This remoteness from the market means that the population (residential and tourist) within travelling distance for a day visit is lower than it would have been if the site had been developed in Cardiff, Swansea or Penhein.

With predicted visitor numbers being half that of the Cardiff option, the level of revenue from visitors was always going to be problematic for the Middleton site. Successful visitor attractions need to be close to the market they are serving (either the residential or tourist population, or both) or provide a product so special or unique that people are prepared to travel a long way to visit it. Unfortunately, the Middleton site is neither close to its market nor able to offer a very strong product offering with a significant reach. The issue of the location of the site being poor in relation to the market is, of course, virtually impossible to rectify after the site has been developed. The site cannot physically be moved. The focus has therefore been on improving the product and enhancing its appeal, in addition to promoting the site more effectively. The poor location of the site will ultimately always restrict its potential for growth and future planning and management needs to reflect this.

The need for funding from the public sector

The initial business plan for the site envisaged that the site would be self-sustaining financially within four years of opening and that the Garden would be able to operate without financial support from the public sector. This was a very ambitious target that should have rung alarm bells with funders at the time. The other two 'national' botanic gardens in Great Britain both receive substantial government subsidy, and these are both well-established gardens located in areas of high population density and with considerable tourist numbers. Table 2 shows the level of public-sector support that these two gardens attracted in 2003/4.

Table 2: Government subsidies for national botanic gardens (2003/4)

Garden	Government support (£ million)	Proportion of operating cost
Royal Botanic Gardens, Kew	24.8	71%
Royal Botanic Gardens, Edinburgh	7.0	75%

Source: Wales Audit Office (2005)

It can be seen that at the time when the NBGW was facing potential closure, the 'competitor' gardens in England and Scotland were reliant on substantial amounts of public-sector funding. The issue of whether governments should subsidise visitor attractions such as these when they do not fund 'private-sector' visitor attractions is a bigger argument than can be tackled here. However, it is clear that WAG has until recently not been prepared to fund the NBGW to a similar extent, with funding largely being in the form of financial bail-out packages. At present, the Garden receives £4 in public funding for every visitor. Kew, in comparison, receives £12. This makes it very difficult for the NBGW to plan the development of the Garden with any financial certainty and potentially leads to a short-term, 'sticking-plaster' management approach being applied.

Small plants!

When the Garden was opened in May 2000, the planting of the Garden was far from complete and the plants that were planted were generally small and had been given little time to establish themselves. The initial swell of visitors that arrived in the first year after the publicity generated by its opening saw much bare brown earth and a garden in its infancy. In comparison with established gardens that people will have previously visited, with fully grown mature plants and borders, and beds bursting with colour, the NBGW seemed a poor relative. The product was not yet fully developed as a garden. As a result, many visitors came for an initial visit and, having been disappointed with what they experienced, chose not to return. In the 11 years since its opening, much hard work has been done to rectify this issue and as a garden it is much improved. However, it has been a harder task to get people who had initially visited and been disappointed to return. Gardens take time to establish and to fully develop may take many decades. Trees grow slowly!

Choice of Mediterranean plants for the Great Glasshouse

The Great Glasshouse is the core and heart of the NBGW, and the centre of any visit. The choice of what species of plants to display in it was therefore a crucial early but also long-term decision. Mediterranean flora was chosen as the plant grouping, with representative plants chosen from the Mediterranean regions of the world, such as Chile, California, Spain and Italy. This choice was dictated by conservation issues. Mediterranean regions only cover 5% of the world's landmass but contain 20% of the world's flowering plants, with many species under threat and endangered. In addition, Mediterranean plants were the speciality of some of the founding botanists involved in the initial establishment of the Garden. Mediterranean plants thrive in hot, dry conditions, in air that is low in humidity. For the visitor entering the Great Glasshouse, this means entering a different climate, distinctly different from the outside of the building. However, it is a climate that many visitors are familiar with, with the European Mediterranean being a popular location for holiday-makers from the UK. Another problem with the choice of Mediterranean plants is that to avoid the dry summer conditions they tend to flower early in the season. This is frequently before the main visitor summer tourism season begins in the UK.

Most other key botanic gardens in Great Britain such as those at Kew, Edinburgh, Wisley and, most recently, the Eden Project in Cornwall, feature 'tropical' plants as a central attraction. Tropical plants grow in hot and humid climates, often characterised by jungles. Visitors entering such greenhouses enter a distinctly different hot and 'sweaty' environment, that is very different to the outside world, and with which most visitors are unfamiliar. As such, it offers a 'different' experience that stimulates the senses and makes visitors perspire. In addition, 'tropical' plants are more dramatic in character than Mediterranean plants, often with large green succulent foliage, and include well-known 'exotic' plants such as banana and palms. This creates dramatic displays of unusual plants and flowers, located in a hot, tropical environment. This makes for a more powerful and interesting visitor experience.

Poor interpretation

Simply described, interpretation translates or brings meaning to people about their natural and cultural environments. Interpreters help visitors better understand and enjoy museums, attractions, cities, historical, archaeological and natural sites (Knudson, Cable and Beck, 2003). At its best, interpretation makes the ordinary seem extraordinary and through careful selection of media and story lines, can give visitors an enhanced experience whilst informing and educating them.

Plants are truly fascinating. They exhibit a myriad of adaptations, uses and forms. However, for most visitors they are inaccessible, often perceived as being dull and little more than outdoor decoration. To bring them to life to a wide range of visitors, including non-gardeners, interpretation is required that highlights their amazing stories and uses. As such, interpretation is increasingly seen as an important component of turning botanic gardens into attractions for a wide range of audiences. The success of the Eden Project illustrates this, with the core function of that project being to tell the story of plants through innovative and creative interpretation. Kew is also spending considerable resources in interpreting the plants in its collection, including, for example, building a tree-top walk that interprets life in the canopy as well as providing an interesting visitor experience.

There is a range of interpretation at the NBGW. This includes individual plant labels, interpretive panels, exhibition areas, the Theatr Botanica and the Apothecary Hall. Much of the initial interpretation was, however, too heavy on text and too scientific, particularly in the Great Glasshouse, and frequently lacked clear and interesting story lines (see Figure 8 as an example). Much of it was concerned with detailed botanical aspects of the plants and generally failed to relate to aspects that the visitor may find interesting. Weak interpretation meant that the stars of the show, the plants, did not shine as brightly as they should have.

Figure 8: An example of an interpretive panel at the NBGW. Photo credit: Ian Keirle

The Garden only attracts 'old people'

The visitor survey carried out by Beaufort Research (2007) showed that the majority of users of the Garden were over 55 years old. Younger people did not see much to attract them. As such, the Garden fails to attract a large number of 'younger' people and so potentially restricts its visitor numbers. To increase visitor numbers, site products, activities and events need to be developed that focus on the under-55 age range and in particular focus on family groups. The children and family market is particularly important for future growth.

Lack of an iconic building

The main building on the site is the Great Glasshouse. Designed by the famous architect, Lord Norman Foster, it is the largest single-span greenhouse in the world. Once inside, the space created and the engineering involved cannot fail to impress the onlooker. From the outside, however, the Great Glasshouse has been designed to fit into the historic landscape (see Figure 9). As such, from the outside it is somewhat underwhelming. Visitor attractions need key features for marketing purposes and iconic buildings frequently provide the focus for site identity. Examples of this could be the Palm House at Kew and the tropical and Mediterranean biomes at the Eden Project.

Figure 9: The Great Glasshouse from the outside. Photo credit: Ian Keirle

The name of the site

Site names are an important element in the promotion and branding of a site. Site names need to be easy to remember, recognisable and convey the essential attributes of what a site is. The name of the Garden is the 'National Botanic Garden of Wales'. This accurately conveys what the site is. However, from a wider visitor perspective this may not have been the best name to have chosen. There are two key words in this title that may put some visitors off from visiting the site: 'botanic' sounds very scientific and dull, and for potential visitors would not be seen as an attractor; 'garden' accurately conveys what the product is but many potential visitors may not be interested in gardens or gardening.

The National Botanic Garden at Kew now promotes itself simply as 'Kew'. This is possible because it is such an established product that people can directly associate the word 'Kew' with the product. The Eden Project in Cornwall makes no mention of plants, botany or gardens. 'Eden' means paradise, while 'project' implies something constructive and ongoing. In March 2003, the name of the NBGW was changed to 'Middleton' as part of a re-branding exercise. However, 'Middleton' had no meaning for visitors and the link between the name 'Middleton' and the Garden had not been sufficiently established to make this name a success. The name of the site was quickly returned to that used at present.

Recovery

Following on from the financial collapse of the site in 2003, much work has been carried out on the Garden to ensure its future viability as an attraction. Without this, any hopes of the Garden fulfilling its role as a centre for scientific research and conservation remain fragile at best. It can be seen in Figure 7 that visitor numbers have stabilised since 2003 and are slowly increasing. What, then, has been done to bring about this change in fortunes?

Development of the gardens

Since the opening of the Garden, when the plants were small and areas of unplanted earth were very visible, much work has been carried out in improving the quality of the Garden and the variety of plants on show. Much of the early planting, particularly in the Great Glasshouse, has now matured and the flower beds around the site are blooming. Feature gardens, such as a Japanese garden, a vegetable garden, a bee garden and a garden of Welsh rare plants, have all been developed. The Double-Walled Garden is fully planted. Consequently, the NBGW now looks like an established and well-cared-for garden. The Garden will continue to develop and improve and as such will slowly become a more mature and better attraction.

Product development

As stated previously, one of the key problems for the Garden is its location. The Garden cannot be moved, therefore to increase visitor numbers an improved product needed to be developed and promoted. Within the constraints of the limited finance at its disposal, the Garden has strived to do this. The opening of the Tropical Greenhouse in 2007 is the largest and most significant development and broadens the experience for the visitor. Another significant development is the opening up of the Waun Las National Nature Reserve. This is adjacent to the site and has a range of interesting walks around it, providing access for visitors to the stunning landscape adjacent to the Garden. This includes the partially restored Regency water features and waterfalls. This development is seeking to broaden the appeal of the Garden away from just being a garden.

Events

Events are important for a number of reasons for visitor attractions. Firstly, they can be used to attract first-time visitors who would not normally come to a garden. Secondly, they help to increase return visits: events provide something new to see and do, which is different from the attraction itself. Finally, events are often covered by the media (newspapers, magazines, radio and television) and as such act as 'free' advertising and help to keep an attraction visible to the public.

The Garden has developed a range of events throughout the year, including guided walks, apple weekends, Christmas-tree decorating, craft and wedding fairs, Easter-egg hunts, orchestral concerts and maypole dancing to name just a few. The Garden is now home to the West Wales Food Festival that attracts approximately 5,000 visitors per year. A new performance space has also been developed, called the Prince's Pavilion. Built by the Prince's Foundation for the Built Environment it provides additional covered space for exhibitions and performances. In addition, a programme of courses has been developed based in the Garden, including gardening skills, crafts skills, medicinal use of herbs, willow work, photography and flower arranging. In the same way as events, these courses bring people back to the garden on a regular basis and help to develop site advocates.

Promoting the gardens

Clearly, people will only come to the Garden if they know about it. The promotion of the Garden is therefore a vital element of ensuring future success. The overall objective of promotion is to keep the Garden 'in the noise'. The budget for the promotion of the Garden is small (about £1 per visitor), so money and effort has to be carefully targeted. Based on market research, five key audience groups have been identified.

- People who reside within a 30-minute drive of the Garden. This includes Carmarthenshire, Pembrokeshire, Swansea and Neath/Port Talbot. People in these areas may return to the Garden on a regular basis, for example to events.

- People who reside outside of the areas specified in 1 above, but that are within a 1½-hour drive of the site. This includes all of south-east Wales (including Cardiff).

- The rest of Wales beyond a 1½-hour drive time.

- People living in the UK and Ireland who may holiday in the area.

- Educational groups

Promotion takes the following forms:

- **Leaflets** – annually, approximately 300,000 are printed and distributed by professional distribution companies to accommodation providers and Tourist Information Centres. Distribution focuses primarily on groups 1 and 2 above.

- **Advertisements** – limited advertising is done due to cost. Several small TV promotional campaigns have been undertaken hosted on regional television channels such as the Welsh-language channel, S4C. In addition, the Garden is advertised on the local radio stations of Swansea Sound and Radio Carmarthenshire.

- **Web site** – the web site for the Garden provides essential information for visitors and seeks to convey what there is to do in the Garden.

- **Coach companies** – promotional material is targeted at coach companies to try to encourage coach tours to include the Garden on their itineraries. Free entry for coach drivers and deals in the cafe help to encourage this market. The Garden has a database of 6,000 coach and tour operator addresses.

- **The media** – media exposure (printed, radio, television and electronic) provides a cheap and effective means of keeping the Garden 'in the noise'. Stories generated in the Garden, such as rare plants flowering, openings, events and other newsworthy items, are communicated to the media via press releases and personal contacts. The media will then cover the stories and in so doing will promote the Garden and keep it in the public eye. The media is one of the most effective ways of reaching target audiences and has the capacity to reach large audiences on a regular basis. The Garden reached the notice of younger audiences in 2009 when it was chosen as a film set for an episode of the popular BBC science fiction series 'Doctor Who'.

♦   **'What's on' flier** – this small flier is produced three to four times a year and highlights events happening at the Garden.

Pricing

Entry prices for the Garden have been given earlier in the case. These prices are considered to be appropriate for the present product offering and to be competitive with other visitor attractions in the area. Special promotions, as outlined below, give opportunities for visitors to enter the site at a reduced cost.

Promotions

To encourage increased use of the site, a range of promotions has been developed. These include free entry for mothers on Mothers' Day and for fathers on Fathers' Day. In addition, in 2011 entry for the whole of January was free. The Garden is not at its best at this time of year and visitor numbers are usually the lowest of the year. The promotion greatly increased entry into the Garden and, although not bringing direct income through admission fees, meant that there were more people on the site to spend money in the café and shop. Furthermore, visitors who came due to the free entry may well return again when the Garden is in full bloom. Another promotion has been a two-for-one offer based upon promotional leaflets sent to accommodation providers in the immediate area.

Membership

The Garden actively encourages visitors to become 'members'. Individual membership is priced at £36 (for 2011) with joint membership being £52. Membership gives visitors free year-round entry into the Garden. The 7,000 members receive a free magazine about the Garden and benefit from free entry into a range of other gardens around the country. Membership provides 'up-front' guaranteed income for the Garden. Furthermore, members visit the Garden more frequently as they do not have to pay entrance fees every time they visit. This increases secondary spending in the café and shop. Members also bring along 'guests' and act as advocates for the site.

Improving interpretation

As stated earlier, plants need to be interpreted to increase their interest to the public. Work has been slowly going on to improve the quality and quantity of the interpretation on site, with some of the older interpretive panels being replaced with newer and higher-quality offerings. The recently opened 'fungi' exhibition (on loan from the National Botanic Gardens in Edinburgh) is clear evidence of this. However, there is still much work to be done and the stories the plants can tell needs to be focused through the development of themes and story lines. Themes could potentially include:

♦   The conservation of plants is vital to the future sustainability of the planet.

♦   Plants have evolved to live in a wide variety of conditions.

♦   Human activities are endangering many plant species.

♦   All life depends upon plants.

Weddings

The wedding market has become a lucrative addition to the normal visitor revenue streams for many tourist sites. People are increasingly seeking interesting places in which to have their wedding ceremonies and receptions. The Great Glasshouse is ideal for such occasions as it is always warm, has considerable atmosphere and has plenty of space outside of it for people to disperse into. At present, the Garden hosts about 40 weddings per year. This brings in considerable income in terms of hire of the venue and catering opportunities. In addition, it brings people (the guests) into the Garden who may not have been before and who may subsequently return.

Use of volunteers

With limited resources at its disposal and much work to be done, the Garden makes significant use of a free and often highly skilled workforce – the volunteer. Approximately 200 people volunteer on a regular basis and play a key role in the maintenance and running of the Garden. Volunteers come with a range of skills that can be utilised and are used for a wide range of jobs including gardening, driving the electric visitor buggies, administration and helping with events. Many volunteers come with considerable skills and the Garden seeks to utilise these by identifying the most suitable tasks for individuals.

Comparisons with the Eden Project

The Eden Project, in Cornwall, has been the most successful purpose-built visitor attraction in the UK of recent years, with visitor numbers of over 1 million in 2009. Situated in Cornwall, it developed as an attraction at the same time as the NBGW and also has plants at its heart. Built into an old china clay quarry, the site comprises two vast greenhouses (the Tropical and Mediterranean Biomes), an education centre (The Core) and outdoor gardens (the Roofless Biome). The Tropical and Mediterranean biomes are vast in scale and can be seen in Figures 10 and 11.

Figure 10: Exterior of the Eden Project in Cornwall. Photo Credit: Ian Keirle

What is it that has made the Eden Project such a success in comparison with the NBGW? There are a number of core differences.

◆   The objective of the Eden Project has a clear and unambiguous mission – the Eden Project was set up from a different perspective than the NBGW. Its mission is to 'tell the relationship between plants and people'. As such, it has a very clear focus that directs everything it does. Eden seeks to make linkages between plants and people through creative and inspirational interpretation. Many of the plants seen are important food sources that are not familiar to the public – such as rice, coffee and cocoa – and have been planted not primarily for conservation reasons but to make the linkage between plants and people, as well as to highlight the importance of plants to the planet and mankind. The emphasis on sustainability transcends all aspects of the organisation and it seeks to make a behavioural difference on visitors once they have left the site.

Figure 11: Interior of the Eden Project in Cornwall. Photo Credit: Ian Keirle

- The plants are the stars but interpretation shows them off – as stated previously, plants mean little to most people unless interpreted through strong themes and story lines. Interpretation is therefore a central part of the Eden Project, from when people first arrive to when they leave. A range of techniques are used including interpretive panels, guides, sculpture and shows.

- Iconic buildings – the scale of the buildings at the Eden Project is much larger than that of those of the NBGW. The Tropical and Mediterranean Biomes are built on a breathtaking scale and their design is different from that which the public will usually have seen before. They make a distinct statement of intent and form an important element of the product offering.

- The location is more suitable for a visitor attraction – situated in the popular tourist destination that is Cornwall, the site is easily accessible to a large tourist market.

♦   Set-up – the Eden Project received a large amount of publicity
     through the press prior to opening. Indeed, it had 500,000 visitors
     before it had even officially opened, with people coming to watch it
     being built. In addition, when planting prior to opening, the Eden
     Project used full sized plants that had already been established in
     other locations. This ensured that when Eden opened it was already a
     well-developed garden.

♦   Events and the press – the Eden Project holds a wide variety of
     large-scale events throughout the year, including ice skating at
     Christmas, concerts with bands such as Snow Patrol and the Kaiser
     Chiefs, circuses and talks. It has also featured on many television
     programmes such as the BBC's Songs of Praise and one of the Live 8
     concerts, as well as being a location in one of the James Bond films.
     This all generates a large amount of media interest and keeps Eden
     visible.

♦   What's in a name? – 'Eden' means 'paradise', while 'project' implies
     something that is constructive and ongoing. As such, it is likely to
     appeal to a wider audience. In particular it makes no mention of
     plants, botany or gardens, all of which may put off a large element of
     the population.

Conclusions

The NBGW has now been open for more than 10 years. Its path has been a
rocky one, from its optimistic opening in the year 2000, through a serious
decline in visitor numbers and near closure in 2003, to the present consolida-
tion of visitor numbers and slow improvement in its financial position. The
principal issue for the Garden has always been where it is located. This has
meant that attracting large visitor numbers has always been and probably always will be challenging. Given this constraint, the Garden has done well in
recent years, especially in view of the severe financial constraints it has been
under, to improve the quality of its product and, through improved promotion and the use of events, to consolidate and improve its visitor numbers.
Its initial central aims of being a site for research, conservation and commercialisation are all slowly emerging again, and with continued development
of the product and support from the WAG, the Garden has a future role as a
visitor attraction, a resource for education, and a focus for conservation and
the scientific study of plants.

Acknowledgements

Thanks to David Hardy and Rob Thomas at the National Botanic Garden for help in compiling this case study.

References

BBC. 2003. No 'quick fix' for botanic garden. http://news.bbc.co.uk/1/hi/wales/3304787.stm

Beaufort Research. 2007. *Visitor Survey of the National Botanic Gardens Wales*. Beaufort Research Ltd.

Berry S, Shepard G. 2001. Cultural heritage sites and their visitors: Too many or too few? *In Cultural Attractions and European Tourism* (G. Richards, ed.), Wallingford: CABI; 159-172.

BGCI. 2010. Definition of a botanic garden. http://www.bgci.org/resources/1528

Connell J. 2004. The purest form of human pleasures: The characteristics and motivations of garden visitors in Great Britain. *Tourism Management* **25** (2): 229-247.

Connell J. 2005. Managing gardens for visitors in Great Britain: A story of continuity and change. *Tourism Management* **26** (2): 185-201.

Eres. 1995. *National Botanic Gardens of Wales Feasibility Study: Summary Report*, Cardiff: Eres Consultancy.

Keirle I, 2002. *Countryside Recreation Site Management: A Marketing Approach*. London: Routledge.

Knudson D, Cable T, Beck L. 2003. *Interpretation of Cultural and Natural Resources*, State College, PA: Venture Publishing.

Royal Botanic Gardens, Kew. 2010. *Annual Report and Accounts for the Year Ending 31st March 2010*, London: The Stationery Office.

Welsh Audit Office. 2005. *Funding for the National Botanic Garden of Wales*. Cardiff: Welsh Audit Office.

VisitBritain. 2006. *Visitor Attraction Trends in England 2005*.

VisitEngland. 2009. *Visitor Attraction Trends in England 2009*. Bdrc-continental.

Ancillary Student Material

Further reading

Dodd J, Jones C. 2010. *Redefining the Role of Botanic Gardens: Towards a New Social Purpose*. University of Leicester: Research Centre for Museums and Galleries.

Fyall A, Garrod B, Leask A, Wanhill S. 2008. *Managing Visitor Attractions: New Directions, 2nd Edition*, Oxford: Butterworth-Heinemann.

Smit T. 2011. *Eden: Anniversary Edition*. Eden: Eden Project books.

Swarbrooke J. 2001. *Development and Management of Visitor Attractions*, Oxford: Butterworth-Heinemann.

Related websites

The following websites offer background information on the NBGW and other comparable garden visitor attractions as well as to some of the organisations mentioned within the case study.

Carmarthenshire County Council: http://www.carmarthenshire.gov.uk

The Eden Project: http://www.edenproject.com/

The National Botanic Garden, Edinburgh: http://www.rbge.org.uk/

The National Botanic Garden, Kew: http://www.kew.org/visit-kew-gardens/index.htm

The National Botanic Garden of Wales: http://www.gardenofwales.org.uk/

The Royal Horticultural Society Gardens at Wisley: http://www.rhs.org.uk/gardens/wisley

The Welsh Assembly Government: http://wales.gov.uk

Visit Wales: http://www.visitwales.co.uk/

Self-test questions

Try to answer the following questions to test your knowledge and understanding. If you are not sure of the answers, please re-read the case study and refer to the suggested references and further reading sources.

1   Describe how the location of the NBGW has influenced visitor numbers.

2   What makes gardens different from other visitor attractions?

3   What are the reasons why national botanic gardens normally require substantial amounts of public funding?

4   What were the key issues that caused the financial difficulties that led to the near closure of the NBGW in 2003?

5   What has been done to improve the NBGW as a visitor attraction?

Key themes and theories

The key themes raised in this case study are:

♦   The role of the marketing mix and in particular the role of place.

♦   Gardens as a particular type of visitor attraction.

♦   Visitor management and product development.

♦   The role of interpretation.

      Scan here to get the hyperlinks for this chapter.

2

South Africa 2010:

Leveraging Nation Brand Benefits from the FIFA World Cup

Brendon Knott, Alan Fyall and Ian Jones

Introduction

The Fédération Internationale de Football Association (FIFA) is the international governing body of association football (also known as 'soccer' or simply 'football' in many countries). Part of FIFA's mandate is to organise a world cup of football, which is hosted in a different member country (or combination of collaborating countries) each time. The FIFA World Cup – often known simply as the 'World Cup' – has taken place every four years since 1930, with the exception of 1942 and 1946 due to the intervention of the Second World War.

The first ever FIFA World Cup on African soil was awarded to South Africa and took place from 11 June to 11 July 2010. In many ways, South Africa appeared to be a very good choice to host this competition. Not only does South Africa represent Africa's most developed economy but it also boasts the wealthiest football league system in Africa and is host to the continent's largest sports media and television companies. The success of South Africa in attracting the FIFA World Cup is, however, particularly remarkable in that it was only re-admitted to FIFA 12 years before the decision was made, following decades of sporting isolation as a result of its 'apartheid' political policies. With Nelson Mandela, the new democracy's first president, in attendance at the final announcement, the hosting of the World Cup appeared to confirm the transformation of the nation from political outcast to one of a new breed of developing countries. Indeed, the success of the bid was celebrated enthusiastically throughout the country and across all of the racial groups that had previously been segregated as a consequence of the nation's apartheid policies.

Although South Africa has had its share of problems, such as rising crime rates, high unemployment, a lack of access to basic services such as hous-

ing and education, and a high HIV infection rate, the hosting of the World
Cup symbolised hope for the country and a chance to prove that this developing nation could host an event of this magnitude as efficiently as the
developed economies who had hosted the previous tournaments. These had
included Germany in 2006, Korea and Japan in 2002 and France in 1998. One
of the principal issues for all concerned with the event was that of legacy.
Not only was it important to leave a positive impression on foreign visitors
and potential investors, but it was also imperative that the South African
society benefited long after the event, especially from improvements to the
country's infrastructure, economic growth through increased tourism and
inward investment, and the wider development of sport across the country
as a whole. An important aspect of the legacy would be the long-term impact
on the nation brand of South Africa. The event would showcase the host nation to the largest global television audience of any single-sport event that
had ever taken place. It was hoped that the global media would show the
world the diversity of cultures, natural beauty and organisational efficiency
South Africa has to offer.

In view of the above, this case begins with a discussion of the relationship
between sport, tourism and mega-events in the South African context. It then
introduces the concept of legacy and, in particular, tourism legacy as it relates
to sporting mega-events. Nation branding is then discussed as an aspect of
tourism legacy. Having established the conceptual framework, the case goes
on to review an empirical investigation of the nation-branding legacy of the
2010 FIFA World Cup in South Africa. Conclusions are then drawn from this
review, and recommendations are made for future practice and discussion
by sport and tourism industry practitioners and academics.

The relationship between sport, tourism and mega-events in the South African context

Increasing attention has been given to sport tourism since the mid-1990s,
both from the sport and tourism industries and from academics (Gibson,
2006), with the two related areas of sport and tourism overlapping to form
a niche sports tourism market. Sport can be broadly defined as "the whole
range of competitive and non-competitive active pursuits that involve skill,
strategy, and/or chance in which human beings engage, at their own level,
simply for enjoyment and training or to raise their performance to levels of
publicly acclaimed excellence" (Standeven and De Knop, 1999, p.12). The
United Nations World Tourism Organization (UNWTO) defines tourism as
"the activities of a person travelling to a place outside his/her usual environ-

ment for less than a specified period of time, with a main purpose other than the exercise of activity remunerated from within the place visited" (cited in Turco *et al.*, 2002, p.17). Sport Tourism could therefore be defined as "leisure-based travel that takes individuals temporarily outside of their home communities to participate in physical activities (active sport tourism), to watch physical activities (event sport tourism), or to venerate attractions associated with physical activities (nostalgia sport tourism)" (Gibson, 2006, p.2).

Sport tourists are visitors to a destination for the purpose of participating, viewing or celebrating sport (Turco *et al.*, 2002). The sport tourism industry involves all the people, places and things that influence and are impacted by sport tourists. It is the collections of business, institutions, resources and people servicing sport tourists (Turco *et al.*, 2002). In this context, sport tourists are those people who visit a destination for the primary purpose of participating in or viewing sport. Gammon and Robinson (2004) distinguish sport tourists by the activities they undertake while travelling and by their primary or secondary motivation to engage in sports while travelling. Travel to a destination may not only primarily be for sport. Tourists may be drawn by the destination's attractions and therefore fit the sporting activities into their plans to visit the destination (Turco *et al.*, 2002). Sport therefore becomes a supplemental or secondary attraction that can further satisfy visitors' needs, extend their length of stay and stimulate economic activity (Turco *et al.*, 2002, p.1).

Sport and tourism have become significant economic activities both in the developed and developing worlds, often making an important contribution to local and national economies (Deery and Jago, 2006; Getz, 2003; Swart and Bob, 2007). Sport events have become an increasingly important component of global tourism economies (Cornelissen, 2007). As a result, interest in hosting sport tourism events has increased worldwide as destinations aim to reap economic, socio-cultural and other spin-offs from hosting such events (Turco *et al.*, 2002). Typically, sport tourism events stimulate investment in infrastructure projects such as airports, roads, stadiums, sporting complexes and restaurants, which can be enjoyed by the local population and tourists alike (Tassiopoulos and Haydam, 2008).

Sport events occur on many different scales or levels, with the largest of these levels being the 'mega-event'. Hall and Hodges (1997, p.3) describe a mega-event as "distinctive, identified by the volume of visitors it attracts, economic revenue generated, and its psychological impact on attendees, that is, whether or not it is a 'must-see' event". They explain that mega-events usually require significant public funds to stage, and are thus unusual or infrequent in occurrence. These events have significant economic and social impact, which is affected by the extent to which the event has an international dimension. Getz (1997) adds that mega-events are loaded with tradition, attract significant media attention at the international level and are often complemented by other smaller events that add to its greatness, such us parades and festivals. The FIFA World Cup is the world's largest single-sport event, which in 2010 attracted a global television audience of over 35 billion people. The FIFA World Cup, hosted by South Africa in 2010, is therefore considered to be a mega-event.

In South Africa, the sport tourism industry is already fairly well established, albeit still growing. Golf tourism, tourism related to mega-events and adventure tourism are key drivers of the overall tourism market. However, as South Africa's biggest ever sports mega-event, the 2010 FIFA World Cup was expected to boost this industry dramatically, with a successful hosting of the competition seen as essential to the future of the sport tourism industry in the country.

Sport and Recreation South Africa's (SRSA) Draft National Strategy for bidding for and hosting major international events identifies three main reasons for the national importance of sport tourism (Kent, 2003, p.4): first, sport events attract tourists to destinations that may otherwise be overlooked; second, the events generate global media exposure, from which the host region inevitably benefits; third, sport event sponsorship can be extremely lucrative, as many companies realise the opportunities events provide to market directly to their target customers. According to the Draft National Strategy (Kent, 2003, p.2), the objectives for sport tourism in South Africa are to:

♦ Establish South Africa as a sport and recreation destination
♦ Provide compelling reasons to visit and to make the country easily accessible in order to do so
♦ Build competitive advantage from other sport and recreation destinations
♦ Build a Sport Tourism South Africa brand that will last, create loyalty and motivate tourism in South Africa.

South Africa had already successfully hosted sports mega-events, such as the 1995 IRB Rugby World Cup and the 2003 ICC Cricket World Cup. Cape Town also bid for the 2004 Olympic Games, ultimately losing out to Athens. South Africa also failed in its initial bid for the 2006 FIFA World Cup, controversially losing out to Germany by a single vote. FIFA then adopted a rotational policy, ensuring an African nation would host the 2010 event. Although South Africa had hosted these and some other 140 major events between 1994 and 2010, nothing could compare to hosting the FIFA World

Cup. The 2003 ICC Cricket World Cup attracted 18,000 international visitors while the 1995 IRB Rugby World Cup attracted over 50,000 international visitors to the country. However, the 2010 FIFA World Cup was far greater in scale than any of these events, attracting a total of around 310,000 international visitors (FIFA, 2010) (see Figure 1).

Sport mega-events and their legacies

Dickinson and Shipway (2007, p.1) describe the event impact literature to date as "rather piecemeal", with a solid body of comparative evidence being slow to develop. They go on to explain that the studies are mostly applied, with economic analysis dominating, driven by a need to examine the positive and negative impacts of hosting events in order to justify public spending and a need to leverage the best possible benefits for communities that host events. This is often termed the 'legacy' of an event, defined by Preuss (2007, p.208) as "all planned and unplanned, positive and negative, tangible and intangible structures created for and by a sport event that remain longer than the event itself". However, given the difficulty of comparing different cases and a tendency to predict economic impacts rather than to undertake confirmatory analysis after events have taken place, there are various claims to the reliability or otherwise of economic impact studies and methodologies (Dickinson and Shipway, 2007). While much of the literature focuses on economic benefits, some authors (e.g. Carlsen and Taylor, 2003; Fredline *et al.*, 2003) suggest more research is needed on the social, physical, environmental and tourism impacts of events and their interrelationships. There have been more advances in establishing knowledge about the effects of the Olympic Games than has been the case thus far with FIFA World Cup competitions (Cornelissen, 2007). For example, the Olympic Games Global Impact (OGGI) project aims to assess the economic and other impacts of Games from their initial conceptualisation, through to the bidding processes and their hosting, with the aim of evaluating the costs, legacies and yardsticks yielded by the experiences of Olympic host cities. However, a similar mechanism does not yet exist for the FIFA World Cup. Nevertheless, Cornelissen (2007, p.248) maintains that "leaving appropriate long-term legacies has become a discourse which has left an indelible mark on the way in which planning for today's sport mega-events takes shape". Dickinson and Shipway (2007) explain that there appears to be a widely held assumption that there is in fact a positive legacy from events. However, recent studies have questioned the positive benefits from events and the equity of their distribution, indicating that a new focus is emerging with an emphasis on leveraging positive benefits of an event (Dickinson and Shipway, 2007). Chalip (2004, p.228) defines leveraging as "the processes through which the benefits of investments are maximized". Leveraging can relate to aspects around the actual event (e.g. visitor spending) or the long-term benefits both before and after the event has taken place (e.g. destination image).

There is a variety of different types of legacy that could result from mega-events. These major areas/types of legacy are summarised below and examples of potential legacies from the 2010 FIFA World Cup are given:

Urban

Urban legacy refers to buildings which were constructed for the mega-event but which serve no sporting function. Included here are changes made to the urban structure of the host city as well as the development of new urban districts and specialised areas. For example, the city of Cape Town developed a 'fan walk' from the main train station in the city centre to the stadium (see Figure 1). This included the pedestrianisation of roads, footbridges, city gentrification, improved security and general beautification of the area. Linked to this was the official 'fan park' in the central business district (see Figure 2). There was also large-scale private investment in accommodation infrastructure, such as new hotels.

Figure 1: The 'fan walk' in Cape Town. Photo credit: Brendon Knott

Infrastructure

Infrastructural legacy refers to the different types of networks, ranging from transport to telecommunications, which are renovated or developed for a mega-event and maintained after the event has ended. New access routes by air, water, road or rail are also part of the infrastructural legacy. For the 2010 FIFA World Cup, the South African government invested heavily in infrastructure upgrades, mainly on new stadiums, airport upgrades and public transport improvements.

Figure 2: Sport tourists at the official fan park in Cape Town. Photo credit: Brendon Knott

Economic

The economic legacy of a sport event includes changes in the number of permanent jobs and changes in the unemployment rate of the host region, economic investment opportunities, attraction of foreign investment, small business development and entrepreneurship. The event represented an opportunity for the country and host cities to engage in high-profile promotion of their products on a global scale (Swart and Bob, 2007). In South Africa, the hosting of the 2010 FIFA World Cup has highlighted the role that sport mega-events can play in promoting economic and developmental agendas. The total capital investment through public funds for the 2010 FIFA World Cup event was US$1.3 billion (Emmett, 2010a), whereas the total overall boost to the South African economy from the event was estimated to be US$13 billion over the six years preceding the event (Domingues, 2011). Sponsorship, television and hospitality revenues from the event were estimated at US$3.2 billion (Emmett, 2010a). The South African government expected to collect €1.1 billion in taxes and the direct tourism spend for the event anticipated to be €1.4 billion (Emmett, 2010a). This translates into a net contribution to the country's GDP of 0.5% (Domingues, 2011).

Social

Social legacies could include nation building and contribution to national pride, changed perceptions of residents of the host city or region, education, racial harmony and increased environmental awareness. The 2010 event was expected to have a large social impact on the host nation, just as the 1995 Rugby World Cup had for the new democratic nation. Football was widely viewed as the sport of choice for the majority black African population. Given South Africa's historic racial divisions and tensions, the event presented an opportunity for racial integration as fans of all racial groups gathered in the stadiums, fan parks, and across the cities to support the national team. It also represented an opportunity for local residents to use the upgraded transport systems in many areas and to allay residents' fears of crime in the inner-city areas.

The event also aimed to change international perceptions of the African continent in general and combat "Afro-pessimism" (Domingues, 2011, p.42). As Africa's World Cup, the slogan for the event was 'Ke Nako (meaning 'it's Africa's time') – Celebrate Africa's humanity'. Danny Jordaan (CEO of the 2010 Organising Committee) claims that the enduring image of the South African people is now that of a "lively people ready to welcome the world". The event will be remembered for its passionate football supporters and their unique style and dress, such as blowing a 'vuvuzela' (plastic trumpet), wearing a 'makarapa' (colourfully decorated headgear) and doing the 'diski' (a vibrant, energetic dance based on football movements) (see Figure 3).

Figure 3: A South African football fan blowing a 'vuvuzela' and wearing a 'makarapa'.
Photo credit: Alric Farmer

Sport

The sport legacy includes the development of international standard sporting facilities and related infrastructure upgrades. These often become 'emblematic symbols' for the host city and depict its link with sports (Swart and Bob, 2007). In South Africa, new stadiums were built in Cape Town (see Figure 4), Port Elizabeth, Durban, Johannesburg, Nelspruit and Polokwane. Existing stadiums in Pretoria, Johannesburg, Rustenburg and Bloemfontein were upgraded for the event and also hosted the 2009 FIFA Confederations Cup. In total, 10 stadiums across nine cities were used for the event.

Besides facilities, a number of sport development initiatives resulted from the World Cup, such as the FIFA 'Football for Hope' projects. An increase in sport participation, support and sponsorship may also result as legacies of a mega-event. Sponsorship of the 2010 FIFA World Cup was mostly by large, multinational companies. However, for the first time, an African company, MTN (a mobile telecommunications company), was a global sponsor of the event.

Figure 4: Fans entering the newly built Cape Town Stadium. Photo credit: Brendon Knott

Tourism

Tourism legacies could include a better-known and understood destination and brand (i.e. nation and destination branding), improved reputation for service delivery, improved public transport systems and improved tourism information systems. The successful hosting of the 2010 event provided a head-start for bidding for other major events after the World Cup and lessons learned by governments, sporting bodies and business will play a major role in the further development of the sport tourism sector (Swart and Bob, 2007). The event also provided an opportunity to expand traditional sport tourism markets for rugby and cricket to include new markets in football-playing nations (Swart and Bob, 2007). Examples of tourism infrastructure upgrades include five new hotels built in Cape Town alone, as well as significant airport upgrades at Cape Town, Johannesburg and Port Elizabeth and a new airport in Durban. There were also improvements to inner-city and airport transport links such as the 'Gautrain' in Johannesburg.

There were an estimated 228,000 tickets sold to overseas fans and 11,000 to African fans (Hazelhurst, 2010). An additional 85,000 non-ticketed African fans were expected to visit the country (Hazelhurst, 2010), possibly a result of ineffective ticket distribution systems and high ticket prices for African fans (Emmett, 2010b). South Africa recorded a 15.1% increase in tourist arrivals to the country in 2010, to record a total of 8,073,552 visitors (Els, 2011). This compares very well in international terms, especially as figures from the UNWTO show that global tourism arrivals are estimated to have grown by an average of only 6.7% in 2010, which means that South Africa greatly outperformed the global market (Els, 2011). The Minister of Tourism for South Africa pointed out that "[i]t is important to acknowledge that the particularly good growth in South Africa's arrivals figures was undoubtedly given a significant boost by the World Cup" and that there was a record peak in tourist arrivals in June and July 2010, which is traditionally the low tourism season (Els, 2011, n.p.). With just under 310,000 visitors travelling specifically for the World Cup event, the World Cup arrivals alone represented about 4% of the total arrivals for 2010. International arrivals to Cape Town International Airport for the FIFA World Cup window were up 24% on 2009 figures for the same period, and some major attractions reported visitor numbers in excess of 2009 peak season figures (Cape Town Tourism, 2010). FIFA World Cup visitors are also reported to have spent up to four times as much as usual winter visitors to Cape Town (Cape Town Tourism, 2010).

Nation branding as a legacy

Having looked at the broad different types of legacies from mega-events, the discussion now turns to the specific aspect of nation branding. The discussion shows that although most commonly included as part of the tourism legacy, nation branding is influenced by (and in turn has an influence on) other aspects of legacy, such as infrastructure changes, economic investment, urban development, social legacies and sport legacy.

In the struggle for competitive advantage, national reputation is becoming more and more significant as countries compete for the attention, respect and trust of investors, tourists, consumers, donors, immigrants, media and governments (Anholt, 2007). Anholt, among other proponents (such as Olins, 2002 and Kotler and Gertner, 2002) supports the notion that nations have a brand image and that this image is made up of a collection of images, symbols, history, perceptions, media, experiences, observations and stereotypes. While some scholars are hesitant that a nation should be considered a brand (e.g. Girard, 2009), Anholt proposes that a powerful, positive nation brand provides a strong competitive advantage for a nation and recommends that a nation's image needs to be skilfully created and carefully managed, just like any other brand. Keller (2008) explains that an important 'building block' of a brand and a source of brand equity is brand image. Brand image refers to "the way people think about a brand abstractly, rather than what they think the brand actually does" (Keller, 2008, p.65). Brand image thus relates to the more intangible aspects of a brand that represent associations formed directly through customer experiences or indirectly through advertising, word of mouth, or other sources of information (Keller, 2008). Keller (2008, p.67) concludes that the challenge for marketers is to create "strong, favourable and unique" brand associations.

There has been a growing awareness of the potentially significant impact that hosting sport mega-events, such as the FIFA World Cup, can have on a country's brand image (Gibson *et al.*, 2008). Sport mega-events have become increasingly important in the contemporary era, with their hosting becoming an object of policy for an increasing number of states in the world, especially "as a means to gain international visibility in some ways" (Cornelissen, 2007, p.242). Sport mega-events represent a "unique publicity platform and opportunity for place marketing" (Essex and Chalkley, 1998, p.201) or, as Berkowitz *et al.* (2007, p.164) put it, "a great branding opportunity" for nations. Such events may provide an opportunity to create or promote an image and also re-brand a nation (Anholt, 2007). Rein and Shields (2006) explain how sports stimulate an emotional heat between the participants and the audiences that can symbolise the energy, vigour, and strength of an emerging nation in ways that eco-branding, museums and other cultural attractions, for example, cannot.

As an illustration of the opportunity created by the World Cup for international visibility through media coverage, the following statistics are telling: 400 media broadcasters and over 15,000 journalists attended the event from all over the world (Emmett, 2010a). There were more than 200 hours of television coverage (Du-Toit-Helmbold, 2011), a figure that does not include for the extensive coverage by independent and 'new media' broadcasters. These figures highlight the global media impact for the nation during the event period, which featured 28 match days and up to 43 days of coverage (including pre-event coverage and opening ceremonies). In terms of television audiences, over 700 million people tuned in to watch the FIFA World Cup final, 100 million more than the number of people who watched the opening ceremony of the 2008 Beijing Olympic Games (Cape Town Tourism, 2010). An excellent broadcast coup for Cape Town was the glass-box studio that the BBC installed on a rooftop near the V&A Waterfront for the duration of the event. Daily commentary came with a backdrop of Cape Town, Table Mountain and the Cape Town Stadium: a priceless global advertisement for the destination. Around 17.5 million viewers in Britain alone tuned into the

BBC to watch their country go up against Germany in their second-round match (Cape Town Tourism, 2010). See Figure 5 for a summary of the media coverage.

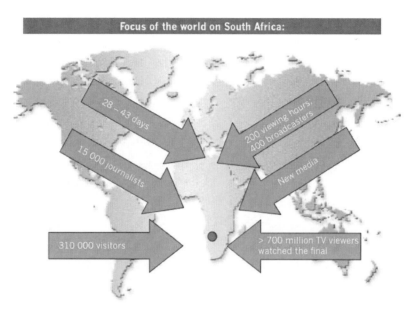

Figure 5: The focus of the world was on South Africa during June-July 2010

Measuring the nation-branding legacy

While it was agreed that the hosting of the 2010 FIFA World Cup in South Africa represented a unique platform and opportunity for creating and managing the host nation's brand, it was unclear exactly what this impact would be. The following section details an investigation that aimed to identify perceptions of international visitors to South Africa during the 2010 FIFA World Cup event regarding the nation brand and its key attributes, as well as to determine any changes in these perceptions as a result of their visit during the event.

Surveys, in the form of mall-intercept questionnaire interviews, were used to gather perceptions of the international visitors in South Africa. Respondents were interviewed at the official fan parks and stadium precincts in two of the major host cities and popular tourist destinations, Cape Town and Durban, on match-days during the event period. A total of 561 international visitors were selected using a spatially based purposive sampling approach at these locations. This method ensured that the survey was not skewed towards a particular area or group of visitors within the fan park or stadium precinct by selecting only one respondent within a particular group of fans/

visitors and ensuring a broad coverage of interviews across the entire de-marcated area. Senior and post-graduate students were used to conduct the interviews (see Figure 6). The questionnaire was mostly structured, using closed-ended questions and Likert-type scales, although three open-ended questions tested prior perceptions, current perceptions and the cause of the change of perceptions related to the South African brand. The questionnaire was pre-tested on international visitors to Cape Town before the event. SPSS for Windows was used to analyse the quantitative data.

Figure 6: International visitors were interviewed at the official fan park and stadium precinct in Cape Town and Durban. Photo credits: Brendon Knott and Alric Farmer

Profile of the sport tourists

A profile of the international tourists surveyed revealed that the vast major-ity of respondents (75%) were first-time visitors, while the World Cup event was the primary reason for travel for 77% of these visitors. A demographic profile of the respondents revealed the following points of interest (see Table 1 for a summary). Most visitors were from Western Europe (United Kingdom

27%; Netherlands 11%; and Germany 10%) and North America (USA 15%). This followed a similar pattern to the official ticket sales profile released by FIFA (2010) and Cape Town Tourism (2010) statistics. However, a number of visitors were from the host's non-traditional tourist markets such as Central and South America (8%), Asia/Australasia (8%) and other African nations (7%). Cape Town Tourism (2010) statistics confirmed that many new visitors came to the city for the first time. Many were from what they consider to be 'new markets', which are viewed as key to tourism growth. These were from South America (Argentina, Brazil and Uruguay) as well as Japan, Mexico, Algeria and Portugal (see Figure 7).

The predominant ethnic origin of respondents (self-rated) was white/caucasian (79%) and the gender was predominantly male (77%). The average age was 32 years, with 77% being younger than 40 years old. This profile is fairly consistent with the 2010 travel statistics issued by Tourism South Africa and FIFA Marketing Research (2010) for this period. Looking at the travel profile of the visitors, it was found that over a third of visitors had attended a previous FIFA World Cup (37%).

Figure 7: International fans from Argentina, seen here at Cape Town Stadium, were among those from 'new markets' that are viewed as key to tourism growth in South Africa. Photo credit: Brendon Knott

Table 1: International visitor profile (n=561)

Nationality:	%
- UK	27
- USA	15
- Netherlands	11
- Germany	10
Ethnic origin (as stated by respondents):	
- White/Caucasian	79
- Black	7
- Latino/Hispanic	5
- Asian and Indian	5
Gender:	
- Male	77
- Female	23
Age:	
- Mean age: 32 years	
- Younger than 40 years	77
Travel profile:	
- Have travelled to a previous FIFA World Cup	37
- First-time visitors to South Africa	75
- World Cup was primary reason for travel	77

Nation-branding perceptions and tourist behaviour

While prior knowledge and perceptions of South Africa for first-time visitors were both rather limited, the unprompted responses tended to focus on the traditional tourism strengths such as the natural beauty, good climate and wildlife. These are generally very positive associations with the nation brand. While the prior perceptions were generally positive, a few negative perceptions were mentioned, mostly related to the much-publicised crime rate or safety and security issues. When asked which factors/sources of information influenced these perceptions prior to travelling and to rate the strength of these factors, respondents noted that the most important were the international media, experiences of friends/relatives and previous sport events in South Africa.

Nearly three quarters (74%) of the first-time visitors agreed that their perceptions of South Africa had changed since attending the World Cup event in the country. This is similar to the findings from a FIFA Marketing Research (2010) study, which stated that 84% of international visitors held the country in higher esteem after attending the event. The new, prompted, perceptions of the brand among all visitors are displayed in Table 2, which used a Likert-type scale to indicate respondents' level of agreement with the different question endings.

Table 2: Nation brand perceptions

'Do you believe that South Africa has/is… ?' (1=strongly disagree; 2=disagree; 3=unsure; 4=agree; 5=strongly agree) in %, n=561	1	2	3	4	5
Beautiful scenery and natural attractions	0.7	0.2	0.9	18.5	79.7
Many friendly, welcoming people	0.9	1.4	3	27.5	67.2
A good climate for tourism and sport	0.7	0.9	6.5	29.2	62.7
Many diverse cultures	1.1	1.1	6.3	39.9	51.7
A competent host of the football World Cup	1.3	1.8	4.7	40.1	52.2
A world-class tourism destination	0.7	1.4	6.4	41.3	50.1
An excellent destination to host future sport mega-events	1.4	1.1	12.9	35.3	49.3
World-class sports facilities	1.3	2.7	11.1	46.9	38.1
A number of successful sports teams and participants	2.0	5.6	23.8	42.5	26.1
A desirable country to live in	3.6	6.5	28.4	37.7	23.9
A safe place to visit	1.8	8.3	23.6	49.5	16.9
A segregated (divided) social society	6.5	10.7	30.2	34.4	18.3
Many business or investment opportunities	6.0	9.7	40.3	28.3	15.7
A stable democratic government	7.4	12.4	54	17.4	8.8
Well-respected political leaders	9.9	14.2	38.6	28.2	9.2

Table 2 shows that the factors scoring most highly are those that have been traditional brand strengths (e.g. natural beauty, friendly people and good climate) and also those that are more experiential in nature for sport tourists/short-term visitors (e.g. related to people, culture, attractions and facilities). The factors that score less well tend to consist of high 'unsure' responses, illustrating a lack of knowledge or understanding related to these issues. This is especially related to aspects of politics and leadership, business/investment opportunities, and social segregation. These are perhaps more nuanced or complex factors that would require greater information or learning to change or create stronger perceptions.

It was also interesting to note that although crime/safety and security had been a major concern for organisers prior to the event, and was mentioned as a negative prior perception, two-thirds of respondents (67%) considered the country to be 'a safe destination to visit'. The most significant reasons given for the change in the perceptions from prior to the event was 'travelling in South Africa' and 'interacting with South Africans'. Linking these perceptions with the reason for travelling, respondents showed a strong support for the nation as a competent host of the World Cup (92%) and as a potential host for future sport mega-events (85%).

In order to gauge whether the travel and event experience would impact on the sport tourist's consumer behaviour, respondents were asked to respond to a series of statements, again using a Likert-type scale to indicate their level of agreement with the statements. These are set out in Table 3 in order of greatest agreement. The responses show a high propensity for repeat travel and word-of-mouth promotion of the nation, two highly valuable tourism-marketing outcomes.

Table 3: Influence of nation brand perceptions on tourists' consumer behaviour

'My visit to South Africa has encouraged me to…' (1=strongly disagree; 2=disagree; 3=unsure; 4=agree; 5=strongly agree)	Mean score (n=561)
Visit South Africa again	4.54
Encourage others to visit South Africa	4.54
Become friends with South African people	4.27
Appreciate South African food, music, art and dance	4.21
Visit other African countries	3.96
Return to South Africa to watch or participate in sport events	3.94
Pay more attention to news or media relating to South Africa	3.85
Buy South African products more easily	3.44
Do business or invest in South Africa	2.93
Emigrate to South Africa	2.55

Table 3 shows that respondents have a high propensity to travel to South Africa again and to encourage others to travel, which represents valuable future tourism income and word-of-mouth marketing. If indeed this turns out to be the case, it could represent a significant tourism legacy for the nation. It will be interesting to note whether the potential tourism legacy for South Africa also involves a tourism legacy for other African nations, with respondents generally 'unsure' whether they would visit these destinations. This is in spite of the fact that the event was promoted as an 'African' World Cup. The behavioural responses that score most poorly were those that required the greatest personal commitment, potential risk or behaviour change, such as emigration, investment and business.

It is important to note three limitations of the study before discussing the conclusions. The now infamous noise created by the 'vuvuzela' (trumpet), and the general congestion and crowding experienced in the venues where interviews took place made the process more difficult and time consuming. The questionnaires were printed in English only, and although the interviewees were often able to speak a number of languages (including French, Spanish, Portuguese and German), respondents were not always able to answer in their preferred language. A further limitation to the survey was that it was extremely difficult to determine prior perceptions once the respondents were already in the country.

Conclusion

This case examines South Africa's efforts to leverage nation-brand benefits from the FIFA World Cup. Sport tourism as well as mega-events were explored within a South African context. The growing importance and recognition of 'legacy' as it relates to mega-events was discussed, and different types and examples of legacies mentioned. This discussion set the background for the more detailed look at nation branding as a particular legacy from the event for the host nation.

From the major findings of this study, it appears that that many visitors who did not have strong perceptions of South Africa now have strong positive perceptions and could be expected to act as 'brand advocates' for the destination. The findings are extremely positive and appear to support the notion that mega-events can be effectively used as nation-branding opportunities, although it needs to be noted that it is difficult to isolate the effect that the World Cup event played in this process from the mere fact that the visitors were able to tour the country. The highly positive support for the hosting of the event may also have influenced perceptions more positively compared to normal. Although more longitudinal studies need to be conducted, from this study it appears that the development of a positive and distinct South African brand has been accelerated through the effective hosting of the 2010 FIFA World Cup.

This study generally supports the nation-branding literature and, in particular, those scholars who promote the concept of the nation as a brand, as discussed earlier. Similar to conventional marketing theory, an improved brand image of the nation leads to an increased brand equity as it translates into positive consumer behaviour (e.g. repeat visits and positive word-of-mouth promotion). Acknowledging the earlier discussion around legacy and leveraging of mega-events, it is recommended that further research be undertaken to determine the degree to which this legacy has been and will be leveraged by nation brand and sport tourism stakeholders. This would assist and support future sport tourism event bids by South Africa as well as by other African nations, for example Egypt and South Africa both potentially bidding for the Olympic Games in 2020.

In summary, the 2010 FIFA World Cup was a hugely significant and symbolic event, not only for South Africa, but for Africa as a whole. The words of Jacob Zuma, South African President, sum up the feelings of the nation at the conclusion of the event:

> "We have been able to show the world that we have what it takes to compete with the best, united in our diversity. It truly is an emotional moment for a nation that had doomsayers warning football fans to avoid coming to South Africa. The world had been told to expect high levels of crime, unfinished stadiums and other infrastructure as well as lack of accommodation. They came and discovered that we are a winning nation of very humble, hospitable people. They learned too that we are very efficient organisers and planners" (Zuma, 2010, n.p).

Echoing this positive assessment, Cape Town Tourism CEO, Mariëtte du Toit-Helmbold says:

> "(South Africa's) efficiency, safety and all-round positive attitude have caught the attention of the world and many a jaded pessimist has been forced to revise [their] views. We believe that this FIFA World Cup has been not only the greatest marketing success story we have ever had, but it has also been an essential and long-overdue turning point for the world's perception of Africa" (Cape Town Tourism, 2010, n.p.).

References

Anholt, S. 2007. What is competitive identity? *African Analyst* 2: 72-81.

Berkowitz P, Germano G, Gomez L, Schafer G. 2007. Brand China: Using the 2008 Olympic Games to enhance China's image. *Place Branding and Public Diplomacy* **3** (2): 164-178.

Cape Town Tourism. 2010. *Tourism Industry Positive about the Impact of the World Cup on Future Tourism Growth for Cape Town.* July 21. http://www.capetown.travel/media/blog/entry/tourism_industry_positive_about_the_impact_of_the_world_cup_on_future_touri/

Carlsen J, Taylor A. 2003. Mega-events and urban renewal: The case of the Manchester 2002 Commonwealth Games. *Event Management,* **8** (1): 15-22.

Chalip L. 2004. Beyond impact: A general model for host community event leverage. In Ritchie B, Adair D (eds), *Sport Tourism: Interrelationships, Impacts and Issues,* Clevedon: Channel View; 226-252.

Cornelissen S. 2007. Crafting legacies: The changing political economy of global sport and the 2010 FIFA World Cup. *Politikon* **34** (3): 241–259.

Deery, M. and Jago, L. 2006. The management of sport tourism. In Gibson H. (ed.), *Sport Tourism: Concepts and Theories,* New York, NY: Routledge; 246-257.

Dickinson J, Shipway R. 2007. *Resource Guide: The Impact of Events.* Hospitality, Leisure, Sport and Tourism Network. The Higher Education Academy. http://www.heacademy.ac.uk/assets/hlst/documents/resource_guides/the_impact_of_events.pdf

Domingues B. 2011. A dream accomplished. *Sport Business International* **164** (1): 42-44.

Du-Toit-Helmbold M. 2011. *Talking Tourism: The Latest Tourism Figures Reflecting Changing Travel Landscape.* Cape Town Tourism e-mail newsletter. 2 March.

Els K. 2011. *Arrivals show record increase in 2010.* Southern African Tourism Update. http://www.tourismupdate.co.za/NewsDetails.aspx?newsId=58303

Emmett J. 2010a. Africa arrives. *Sportspro* **19**: 43-46.

Emmett J. 2010b. The whole world in his hands. *Sportspro* **19**: 48-56.

Essex S, Chalkley B. 1998. Olympic Games: Catalyst of urban change. *Leisure Studies* **17** (3): 187-206.

FIFA. 2010. Study reveals tourism impact in South Africa.

http://www.fifa.com/worldcup/archive/southafrica2010/news/newsid=1347377/index.html

FIFA Marketing Research. 2010. Onsite fan research. http://www.fifa.com/worldcup/archive/southafrica2010/organisation/media/newsid=1305767/index.html

Fredline L, Jago L, Deery M. 2003. The development of a generic scale to measure the social impacts of events. *Event Management* **8** (1): 23-37.

Gammon S, Robinson T. 1997. Sport and tourism: A conceptual framework. *Journal of Sport and Tourism* **4** (3): 11-18.

Getz D. 1997. *Event Management and Event Tourism,* New York: Cognizant Communications.

Getz D. 2003. Sport event tourism: planning, development and marketing. In Hudson S (ed.) *Sport and Adventure Tourism.* New York: Haworth; 49-88.

Gibson, H. 2006. *Sport Tourism: Concepts and Theories,* New York: Routledge.

Gibson H, Qi C, Zhang J. 2008. Destination image and intent to visit China, and the 2008 Beijing Olympic Games. *Journal of Sport Management* **22** (3): 427-450.

Girard, M. 1999. States, diplomacy and image making: What is new? Reflections on current British and French experiences, paper presented to conference in Image, State and International Relations, London School of Economics, 24th June.

Hall CM, Hodges J. 1997. The politics of place and identity in the Sydney 2000 Olympics: Sharing the spirit of corporatism. In Roche M (ed.) *Sport, Popular Culture and Identity.* Germany: Meyer & Meyer; 95-112.

Hazelhurst E. 2010. Projected African attendance at World Cup falls as ticket sales stall. *Cape Times Business Report*. 22 April.

Keller KL. 2008. *Strategic Brand Management: Building, Measuring and Managing Brand Equity*, 3rd Edition, Upper Saddle River, NJ: Pearson.

Kent J. 2003. *Draft National Strategy for Bidding and Hosting for Major International Events*. Sport and Recreation South Africa (SRSA), Pretoria.

Kotler P, Gertner D. 2002. Country as brand, product, and beyond: A place marketing and brand management perspective. *Brand Management* **9** (4-5): 249-261.

Olins W. 2002. Branding the nation: The historical context. *Brand Management* **9** (4-5): 241-248.

Preuss H. 2007. The conceptualisation and measurement of mega sport event legacies. *Journal of Sport and Tourism* **12** (3-4): 207-228.

Rein I, Shields B. 2006. Place branding sports: Strategies for differentiating emerging, transitional, negatively viewed and newly industrialised nations. *Place Branding and Public Diplomacy* **3** (1): 73-85.

Standeven J, De Knop P. 1999. *Sport Tourism*, Champaign, IL: Human Kinetics.

Swart K, Bob U. 2007. The eluding link: Toward developing a national sport tourism strategy in South Africa beyond 2010. *Politikon* **34** (3): 373-391.

Tassiopoulos D, Haydam N. 2008. Golf tourists in South Africa: A demand-side study of a niche market in sports tourism. *Tourism Management* **29** (5): 870-882.

Turco DM, Riley R, Swart K. 2002. *Sport Tourism*, Morgantown, WV: Fitness Information Technologies.

Zuma, J. 2010. *Media Statement by President Jacob Zuma Marking the End of the 2010 FIFA World Cup Tournament*. SABC broadcast centre, Johannesburg, 12 July. http://www.info.gov.za/speech/DynamicAction?pageid=461&sid=11413&tid=11877

Ancillary Student Material

Further reading

Alegi P. 2010. *Laduma! Soccer, Politics and Society in South Africa, from its Origins to 2010*, Scottsville, South Africa: University of KwaZulu-Natal Press.

Anholt S. 2003. *Brand New Justice: The Upside of Global Marketing*, Oxford: Butterworth-Heinemann.

Anholt S. 2007. *Competitive Identity: The New Brand Management for Nations, Cities and Regions*, New York: Palgrave Macmillan.

Morgan N, Pritchard A, Pride R. 2011. *Destination Branding: Creating the Unique Destination Proposition, 3rd Edition*, Oxford: Butterworth-Heinemann.

Nauright J. 2010. *Sport, Cultures and Identities in South Africa, 2nd Edition*, Morgantown: Fitness Information Technology.

Weed ME, Bull CJ. 2009. *Sports Tourism: Participants, Policy and Providers, 2nd Edition*, Oxford: Elsevier.

Related websites and audio-visual material

The following websites offer background information, analysis and greater understanding of the South African sport tourism and nation-branding context:

Association of National Olympic Committees of Africa: www.anoca.info

Cape Town Tourism: http://www.capetown.travel

FIFA World Cup: http://www.fifa.com/worldcup

International Marketing Council of South Africa: www.brandsouthafrica.com/

Premier Soccer League, South Africa: http://www.psl.co.za

Soccer Laduma, Football newspaper website, South Africa: http://www.soccer-laduma.co.za

South African Sports Business, local sport industry news: http://www.sasports-business.co.za

South African Tourism: http://www.southafrica.net

Sport and Recreation South Africa, Government Department website: http://www.srsa.gov.za

Supersport International, television and media company: http://www.super-sport.co.za

Self-test questions

Try to answer the following questions to test your knowledge and understanding. If you are not sure of the answers then please refer to the suggested references and further reading sources.

1   Define the niche area of 'sport tourism'.

2   Explain what is meant by a 'mega-event' and give examples of events that can be considered mega-events.

3   Explain what is meant by 'legacy' and discuss the main types of legacy that result from mega-events.

4   Explain the importance of nation branding within the tourism industry.

Key themes and theories

The key themes raised in the case study relate to the following areas:

◆ Sport tourism:
  ◆ Understanding the relationship between sport and tourism.
  ◆ Defining this tourism niche area.
◆ Mega-events:
  ◆ Identifying and understanding different levels/scales of events.
  ◆ Understanding impacts and legacies of mega-events.
◆ Legacy and leveraging of mega-events:
  ◆ Defining legacy.
  ◆ Understanding the key aspects of legacy from events.
  ◆ Distinguishing between 'legacy' and 'leveraging' of events.
◆ Nation-branding:
  ◆ Defining nation-branding.
  ◆ Understanding the development of nation-branding, from branding and place branding theory.
  ◆ Understanding the role and significance of nation-branding within tourism.

If you need to source further information on any of the above themes then these headings could be used as key words to search for materials and case studies.

Key theories

◆ The overlap of 'sport' and 'tourism' to form the niche area of 'sport tourism'.
◆ Categorisation of events by scale and media exposure.
◆ Impacts and legacies of mega-events.
◆ Leveraging the impacts of mega-events.
◆ The marketing and branding of places, cities and nations.

Scan here to get the hyperlinks for this chapter.

3

Definitely Dubai: Destination Branding in Action

Paul Williams and Nick Ashill

Introduction

This case study looks at the destination branding of Dubai, one of the world's fastest growing tourism destinations. The case study explores the tourism industry in Dubai and then reviews the background to its destination branding, including the latest branding campaign: 'Definitely Dubai'. It also outlines some of the reasons for Dubai's growth as a tourism destination, the primary driver of which has been the need to diversify the economy and reduce the reliance on its dwindling stock of oil. The challenges faced in creating the brand are also examined.

Figure 1: Map of the United Arab Emirates: *Source*: CIA World Factbook (2010)

Dubai is one of the seven emirates of the United Arab Emirates (UAE), a country located in the Middle East region. As can be seen in Figure 1, Dubai lies on the coast of the Persian Gulf and is sandwiched between the emirates of Abu Dhabi and Sharjah. The emergence of Dubai into an economic powerhouse has been quite remarkable, with international trade, regional financial services, ambitious real-estate projects and unprecedented tourism growth all driving Dubai forward. Since the early 1990s, Dubai has grown from a relatively small trading port into an international destination of high repute, for both business and leisure tourists. Dubai has seen significant investments in tourism, including attractions, hotels, airports, airlines and other tourism amenities. Most of this development has been in the luxury segment of the market, with opulence and ostentation the primary positioning of the destination to attract high-spending tourists (Henderson, 2006; Balakrishnan, 2008).

The discovery of oil and gas in the region in the 1950s and 1960s was the catalyst for the enormous economic growth and investment in the UAE. The Federal Emirate of Abu Dhabi, where most of the oil and gas is located, has reaped the benefits of worldwide demand for oil and built up enormous wealth that has been re-invested back into the UAE. This investment has resulted in some of the best roads, airports, hotels, hospitals, universities, schools and utilities infrastructure in the world. With an average per-capita income of around US$ 36,973 per annum for its citizens (IMF, 2010), the UAE is ranked as one of the world's top-15 wealthiest economies.

With the long-term supply of oil uncertain, and with the majority of the supply of oil resting within the emirate of Abu Dhabi, Dubai has autonomously invested in several ambitious projects within the emirate. These are intended to help ensure its long-term survival and diversify its economic portfolio away from oil and gas. For example, it has invested into transportation infrastructure, such as the brand new Maktoum airport, which will be the world's largest by 2017 with an estimated 120 million passengers. In addition, the Dubai government has extended the present Dubai airport with two new terminals, built a new city-wide monorail system and developed a brand new cruise-ship terminal.

Other investment examples include real estate, shopping malls, hotels, industry clusters, a regional financial services hub and a myriad of commercial/office projects, all of which have been built since the early 1990s. Dubai has also built the world's largest man-made port at Jebel Ali, in order to strengthen its development as a major player in worldwide trade and logistics. Figure 2 highlights the glitzy, modern, business-like and high-rise images of Dubai, which are in stark contrast to the more traditional Arabesque images often portrayed in the media.

Figure 2: Dubai's modern skyline. Reproduced courtesy of DTCM

From a tourism perspective, many of these commercial infrastructure developments have facilitated growth in visitor arrivals to the country. Increased tourism demand has led to an increased supply of new hotels, restaurants, shops and tourism attractions. In addition to its natural tourism resources, Dubai has built several man-made tourism attractions and facilities to the envy of other tourism destinations around the world. Examples include the Burj Khalifa, the world's largest building and the Burj-al Arab Hotel, with its unique sail-shaped design and fame as the self-proclaimed, and self-marketed 'world's only seven-star hotel'. When these iconic symbols are combined with Dubai's other tourism pull factors of sunshine, beaches, oceans, deserts and friendly Arabian hospitality, it is clear to see how Dubai has emerged as a 'Star in the East' (Balakrishnan, 2008) of successful tourism development.

Dubai's tourism growth

Tourism has risen to become the largest contributor to Dubai's economy, its share being around 30% of GDP (Economist, 2008) at an estimated AED[1] 57 billion (US\$ 15.5 billion) per annum. In contrast, the previously dominant oil and gas revenues contributed only 9% of the GDP for Dubai in the same year. Tourism has thus grown rapidly in Dubai, with now approximately 7.5 million international visitors arriving each year at Dubai airport. From 2000 until the worldwide economic downturn in 2008, Dubai had enjoyed double-digit growth rates of around 15% per annum in visitor arrivals (Deloitte, 2008).

---

1   Arab Emirate Dirham.

Table 1: International visitor arrivals at Dubai Airport

Year	International tourist arrivals (million)
1990	0.63
2000	3.03
2002	4.76
2008	7.56
2009	7.61

Source: DTCM (2011)

The data given in Table 1 show the prolific growth of international tourism since the early 1990s. It is even estimated that Dubai is aiming for 15 million tourists by 2015 (WTTC, 2005). There are also a significant number of tourists who visit the emirate via other ports of entry. For example, the neighbouring emirates of Abu Dhabi and Sharjah also have international airports. In addition, the geography of the country means that land access is possible via Oman and Saudi Arabia, and also via boats and cruise-ships docking in Dubai. Unfortunately, statistics are not available on visitors through these other ports of entry to provide accurate estimates, but it is likely that the visitor numbers are substantial to add to those statistics in Table 1.

Back in 2002, the largest markets were from the regional Gulf Cooperation Council (GCC)[2] countries, making up around 34% of visitors, with South Asia (25%) and Europe (15%) also being significant markets. More recently, the profile of visitors has changed, with the largest markets now coming from Europe and South Asia in 2009, with around 32% and 29% of visitor arrivals respectively. Table 2 shows the international profile of visitors who stayed in hotels during 2009.

Table 2: International profile of hotel visitors (thousands)

UAE	GCC	Arab	Asia	Europe	US	Oceania	Total
535	679	481	1,800	1,932	497	151	6,105
9%	11%	8%	29%	32%	8%	2%	

Source: DTCM (2011)

The key to the success of Dubai has been the leadership and vision of His Excellency Sheikh Rashid Bin Saeed Al Maktoum and his son His Excellency

---

2   GCC Gulf Co-operation Council is an economic union of several Arab states, namely Bahrain, Kuwait, Oman, Qatar, Saudi Arabia and the United Arab Emirates.

Sheikh Mohammed Bin Rashid Al Maktoum, the present Ruler of Dubai and Vice President of the UAE. Their leadership has been instrumental in driving the Dubai emirate forward into a modern city with an exciting blend of traditional and modern architecture. Sheikh Mohammed in particular has promoted a diversification strategy for the Dubai economy and has ambitiously driven forward new projects and ideas that many thought impossible. He has a hands-on approach and is often seen visiting new projects unannounced to ensure they are kept on track (Balakrishnan, 2008).

Dubai's success has also hinged on its geographic location as a strategic link between the East and the West. Accessibility is one of the key criteria for successful tourism destination development (Henderson, 2006). Dubai is a popular transit point for Europeans en route to the Far East and Australasia, and also as a hub for Asian visitors from the booming economies of China and India to their wealthier partners in Europe. The relatively short flying times from Asia (6 hours), Europe (7 hours) and India (3 hours) also means that Dubai is an easy access point for large populations of people, many of whom have the desire, money and propensity to travel overseas on holiday. Dubai aims to fulfil these desires for holidays from such countries with large populations. In addition, Dubai serves as a regional hub between the western Middle-eastern countries (e.g. Lebanon, Egypt, Saudi Arabia, Bahrain, Kuwait and Iraq) and their eastern neighbours (e.g. Iran, Pakistan, Oman and India). This accessibility not only provides tourists with a transit and stopover destination, it also serves as an accessible destination for a large numbers of tourists from around the region and beyond who want to travel overseas on holiday.

Dubai is also seen as a liberal country in comparison to its more traditional and conservative neighbours, both within the UAE and in the wider region. Strategically, Dubai has promoted itself as a blend of 'East meets West', using traditional images of Arabian culture and architecture in combination with more modern cosmopolitan and modern images of a typical 'Western' destination. While the population of Dubai is predominantly Muslim and is governed under the strict Sharia Islamic legal principles, it has generally taken a more tolerant and liberal attitude towards people of other religions or none at all. This tolerance has helped to promote tourism products to many consumers who desire hedonistic holiday pleasures such as alcohol consumption, sunbathing in swimming costumes and mixed-gender social interaction, many of which are forbidden in Islamic countries (Henderson, 2006). Dubai has thus emerged as a free, safe, open and tolerant tourism destination with a harmonious mix of nationals, expatriates and tourists from outside the region.

Another factor in its success has been Dubai's diversity of natural and man-made attractions to promote itself as a year-round destination. For most of the year, the sun shines and this enables visitors to enjoy the sandy beaches and clear waters of the Gulf, in combination with outdoor pursuits such as sailing, scuba diving, golf and desert safaris. When it gets too hot, visitors can head indoors to attractions such as the shopping malls (with their tax-free retail opportunities), Ski Dubai an indoor ski facility; Atlantis the Palm, a water-based theme park; the Dubai Heritage Village and souks; and the Burj Khalifa, the world's highest building, rising 828 metres (2,716.5 feet) and more than 160 stories above sea level. Figure 3 shows the symbolic Burj Khalifa rising above all the other buildings.

Figure 3: Burj Khalifa: Tallest building in the world. Reproduced courtesy of DTCM

Dubai is also perceived as being a safe destination (Henderson, 2006). For the investor, the attractiveness of Dubai is equally apparent. With opportunities such as the Jebel Ali Free Zone (which has a number of significant benefits including 100% foreign ownership and full repatriation of profits), investors find it safe and attractive to open up headquarters in Dubai. Dubai's image also includes a clear projection of the importance of education and the knowledge economy. In 2003 the city launched Dubai Knowledge Village (DKV), which placed the Middle East on the map as a destination for education. Today it boasts a growing number of internationally renowned overseas Universities from such countries as England, Australia, Scotland, India, Russia and the United States.

The diversity of attractions has the added benefit of attracting many different customers from a broad range of markets. The investment in a wide range of tourism attractions and amenities means that most tourists will have their needs met whether they are from leisure markets or business markets. For example, Dubailand, which is a theme park, tourism and entertainment complex divided into seven theme worlds like Disneyland, is aiming to attract approximately 15 million visitors a year. There are also investments in special-interest tourism, such as medical tourism with Dubai Healthcare City; golf tourism, with 17 golf courses completed or planned; cruise tourism, with a new cruise terminal; shopping tourism, with a large number of shopping malls and the Dubai Shopping Festival, which includes special events such as 'Dubai Summer Surprises' to boost tourism in the off-peak summer period. There is also sports tourism, which includes events such as the Rugby World Cup Sevens in 2009, the annual Dubai World Cup (the world's richest horse race), the Race to Dubai golf tournament for the European Tour, and the annual Dubai Tennis Championships. Finally, Dubai Sports City has also been built as a huge multi-sport venue, including motor sports, cricket, football and rugby. In essence, Dubai offers a broad spectrum of attractions and events for many different tourist and business markets.

Finally, it is important to mention the role of Emirates airline as the flagship carrier for Dubai, as it has also been instrumental in promoting tourism growth in the emirate. This premium-quality airline has generated enormous publicity and favourable images around the world to attract tourists to the emirate. The airline has won many awards for its excellent service and has expanded to around 2,400 flights a week to over 100 destinations around the world, carrying over 25.9 million international passengers (IATA, 2010). In combination with the destination management organisation, the Department of Tourism and Commerce Marketing (DTCM), the airline has invested significant amounts of money in marketing Dubai, which has clearly helped Dubai's visitor numbers. For example, Emirates airline has sponsored several key worldwide sporting events (e.g. the Melbourne Cup, the World Rugby Sevens, the World Cup of Golf, the Cricket World Cup, the FIFA Soccer

World Cup and the Dubai World Cup of horse racing). In addition, the airline has sponsored the Emirates Stadium (Arsenal's soccer ground in London) to create publicity in the UK, its largest market. Another clever initiative was to buy the lease for the former Concorde Roundabout at London Heathrow Airport, which now models an Emirates Airline A380 for travellers to see as they arrive at or depart from the airport. These marketing initiatives have created international awareness and profile for the airline, and concurrently the emirate of Dubai. As such, Dubai as a tourism destination has gained significant spin-off effects from the marketing muscle of its airline.

Background and historical development of 'Brand Dubai'

Destination branding characterises those marketing activities that (a) both identify and differentiate a destination, (b) convey the promise of a memorable travel experience that is uniquely associated with the destination, (c) consolidate and reinforce the recollection of pleasurable memories of the destination experience and (d) reduce consumer search costs and perceived risk. All this has the intent of creating an image that influences consumers' decisions to visit the destination and not an alternative one (Blain, Levy and Ritchie, 2005). Destination branding creates awareness of the destination through the brand's imagery, such as a brand slogan, and these images reflect the 'essence' of the destination (Henderson, 2006). Prospective customers can then, if they wish to, associate with these brand images and create expectations that are confirmed or disconfirmed on their visit.

Lee and Jain (2009) analysed Dubai's branding strategy prior to the 2008 global economic downturn. Their findings suggest that instead of replicating what other competitor destinations have already achieved, Dubai deliberately followed a strategy of offering innovative products and services to both tourists and investors: Ski Dubai (skiing in the desert), Burj Al-Arab hotel (the luxury 'seven-star' hotel on the Dubai coastline), and Burj Khalifa (the world's tallest building) being just a few innovative examples of what the city has to offer. According to leading branding experts, customer value is made up of three value components: economic, functional and psychological[3]. The different experiences and attractions available in Dubai can fulfil these three different customer value components according to Lee and Jain (2009). For example, the functional dimension includes both indoor and out-

---

3   For economic value, customers equate the perceived quality of the product offering with the price they have to pay. Functional value is determined by evaluating the product offering in terms of a set of features they possess. Psychological value is determined by a set of intangibles such as service, brand name, trust and reputation.

door activities; the psychological dimension includes perceptions of feeling safe and welcome; and the economic dimension from the trading and free zone commercial incentives.

While there is some debate about the benefits of destination branding (Henderson, 2006; Morgan, Pritchard and Pride, 2011), in part due to the complexity and challenges of bringing divergent stakeholders together and obtaining consensus as to the overall destination 'image' sought in the marketplace, many places around the world have invested considerable sums of money in destination branding campaigns. The purpose of such campaigns is to allow the destination to shape how they wish to be seen in the marketplace. Most have had positive outcomes. Some examples include branding campaigns such as PURE NZ in New Zealand, Uniquely Singapore, Amazing Thailand and Incredible India. These campaigns have created awareness of the destinations by promoting the unique characteristics and essence of each destination. For example, the PURE NZ brand helps the country to promote its embedded core brand values of un-spoilt natural environments and being adventurous (Morgan, Pritchard and Piggott, 2002). Dubai has also embarked on a campaign of destination branding to help create positive perceptions of the country to prospective visitors.

In the early 1990s, Dubai was largely a desert city and survived on limited oil and trading. The then Deputy of Dubai, His Highness Sheikh Mohammed Bin Rashid Al Maktoum, realised something needed to be done to change this and sustain the economy. It was at this time that 'Brand Dubai' was born. The team responsible for creating the master umbrella[4] 'over-arching' brand consisted of the Emirates airline, the Airport and Civil Aviation Authority, the government and tourist board, various hotels and the destination management organisations.

The first step in the development of the brand was the realisation that access was a strategic priority. Dubai airport became an international hub and experience offering highly acclaimed duty-free. The second step was the major redevelopment of one of Dubai's beachfront hotels which, because of its unique design, became the first visible icon of Dubai (the Jumeirah Beach Hotel). These two initial branding tools were further enhanced by the launch of one of Dubai's most famous sub-brands and its mystical persona (it opened in 1999): The Burj Al Arab Hotel, as mentioned previously and shown in Figure 4.

---

4 Although such brands neatly encapsulate all desired attributes and brand values under a single umbrella, one of the disadvantages of such an approach is that any negativity attached to one attribute or value can have serious repercussions for all other attributes and brand values which may severely damage the overall credibility and sustainability of the brand.

Department of Tourism and Commerce Marketing

Figure 4: The Burj Al Arab 'seven-star' hotel. Reproduced courtesy of DTCM

Further branding developments that followed focused largely on increasing the awareness of Dubai as a destination and widening distribution channels. Central to achieving this objective was the establishment by the Dubai government of the DTCM in 1997. Its initial mandate was to work very closely with the Emirates airline and develop the route networks of the airline, thereby enhancing Dubai's visibility in the global marketplace. The role of DTCM has broadened significantly since 1997 and today it has specific responsibility as the principal authority for the planning, supervision and development of the tourism sector in the emirate, including the licensing of hotels, hotel apartments, tour operators, travel trade companies and travel agents. Its supervisory role also covers all tourist, archaeological and heritage sites, tourism conferences and exhibitions, the operation of tourist information services and the organisation and licensing of tour guides. In addition to its head office in Dubai, the DTCM has 18 overseas offices. They are located in New York (USA), London (the UK and Ireland), Paris (France), Frankfurt (Germany), Stockholm (Scandinavia), Milan (Italy), Moscow (the Russian Federation, CIS and Baltic States), Sydney (Australia), Johannesburg (South Africa), Mumbai (India), China (Beijing, Guangzhou and Shanghai), Hong Kong (Far East), Tokyo (Japan), Saudi Arabia (Jeddah and Riyadh) and Zurich (Switzerland and Austria).

In the late 1990s, the Dubai Government also encouraged local tourism through major hotel companies by actively cooperating with DTCM to promote Dubai both regionally and globally. Marketing and branding efforts included international travel and tourism exhibitions, Dubai's own road shows, international advertising campaigns, brochure production and distribution, media relations, the hosting of international airlines and hotel chains in Dubai as part of a 'familiarisation' visit strategy, and government-led approaches to investors from the tourism and commercial sectors.

In June 2009, the Dubai government created the Dubai Media Affairs Office (DMAO) to coordinate Dubai's media affairs regionally and globally. Its primary goal was to achieve maximum exposure for Dubai's achievements on economic, cultural and social matters and in doing so work closely with all Dubai government departments and authorities as well as non-government stakeholders. The DMAO recognised that greater communication coordination was needed among different organisations directly and non-directly responsible for Dubai's image and greater accessibility to more accurate information on various subjects related to Dubai was needed for regional and international media.

In 2010, DTCM launched 'Definitely Dubai', a new visual, consumer-facing brand identity, which has been rolled out across all marketing collateral and advertising campaigns globally. The new brand identity comprises of a new logo inspired by Arabic calligraphy, Thuluth script, which pays homage to the existing Government of Dubai logo. The logo has been designed so as to balance the Arab cultural roots of Dubai with a more contemporary style (to convey the message that Dubai is a modern, cosmopolitan holiday destination). This is consistent with the marketing messages and brand values previously conveyed to prospective tourists. It is written in English with an Arabic hand to reflect Dubai's inter-cultural and cosmopolitan nature (see Figure 5).

Figure 5: The 'Definitely Dubai' logo. Reproduced courtesy of DTCM

The release of the website portal is significant for brand visualisation, and highlights DTCM's continued focus on promoting Dubai to new and repeat visitors. The strategic direction behind the Definitely Dubai portal was based on the need to distinguish between a government entity and consumer brand, and ensure consistency of message across representative offices overseas.

The growth of 'Brand Dubai' as an umbrella or master brand has been supported by many sub-brands including the Emirates airline, the Dubai Shopping Festival, Ski Dubai, Dubai Metro, Burj Al Arab, Dubai Desert Classic Golf Tournament, the Dubai World Cup and many others. The utilisation of different sub-brands has proved an economical means of communicating common or shared information, and of reinforcing a strong connection to the umbrella brand, 'Brand Dubai', and all the associations that come along with that. The development of these sub-brands has also allowed tourists to understand better how Dubai's product offerings vary and which particular product or products might be right for them. For example, the Emirates 'Meet Dubai' campaign and webpage (see Figure 6) shows 14 television commercials along with print advertisements that talk about meeting the multicultural people of Dubai and the diverse culture of the city. The commercials reflect the views of citizens and residents about what it is like to live and work in Dubai.

Figure 6: Emirates 'Meet Dubai' webpage. Reproduced courtesy of Emirates Airlines

The reality of branding Dubai: Difficulties and challenges

The efforts of the Dubai government and various tourism stakeholders since the mid-1990s have been very successful in increasing destination awareness for Dubai and communicating a clearly defined and appealing image. Like all destinations, however, its destination marketers have faced some common and unique challenges. Dubai as a destination brand is a multidimensional and complex entity. There are many actors participating in the ongoing development of Brand Dubai and these actors have many different goals and objectives, resources and capabilities. The complexity of their interrelationships raises potential concerns about dysfunctionalism and inconsistency of brand values.

Brand Dubai is a composite product consisting of a bundle of different products and services such as accommodation, hospitality, attractions, arts, entertainment, culture, heritage and the natural environment. Although Dubai has identified its key stakeholders well and is actively engaging with them, the DTCM have had little direct control over these different sectors. Similarly, it cannot control the elements of the marketing mix employed by organisations in these different sectors, even though they all represent stakeholders of the destination brand. Finding a common opinion can therefore be very challenging, especially given that destinations comprise many companies from different industries and a diverse set of interest groups from both the private and public sectors. On the one hand, it is critical for destination marketers to bring the brand alive so that visitors experience the promoted brand values and 'feel' the authenticity of the destination. On the other hand, in achieving this task destination marketers also have to promote an image acceptable to a range of public and private sector stakeholders. Separate tourism entities and enterprises have their own individual images and their own brands, which may conflict and be problematic to subsume in an all-embracing, master-brand concept.

Although tourism accounts for a third of the Dubai economy (Kerr, 2011), the multidimensional nature of Brand Dubai will inevitably imply difficulties in managing and controlling it over time. Keller (2008) suggests that the most important consideration in reinforcing a brand is the consistency of the nature and amount of marketing support the brand receives. Brand consistency is critical to maintaining the strength and favourability of brand associations. But managing brand equity with consistency will inevitably require making numerous tactical shifts and changes in order to maintain the strategic direction of the brand. The global financial crisis has thrown up severe challenges to hotel managers and owners who have had to make staff redundant and yet also cope with a continuing wave of new hotel openings. A tide of impending hotel room supply will present Dubai's hospitality industry with additional pressures. Indeed, Dubai has absorbed an extra 20,000 rooms during the period 2008-2010, but another 60,000 rooms are planned over the following five years (Kerr, 2011). Excess supply, due to lower demand, is a significant challenge to be faced.

Another challenge for Dubai's destination marketers is to understand the nature of the consumption process involving tourism products. Tourism 'products' consumed in any destination represent a collection of products and services: for example, a tourist visiting Dubai for the first time will probably visit such attractions as the Burj Al Arab and Mall of the Emirates. This collection of products and services is selected by the consumer, which means all destinations are being marketed without the marketer knowing what exactly the product 'experience' will be. Tourism products must therefore be marketed with tangible evidence (known as 'tangibilising the intangible'). The danger is that by emphasising the tangible elements one may fail to differentiate oneself from other destination places, and since the intangible elements are abstract, emphasising the abstract only serves to compound the intangibility of the destination. It is therefore critically important for all of Dubai's tourism sub-brands to remain focused on enhancing and differentiating 'abstract realities' by manipulating tangible cues.

The ongoing development of Brand Dubai must also be consistent with the essence of the destination. There is general consensus that destinations with clearly defined and appealing images are better positioned than those about which little is known or that are perceived as being less attractive. Recognising this, Dubai has been very successful in creating an emotional appeal capable of being chosen by potential tourists over other destinations. 'Image' here is defined as "an amalgam of the knowledge, feelings, beliefs, opinions, ideas, expectations and impressions that people have about a named location" (Henderson, 2007, p.262). Of course, it is not just the images held by the tourist that are important but also those of investors and managers of tourism businesses such as tour operators, hotel companies and airlines, whose decisions inevitably impact on consumer travel opportunities and the development of tourism more generally.

Ekinci (2003) and others (e.g. Groves and Go, 2009) suggest that one of the most important components of branding a destination is brand personality, which represents the human side of brand image. Brand personality uses human personality traits to describe a destination image (e.g. 'family orientated', 'friendly', 'exciting', 'interesting' or 'original'). Arguably, it is brand personality that brings destination image alive. Positive associations with the destination experience and its people contribute to positive word of mouth, which enhances the brand image of the destination. Below are a few examples of consumer experiences and perceptions of Dubai that can be found on the lovemarks.com website. Developed by Saatchi and Saatchi, the term 'lovemark' was created to answer the question 'what makes some brands inspirational why others struggle?' A 'lovemark' is a brand that delivers beyond consumer expectations of great performance but also one that reaches the heart of consumers as well as their minds, creating an intimate emotional connection (Saatchi and Saatchi, 2011). These consumer quotes clearly reinforce the fact that Dubai has successfully created a mythical story: a fairly tale for many who live in the desert.

A Dream Coming True

Dubai is a dream coming true. I've witnessed it first hand. No place on earth I can think of is as ambitious as this city. I do hope that it continues with its success and expands it beyond the material dimensions to include social, cultural and spiritual growth.

Dergham, United Arab Emirates - 08 January 2006

Still a Dream

Dubai - final destination for anyone working in Arab countries. It's still a dream for so many: a city of festivals, a city of cities - shopping, gold, cinema, internet, sport, kids' festival - I am bound to be there. Dubai calling me!

Unnikrishna, India - 01 November 2004

Waiting To Be Trekked!

From a desert to a metropolis that holds some of the wonders the world has witnessed, surely marketing the city of Dubai has been one of the most innovative of endeavors I have ever seen! This city that is part of the United Arab Emirates has an eclectic mix of entertainment, shopping, festivals, culture, desert dunes, and local delicacies that will simply delight you. Take a look at how this visionary city exceptionally markets itself! Burj Al Arab – the only 7-star hotel; Palm Islands – the largest man-made island; Hydropolis – the first underwater hotel; Burj Khalifa – to be the tallest building in the world; Dubai Land – has the Mall of Arabia, future largest mall in the world; The World – a collection of man-made islands forming an image of the world map. This desert beauty is waiting to be trekked!

Sara, United Arab Emirates - 13 September 2004

Since the end of 2007, Dubai has been hit by the worldwide economic down-turn, as have most destinations. Visitor arrivals and hotel occupancies have either dropped or growth has slowed significantly. Less disposable income across the main markets in Europe and the GCC has meant that Dubai has also been aggressive in new markets which are more stable but cheaper, such as India and China. This may threaten the brand positioning somewhat, or at least be perceived as a threat to the luxury image it portrays. It is interest-ing to note that demand for holidays from these value-for-money markets is growing, despite the downturn. Even Emirates has set up its own budget airline, Fly Dubai, to compete with its budget competitors: Air Arabia, Al Jazeera Airways and BMI from the UK. The budget airline brand protects the 'premium' brand image of its parent, Emirates, from any brand dilution effects. However it potentially sends mixed messages, as Dubai as a holiday destination also markets itself heavily as a luxury brand.

Tourists today are less interested in an experience based purely on 'sun and sand' and are demanding more culture and adventure experiences. This means preserving and enhancing Dubai's image as an Arab city of inter-national spirit and sensibility, and ensuring a greater focus on authenticity by promoting such as values as integrity, honesty and trust. Keeping Brand Dubai fresh and relevant will remain an ongoing challenge. The Dubai brand quickly established itself on the basis of being the 'biggest, highest, tallest, fastest, whatever-est'. However, since the economic downturn, there has been less of an appetite for this kind of offering.

Another threat to the development of Brand Dubai is the political instability in the region. Recent conflicts in neighbouring countries such as Bahrain, Libya, Iraq, Afghanistan, Pakistan, Sudan and Iran are constraining factors to the region and Dubai is likely to feel this. Events in other volatile nations such as Syria, Egypt, Yemen and Lebanon are likely to have a negative dom-ino effect on visitors to the region, in particular from North America. While Dubai portrays itself as a peaceful and safe destination, the media images portrayed from its warring neighbours create negative perceptions in the consumer's mind about tourist security, particularly Westerners who may be distant and unfamiliar with the region (Henderson, 2006).

Finally, the challenge from new competition from other tourism destinations in the region has the potential to upset the Brand Dubai initiatives. While competition is generally healthy, especially for consumer choice and prices, it can have a negative effect on the brand. There has been significant compe-tition from other countries in the region such as Qatar with its successful bid for the 2022 FIFA World Cup and Bahrain with its contract for the Formula 1 Grand Prix. Even within the UAE, there appears to be significant competition from other emirates such as Abu Dhabi, Sharjah and Ras al Khaimah, which are also investing autonomously into a diversified portfolio of economic and tourism projects, competing for many of the same consumers. Admittedly these destinations are emerging more slowly that of Dubai, but they can be viewed as potential threats to the brand's overall development.

It is also important to acknowledge the importance for a destination brand to reach out to people and manage public opinion in today's increasingly digital society. In the year up to now, late 2011, Dubai has enjoyed resurgence in terms of positive brand associations, largely because of its efforts to incorporate social media networks into its global communications platform. A recent report by Digitial Daya (2011) that tracks new media identified positive to negative sentiment (favourable versus negative media mentions) as being 1:3 during December 2009, when concerns about Dubai's mountain financial debt and the meltdown of the city's property market were at its peak. For the period July-December 2010, however, the ratio of positive to negative sentiment was reported at 5:2. During this six-month period, Dubai achieved an average of 386,000 mentions a month. These positive associations are being heard on the web on the many blogs and social media networks that populate it. Use of YouTube and Twitter is also evident. Ian Scott (Director UK & Ireland, DTCM) and Simon Calder (a travel and tourism expert) talk about Dubai's appeal as a family destination on YouTube (2011). DTCM also has a presence on Twitter (Scott, 2011).

Conclusions

If Dubai can maintain its position as the cultural centre of the Middle East, its tourism industry may still thrive even without periodic astonishing construction projects. Foreigners will still be attracted to Dubai for its business activities, its sporting events, its shopping and many cultural attractions. The 'glue' will remain the cultural strengths that have turned the emirate into a tourist paradise. By fostering diverse industries, and by exercising more prudence with government finances, Dubai should be able to retain its rapid growth and economic vitality of previous years. Such a vibrant economy would be much more lasting and appealing than yet another luxury hotel. Perhaps Dubai should now join forces with Abu Dhabi to create an awareness of 'Brand UAE'. With the capital's cultural tourism strategy now firmly in place, the potential for crossover is growing, making it possible for Dubai's 'sun-and-sea leisure' to complement Abu Dhabi's business and cultural tourism.

The identity of Dubai is constructed through historical, political and cultural discourses (Govers and Go, 2009). The UAE is a highly varied nation and it brings with it the volatility of the Middle-east, in contrast to a peaceful and harmonious city of cultural and ethnic diversity. Foreign residents represent about 80% of Dubai's population (Lee and Jain, 2009), and they live peacefully with the local population and incoming visitors. Dubai has developed a brand identity through a unique value proposition, attraction and brand promise. Central to the branding process has been the effort of the city's decision makers to position the city in the upper echelon of markets such as tourism, real estate and education. This positioning for the ostentatious could backfire now that the global economic downturn is reducing overall consumer expenditure, especially on luxury goods such as holidays in five-star hotels. Dubai is also a destination with a past and a contemporary society which is made up of numerous ethnic groups who have their own sub-culture and heritage. Capturing these ingredients in a brand is not an easy task.

References

Balakrishnan MS. 2008. Dubai – star in the east: A case study in strategic destination branding, *Journal of Place Management and Development* **1** (1): 62-91.

Blain C, Levy SE, Ritchie B. 2005. Destination branding: Insights and practices from destination management organizations. *Journal of Travel Research* **43** (May): 328-338.

CIA. 2010. *Central Intelligence Agency World Factbook.* https://www.cia.gov/library/publications/the-world-factbook/maps/maptemplate_ae.html

Deloitte. 2008. *Hospitality Vision: Middle East Performance Review.* http://www.deloitte.com/assets/Dcom-Shared%20Assets/Documents/UK_THL_HospitalityVisionMiddleEastPerformanceReview2008.pdf

Digital Daya. 2011. Brand Dubai shining on social networks. http://www.digitaldaya.com/press-release/wp-content/uploads/2011/01/Brand-Dubai-Pulse-Report-Final-PV-Opt.pdf

DTCM. 2011. Department of Tourism and Commerce Marketing. http://www.dubaitourism.ae/trade-resources/statistics

Economist. 2008. Travel and tourism: A new itinerary. *The Economist,* May 15, n.p.

Ekinci Y. 2003. From destination image to destination branding: An emerging area of research. *E-Review of Tourism Research* **1** (2): 21-24.

Govers R, Go F. 2009. *Place Branding: Glocal, Virtual and Physical Identities, Constructed, Imagined and Experienced*, Basingstoke: Palgrave MacMillan.

Henderson JC. 2006. Tourism in Dubai: Overcoming barriers to destination development. *International Journal of Tourism Research* **8** (3): 87-99.

Henderson JC. 2007. Uniquely Singapore? A case study in destination branding. *Journal of Vacation Marketing* **13** (3): 261-274.

IATA. 2010. World Air Transport Statistics, 54th Edition. International Air Transport Association. http://www.iata.org/ps/publications/Pages/wats-passenger-carried.aspx

IMF. 2010. International Monetary Fund. The World Economic Outlook Database. http://www.imf.org/external/pubs/ft/weo/2010/02/weodata/index.aspx

Keller K. 2008. *Strategic Brand Management: Building, Measuring, and Managing Brand Equity*, Upper Saddle River, NY: Pearson Prentice-Hall.

Kerr S. 2011. Dubai heads downmarket to lure visitors. *Financial Times*, January 25: 13

Lee H, Jain D. 2009. Dubai's brand assessment success and failure in brand management: Part 1. *Place Branding and Public Diplomacy* **5** (3): 234-246.

Morgan N, Pritchard A, Piggott R. 2002. New Zealand, 100% Pure: The creation of a powerful niche destination brand. *Journal of Brand Management* **9** (4): 335-354.

Morgan N, Pritchard A, Pride R. (2011) *Destination Brands: Managing Place Reputation*, Oxford: Elsevier Butterworth Heinemann.

Saatchi and Saatchi. 2011. The Future Beyond Brands. Lovemarks. http://www.lovemarks.com.

Scott I. 2011. DCTM on Twitter. http://twitter.com/#!/ianDTCM

WTTC. 2005. World Travel and Tourism Council. Press Release. http://www.wttc.org/eng/Tourism_News/Press_Releases/Press_Releases_2005/2015_forecasts_for_UAE_Travel_and_Tourism_/

YouTube. 2011. DTCMUKI's Channel. http://www.youtube.com/dtcmuki

Ancillary Student Material

Further reading

Balasubramanian A. 2010. *Rebuilding Dubai: Post-bubble economic strategy*,
  http://hir.harvard.edu/big-ideas/rebuilding-dubai

Hankinson G. 2007. The management of destination brands: Five guiding principles
  based on recent developments in corporate branding theory. *Journal of Brand
  Management* **14** (3): 240-254.

Keller K. 2008. *Strategic Brand Management, International Edition* (3rd ed.), Prentice-
  Hall.

Konecnik M, Gartner WC. 2007. Customer-based brand equity for a destination. *Annals of Tourism Research* **34** (2): 400-421.

Moilanen T, Rainisto S. 2009. *How to Brand Nations, Cities and Destinations: A Planning
  Book for Place Branding*. Basingstoke: Palgrave MacMillan.

Marzano G, Scott N. 2009. Power in destination branding. *Annals of Tourism Research*
  36 (2): 247-267.

Related websites

The following websites offer background information on Dubai and its sub-
brands. The key resources also include those listed in the reference section of
the case study.

Tourism Dubai, Dubai's main tourism portal: http://www.dubaitourism.ae/

Definitely Dubai Branding Campaign website: http://www.definitelydubai.
com/

Emirates airline main homepage, with links to many other Dubai tourism
sites:

http://www.emirates.com/ae/english/

Self-test questions

To reflect on what you have learned in the case study, answer the following questions. While the answers can be found in the case study, you may also refer to other references and further reading for more detailed background.

1   What are the benefits and drawbacks of destination branding?

2   What are the main brand images (attributes) of Brand Dubai?

3   What are the main challenges presently faced by Dubai's destination marketers?

4   Critically examine the 'Definitely Dubai' website from the perspective of the consumer.

Key themes and theories

The key themes raised in the case study relate to the following areas:

- ♦   Destination branding
- ♦   Dubai tourism development
- ♦   Challenges in developing destination brands.

The key theories relate to:

- ♦   Branding
- ♦   Destination marketing
- ♦   Tourism development
- ♦   Government involvement and destination marketing.

If you need to source further information on any of the above themes and theories then these headings could be used as key words to search for materials and case studies.

     Scan here to get the hyperlinks for this chapter.

SUSTAINABLE
TOURISM

4

Visitor Management at a World Heritage Site:

Skara Brae Prehistoric Village

Anna Leask and Brian Garrod

Introduction

The UNESCO World Heritage List (WHL) sets out to represent the very best of the world's natural and cultural heritage, comprising a collection of sites that are of such outstanding universal value to humanity that it would be unconscionable for them not to be protected for the benefit of future generations. As of July 2011 there were 936 sites inscribed on the List, located in 153 different countries, and these are titled World Heritage Sites (WHS). Examples include world-famous tourism attractions such as Stonehenge in the UK and the Great Wall of China, as well as many less well-known properties and monuments. The List includes large-scale cultural landscapes, such as the city of Bath in the UK or the historic town of Sintra in Portugal. There are also natural areas inscribed on the List, such as the Serengeti National Park in Tanzania and Australia's Great Barrier Reef.

The WHL began in 1976 and is still being built up, with a number of successful nominees being added every year. As a result, the range of sites represented on the List also continues to expand. Nevertheless, it can be said that all of these sites share a common problem, which is that they all require effective visitor management strategies. This purpose of case study is to examine visitor management at the Skara Brae Prehistoric Village, which is part of the Heart of Neolithic Orkney WHS in Scotland. Following a brief description of the site, its context and its presentation, the case study identifies the need for visitor management at the site and outlines the various visitor pressures that are faced. In doing so, the case study considers how these pressures have been managed. It concludes by drawing lessons for visitor management at heritage sites more generally.

Visitor management

There are a number of reasons why visitor management is becoming an increasingly important task to be undertaken by those responsible for heritage sites, particularly those that have achieved WHS status. As Shackley (2006) notes, many such sites have seen a significant growth of visitor numbers, promoted by a range of factors including the more diverse use of discretionary time in many Western societies, increased car ownership and reduced travel costs (for example, the emergence of the low-cost airlines) and the extensive media publicity given to sites on the WHL. Furthermore, the market for visits to heritage sites has matured and visitors are generally more discerning, having ever greater expectations about access to the site and the quality of its interpretation. Visitor pressure on heritage sites has probably never been higher, and this is especially true of those that have been awarded WHS status.

Managers of heritage sites therefore find themselves on the horns of a dilemma. On the one hand visitors are needed, not only because they are likely to represent an important source of revenue for the site, through for example admission fees or secondary spending at the site, but also because there is an increasing expectation that heritage sites should provide both educational and recreational opportunities for the general public. On the other hand, visitors bring the risk of harmful impacts to the site and to the various artefacts located there. The range of possible visitor impacts is well documented (e.g. Garrod, 2008; Shackley, 1998) and includes, for example, overcrowding on the site and people congestion at particular bottlenecks; physical stresses on the site due to visitors trampling on sensitive parts of the site or handling sensitive artefacts; litter, graffiti and vandalism; traffic congestion on the site and in the local area, and possible vibration damage from cars and coaches. In most cases, both the risk of occurrence and the potential magnitude of such impacts are likely to rise as visitor numbers increase. Winning more visitors may therefore be at the same time both a blessing and a curse for a typical heritage site.

While some sites are relatively robust and can withstand increased levels of visitation, others will be more susceptible to damage. Some will be visited regularly by large numbers of people, while others will only have a small number of visits on an irregular basis. Some sites will only experience visitor pressure at peak times, while others will be subject to some degree of visitor impact all of the time. It is important, therefore, that the managers of each site examine the visitor-impact balance carefully and design visitor management strategies that will be appropriate to the particular context of their site. The visitor management imperative is particularly important to sites that are inscribed on the WHL, especially given the potential for WHS status to result in greater awareness on the part of prospective visitors and for higher visitation levels to result (Shackley, 1998; Fyall and Rakic, 2006). Since 1996, all sites that are nominated for WHS status must first develop a Management Plan. Typically such documents include consideration of the various impacts that visitors are already having or may potentially have on the site, and detail the policies that have been or will be introduced in order to address them. Management Plans are also intended to specify how the site will be maintained, how the needs of visitors will be met (including visitor safety and access for disabled people), and how the site will be interpreted to visitors, for example through the use of guides, booklets and information boards.

The Skara Brae Prehistoric Village

In the winter of 1850, a great storm battered Orkney. There was nothing particularly unusual about that, but on this occasion the combination of Orkney's notorious winds and extremely high tides stripped the grass from a large mound known as Skerrabra. This revealed the outline of a series of stone buildings that intrigued the local laird, William Watt of Skaill, who began an excavation of the site.

Located on the main island of Orkney in the Northern Isles off the coast of Scotland, Skara Brae is now recognised as one of the best-preserved group of prehistoric houses in Western Europe. The village was inhabited from around 3100BC to 2500BC and appears to have been continually modified throughout this period of time. Six houses are presently visible, although there were almost certainly more than this originally: the north side of the settlement has been lost to the sea, a retaining wall having been built in 1920s in an attempt to prevent further loss. Recent geophysics also suggests that there may be further remnants of the village still buried to the south-east. Figure 1 provides an overview of the site.

The houses appear to have been linked together by narrow, roofed passages. They contain stone furniture, hearths and drains, and give a remarkably vivid picture of life in prehistoric times (see Figure 2). Successive excavations also uncovered a wealth of artefacts and ecofacts, including hand tools, pottery, jewellery and gaming dice. No weapons were found and the houses do not seem to have been fortified, suggesting that the inhabitants led a relatively peaceful way of life. Many of the items to be unearthed are now on display in the site's purpose-built visitor centre. The importance of Skara Brae is widely acknowledged and in 1999 it was inscribed on the WHL as part of the Heart of Neolithic Orkney World Heritage Site.

Figure 1: The Skara Brae Prehistoric Village. Photo credit: Jim Schlater

Figure 2: Prehistoric house interior. Photo credit: Jim Schlater

The Heart of Neolithic Orkney WHS designation

The Heart of Neolithic Orkney WHS was inscribed onto the WHL in 1999, following its nomination in 1998. Several properties combine to present the WHS, including Maeshowe, the Stones of Stenness, the Ring of Brogar and Skara Brae. The sites combine to form a 'group of buildings', one of the types of site that can be nominated to UNESCO for listing. They are separated from each other, though the first three form part of the Brodgar Conserva-tion Area, while Skara Brae is situated approximately 6 km north-west of this. The sites are listed as a consequence of Criterion 24 (a) of the World Heritage Convention, in that "(i) the monuments represent masterpieces of human creative genius …(ii) in that they exhibit an important interchange of human values during the development of the architecture of major cer-emonial complexes in Britain … (iii) in that they bear unique or exceptional testimony to an important indigenous cultural tradition … and … (iv) as an outstanding example of a type of architectural ensemble and archaeological landscape" (Historic Scotland, 1998). Moreover, UNESCO recognises the site to be "an outstanding testimony to the cultural achievements of the Neo-lithic peoples of northern Europe" (UNESCO, 2008, n.p.).

UNESCO guidelines state that each WHS should have effective management processes in place and these are often formalised into a Management Plan. At the time of nomination, a Statement of Intent was signed by the four or-ganisations that were represented on the Heart of Neolithic Orkney WHS Steering Group: Historic Scotland, the Orkney Islands Council, Scottish Natural Heritage and the Orkney Archaeological Trust. These groups had responsibility for the management of the site and its immediate surround-ing area. The partners committed themselves to work together to "safeguard the special values, qualities, authenticity and integrity of the Site" (Historic Scotland, 2008a, n.p.). The Management Group presently comprises Histor-ic Scotland, the Orkney Islands Council, Scottish Natural Heritage and the Royal Society for the Protection of Birds (RSPB), the Orkney Archaeological Trust having been merged into the Orkney Islands Council and the RSPB having been added to the group when it acquired the neighbouring Brodgar Reserve in 2001.

In 2001, the first Management Plan for the Heart of Neolithic Orkney WHS was introduced, covering the period 1999 to 2006. The Plan set out a series of 52 actions intended to ensure the conservation and presentation of the site, along with the parties responsible for implementing them. Crucially, provision was made for a buffer zone around the site in order to assist in the protection of the site. While the zone itself confers no additional protection to the site, the WHS and its buffer zone are considered together as a single entity in local policy making and planning, helping to protect the site from impacts that affect the area as a whole and to maintain the overall visual coherence of the site. The Management Plan also sought to identify ways in which the different elements of the WHS could be presented in an integrated way, and one of the first actions to be undertaken was for Historic Scotland to develop an overall interpretation plan for the WHS. New interpretation panels were erected in order to place each part if the site in its wider context and to ensure that the natural heritage at each site was interpreted as well as the cultural heritage. Revised guide books were introduced to ensure consistency in the interpretation of the WHS as a whole.

Another important measure resulting from the implementation of the Plan was the instigation of a site resource monitoring programme in order to gauge the impacts of visitors at all of the sites. An article in the press raised fears that this might lead to a limitation being placed on visitor numbers to Skara Brae, or even to parts of the site being closed due to the considerable pressures that visitors put upon it (Johnston, 2003). However, even though timed tickets have recently been introduced at Maeshowe, visitor numbers have not been constrained at the Skara Brae site, the preference being to manage how visitor use the site rather than to set quantitative limits. The Plan also provided for the appointment of a WHS Co-ordinator tasked with the development of the Heart of Neolithic Orkney WHS Management Plan (Historic Scotland, 2008b).

A second Management Plan for the WHS was published in 2008 (Historic Scotland, 2008b). This provided a review of the achievements of the 2001 Management Plan and an analysis of the main issues for the WHS over the long term (2008 to 2038). A detailed Management Plan for 2008 to 2013 was then developed within this context. A total of 46 objectives were set out for the management of the WHS as whole, relating for example to the further monitoring of visitor activity, addressing the on-going problem of coastal erosion and the development of existing on-site and off-site educational activities. It should be noted that relatively limited attention is given to the role of tourism in the Management Plan, with the most frequent references being made to the economic contribution made by the WHS. The Heart of Neolithic Orkney WHS Setting Project also highlights several additional concerns regarding the management of the wider WHS setting.

Visitors to Orkney and Skara Brae

According to the Orkney Visitor Survey, tourism contributed £31.8 million to the Orkney economy in 2008/9, with around 142,000 visitors per annum coming to the islands (A. B. Associates, 2010). The survey also showed that 49% of visitors were from Scotland, while 33% were from elsewhere in the UK and the remaining 18% were from overseas. This represented a continuing drop in the number of overseas visitors, from 38% in 1996, 32% in 2000 and 21% in 2005. Over 60% of visitors were on holiday, with 17% visiting friends and relatives, and 16% on business. The average length of stay was 4.4 nights in Orkney, with the majority of visitors travelling by combination of car and ferry (70% and 77% respectively). A total of 71% of visitors had visited Skara Brae as part of their trip, up from 51% in 2005, despite the fact that just 57% of visitors in 2009 had previously 'heard of' the site. Many visitors listed walking as a popular activity, alongside visiting archaeological sites. Only 28% of visitors travelled as families, with just over one-third travelling with one other adult. Key market segments were the 45 and above age group (61%), especially those aged 55-64 (24%) – this was, however, a decrease on the 2005 figure of 34%. In 2009, a total of 26,978 cruise passengers visited. Hotels and bed-and-breakfast accommodation were used by 23% and 19% of visitor respectively in 2009, compared to 27% and 21% respectively in 2005. This downward trend is thought to be as a result of more visitors now preferring to use self-catering accommodation, its usage increasing from 16% of visitors in 2005 to 19% in 2009. The Orkney Tourism Group was formed in 2005 and has published the Orkney Tourism Strategy 2006-2015 and the Orkney Tourism Action Plan.

Visitor numbers to Skara Brae show that this is the busiest paid-entry attraction on Orkney, although the site records fewer visitors per annum than the busiest free sites of the Italian Chapel and St Magnus' Cathedral (VisitScotland, 2010). Visitor numbers to Skara Brae have grown from 52,400 in 1995, to 61,056 in 1998 when the new visitor centre was opened, with 69,361 visitors being recorded in 2009 (British Tourist Authority, 1996; VisitScotland, 2010). Revenue is in the region of £375,000 per annum (Historic Scotland, 2009). On its busiest day in 2005, the site received an estimated 1,700 visitors in one day. Meanwhile, visitors to the nearby Skaill House (see Figure 3) totalled 49,975 in 2009 (Visit Scotland, 2010). Around 70% of visitors to Skara Brae also visit Skaill House.

Figure 3: Skaill House. Photo credit: John Findlay

Visitors to Skara Brae are a combination of locals, holiday visitors, cruise ships – with 67 in 2003 making Kirkwall one of the UK's busiest ports for cruise ships – and day visitors taking trips from the mainland via John O'Groats and South Ronaldsay. The local population is relatively small. Visitor numbers peak during the summer months and decline in the off-peak winter months, where inclement weather can also make visiting the site difficult.

The Skara Brae visitor experience

A purpose-built visitor centre was opened at Skara Brae on 1 April 1998 at a cost of £1.3 million. It is located just outside the WHS buffer zone, near Skaill House which is situated next to the site (see Figure 3). It houses a five-minute audio-visual presentation, a museum with many of the original artefacts found on the site, an exhibition area, an interactive exhibit where visitors can try to build a model of a Neolithic house from blocks, and five touch-screen computer stations. There are also educational facilities. The old interpretation centre at Skara Brae can be used for educational visits by prior arrangement. In keeping with other Historic Scotland sites, pre-booked educational visits are free of charge. A schools pack is available and can be used by teachers before and during visits. A limited events programme is run from the visitor centre. A series of ranger tours and activities run from this and other sites within the Heart of Neolithic Orkney WHS. A replica Neolithic house (see Figure 4), opened in July 1998, is connected to the interpretation centre, with paths across the grass to Skara Brae itself. The purpose of the replica is to allow people to experience the space and layout of one of the houses without damaging the resource.

Figure 4: The replica house. Photo credit: Jim Schlater

The visitor centre has been awarded a 5* VisitScotland grading plus a Gold Green Tourism Business Scheme award. The site is open all year round (Historic Scotland, 2008c) and has a magnificent setting next to the sea, though the exposed nature of the site makes it a bracing environment at some times of the year. There are some external interpretation boards on the monument, with duty staff at peak times. The site is linked to the nearby Skaill House, which was opened to visitors in 2001 in an attempt to spread visitors around the site. This is Orkney's finest mansion and was built in 1628 for the Bishop of Orkney. It operates a joint-ticketing arrangement in peak months and is closed in the off-peak months. Coastal walks lead out from the site to Yesnaby or Stromness, although these are not developed to any great extent.

There is a small retail outlet on the Skara Brae site, where visitors may purchase guidebooks, Explorer tickets (see below) and general Historic Scotland memorabilia. There is also access to retailing opportunities through the extensive Historic Scotland on-line shop, where videos and CD-Roms of Skara

Brae may be purchased and advance-ticket purchases made. There is a café in the visitor centre that is open year round, but no on-site accommodation is available. Approximately 50% of the site is wheelchair accessible. Wheelchair access to the visitor centre and replica house is straightforward, with ramped access and all exhibitions and services being on one level. Access to the site itself is 400 metres from the visitor centre and can be managed by wheelchair or for those with limited mobility.

Summer admission charges in 2009, comprising a joint ticket with nearby Skaill House, were £6.90 for adults and £4.10 for children. Concessional tickets for the over 60s cost £5.50 while the under-5s entered for free. Winter admission charges (comprising Skara Brae only) were £5.90 for adults, £3.50 for children, £4.70 for concessions and free for the under 5s. There is an Orkney Explorer Pass available for visits to all staffed Historic Scotland sites on Orkney, although this is only available from April through to October, as some sites close in the winter months. General 'Explorer' tickets may be bought for three- or seven-day periods, allowing free access to all HS sites visited during the nominated period. Tickets may be purchased on-site or in advance via the Historic Scotland website. Members of Historic Scotland and English Heritage are entitled to free access to the site.

Management issues

Any discussion of visitor management at Skara Brae needs to be set within the context of the site itself, with its association with the nearby Skaill House (see Figure 5) and also in terms of the role it plays within the wider Heart of Neolithic Orkney WHS.

Visitor access

Visitor access to the original settlement site has been gradually restricted over time due to the concerns about the damage that visitors can cause. Visitors are therefore no longer able to access the site buildings directly, although until recently they were still allowed to walk along the wall heads. Various efforts have been made over the years in order to try to manage physical access, including buttressing of the wall heads, paving of the narrower parts of the paths and erecting handrails at critical points, although there are still some exposed drops. These measures have not always prevented visitors from occasionally falling into the houses, so action was taken in 2006 to prohibit visitors from walking on the wall heads at all, restricting them to a set path around the perimeter of the settlement site (see Figure 6). In order to protect the best-preserved house from the elements, a toughened glass roof was constructed over it. This has now been replaced with a solid structure in order to provide more stable environmental conditions within the house.

Figure 5: Relationship between Skara Brae and Skaill House. Photo credit: John Findlay

Figure 6: A vsitor to Skara Brae on the set path. Photo credit: John Findlay

Visitors have therefore found themselves progressively distanced from the central focus of site: the prehistoric houses themselves. This has undoubtedly reduced visitor satisfaction for some people. For example, a contributor to a BBC 'blog suggested that "the magic and the mystery of a visit to Skara Brae in the 1950s and 1960s are gone ... it is no longer a place of freedom and exploration and the village is now so full of protective roofing, walkways, fences and buttresses that it can be difficult to discern 3000BC from 2000AD". While the construction of the replica house is clearly intended to help to mitigate this effect and allow visitors a close-up physical experience with the site, it can be argued that this is not a realistic substitute in terms of providing a truly authentic, close-up visitor experience. Plans have also recently been made to install a camera inside one of the houses so that it can be viewed from the safety of the visitor centre. This will be doubtless be of benefit to disabled visitors and to those who do not wish to venture outdoors in inclement weather, but it may be unrealistic to imagine that every visitor will be happy with this arms-length experience.

Monitoring is being undertaken to establish the extent to which visitors walking around the site are affecting the resource. It is important also to recognise that visitors are not the only source of impacts on the resource. For example, recent studies suggest that the site is vulnerable to erosion due to its coastal location (see Figure 7), with salt crystals being suspected of causing damage to the stones. Visitors are clearly only one piece of the overall jigsaw.

Figure 7: Coastal erosion at the Skara Brae site. Photo credit: Jim Schlater

People congestion

People congestion at Skara Brae can be a problem, particularly at peak times when the site can easily reach full capacity. The pattern of visitation to the site is highly seasonal, as it is for many Scottish visitor attractions, and this results in periods of intense activity which not only create additional pressure on the fabric of the site but can also negatively affect the visitor experience, for example when visitors have to compete with each other to see the exhibits properly. A particular issue is that many visitors come on organised coach tours and these are sometimes poorly scheduled. For example, it has been common practice for the cruise companies to arrange for the coaches carrying excursionists to travel in convoy, with up to four large coaches arriving at Skara Brae at almost exactly the same time (Historic Scotland, 1998). The convoys of coaches have also led to traffic congestion around the site: there is only limited car parking for cars and coaches close to the site, and the access roads are narrow. This situation is now being addressed through working with the cruise companies to ensure a more efficient scheduling of coach arrivals and departures. Such measures have proven hard to put into practice, however, as the cruise operating companies are based on the Scottish mainland and tend not to use local guides. WHS staff members are also liaising with the local tourist guide association in order to try to even out the distribution of visitors on days when the cruise ships are expected to be in port.

While it is recognised that cruise passengers bring important economic benefits to Orkney, the Orkney Islands Council aspires to increase quality tourism rather than the numbers of people passing briefly round the island. The Heart of Neolithic Orkney WHS Management Plan also seeks to emphasise quality tourism, to encourage tourists to stay longer in Orkney and to increase visitor spending (Historic Scotland, 2001). This will, of course, require that Orkney is able to keep improving the visitor experience: people will only pay more for their visit if they believe they are getting a higher-quality product, and visitor congestion can have a negative effect on people's perception of the quality of the visit. Part of the solution, it is argued, is to achieve a more evenly spread distribution of visitors around the many tourist attractions that Orkney has to offer. However, while some specific sites, such as the Broch of Gurness, could readily accommodate more visitors, others clearly cannot without risking damage to the resources concerned. The overall strategy must therefore be to accept fewer visitors but to attract those who are willing to spend more money per person. This implies a strategy of focusing on quality rather than volume.

Visitor congestion could also be reduced by encouraging visitors to explore all of various sites which make up the Heart of Neolithic Orkney WHS, rather than just the more well-known ones (those being Skara Brae and Maeshowe, a spectacular chambered tomb build around 5,000 years ago). Other components of the WHS include the Barnhouse Stone, a three metre-tall monolith located almost a kilometre from Maeshowe; the Standing Stones O' Stenness, an early example of a stone circle, and the Watchstone, a monolith standing over five metres tall located near the Bridge of Brodgar; and the nearby Ring o' Brodgar, one of the most impressive and best-preserved henges in the British Isles. Efforts have recently been made to spread visitors around the entire WHS; for example the ranger service, which is based at Skara Brae, offers regular guided tours of the other sites.

In terms of Skara Brae specifically, it is notable that visitors tend not to venture very far away from the site in order to see it in its wider context, but to stay close to the visitor centre and the Neolithic village itself. The visitor centre has been successful in allowing visitors to be better informed about the site's resources and encouraging less-damaging behaviour. It also acts as an alternative to visiting the site for some visitors not wishing to access the weather-exposed site. However it can be argued that it also serves to concentrate visitors in one place. Furthermore, coach tour itineraries do not always allow visitors very much time at the site, which means that they do not have the opportunity to explore much further than the visitor centre and the replica house.

Conclusions

Visitor management is clearly a critical issue for Skara Brae and this case study illustrates a number of important issues in devising and implementing an effective visitor management strategy. The first relates to the need to take a joined-up approach. Indeed, there are several reasons why visitor management at Skara Brae cannot be considered in isolation from the wider tourism offer of the Orkney. The site is not managed by a single authority (even though in many respects Historic Scotland takes the lead) but by a consortium of organisations, each of which has specific interests and responsibilities in terms of protecting the site and managing access to it. This implies that they must work together in order to ensure that their efforts are complementary rather than contradictory. It is also notable that Skara Brae did not receive WHS designation in its own right but as part of a multi-site designation involving several other prehistoric sites on the main island of Orkney. WHS designation requires that each site has an effective Management Plan, which should include consideration of visitor management. In case of the Heart of Neolithic Orkney WHS, of which Skara Brae is but one part, this has meant developing a Management Plan for the site as a whole. Such plans are inevitably more complex, as they need to take account of the needs of each constituent site as well as the WHS as a whole. On the other hand, a particular benefit of the multi-site approach is that policy makers and planners are forced to consider the site as a single entity, which gives the various sites that make up the Heart of Neolithic Orkney WHS a considerably higher profile in land-use decisions, applying for funding for conservation and visitor education work from various sources, and so on.

This leads on to a second important issue illustrated by this case study, which is the frequent need to disperse visitors around and between sites in order to reduce visitor pressure. Overcrowding of sites is a common phenomenon and arises for a number of reasons, including temporal variations in demand (over the course of each day and the year as a whole) and supply-side factors, such as the itineraries of coach tour operators in the case of Skara Brae. The result is the capacity of the site to receive visitors is over-reached, resulting in the increased risk to physical damage occurring to the site, the safety of visitors being compromised and, importantly, the quality of the visitor experience being reduced. In the case of Skara Brae, one step that has been taken has been to work with the cruise ship companies in order to rationalise their excursion schedules in order too avoid too many visitors arriving at the site at the same time. A number of initiatives have also been put into place to try to disperse visitors to other parts of the WHS site and to other tourist sites in Orkney.

A third major issue illustrated by this case study is the difficult relationship between the desire to allow open visitor access and the need for effective conservation measures to be put in place to protect the site. These demands are often seen as contradictory: visitors are often a source of pressure on the physical resources of the site, so that restricting visitor access is seen as entirely compatible with conservation priorities. It is notable that visitors have been progressively required to retreat from the actual Skara Brae site over the years. Various measures are being used in an attempt to compensate for the reduced physical access to the site, for example the provision of a full-scale replica house and the introduction of a remote-control camera. There is also a range of state-of-the-art interpretive materials available in the purpose-built visitor centre. These are intended to help visitors to understand and better appreciate what they are looking at, albeit from an increasing distance. Yet while this approach has a clear rationale from a conservation perspective, it is important to recognise the potential impact this may have on the visitor experience, particularly if visitors are no longer able to experience the 'magic' of this very special place. WHS status requires that sites not only secure the physical protection and conservation of the site but also ensure that it is presented to the public in an effective manner by allowing them access to it, and by providing suitable education and interpretation. Clearly this is a difficult balance to attain.

References

A. B. Associates Ltd. 2010. *Orkney Visitor Survey 2008/2009: Final Report.* http://www.orkney.gov.uk/Files/Council/Publications/2010/OrkneyVisitorSurvey_2009_FinalReport.pdf

British Tourist Authority. 1996. *Visits to Tourist Attractions 1995.* London: BTA.

Fyall A, Rakic T. 2006. The future market for World Heritage Sites. In Leask A, Fyall, A (eds). *Managing World Heritage Sites,* Oxford: Elsevier; 159-176.

Garrod B. 2008. Managing visitor impacts. In Fyall A, Garrod B, Leask A, Wanhill S. (eds). *Managing Visitor Attractions: New Directions,* 2nd Ed. Oxford: Elsevier; 165-180.

Highlands and Islands Enterprise. 2005. *Orkney Enterprise Visitor Survey.* Kirkwall: Orkney Enterprise.

Historic Scotland 1998. *Nomination of the Heart of Neolithic Orkney for Inclusion in the World Heritage List.* http://whc.unesco.org/en/list/514/documents/

Historic Scotland. 2001. *Management Plan for Heart of Neolithic Orkney World Heritage Site.* Edinburgh: Historic Scotland.

Historic Scotland. 2008a. http://www.historic-scotland.gov.uk/neolithic-orkney

Historic Scotland. 2008b. *Heart of Neolithic Orkney World Heritage Site Management Plan 2008-13* http://www.historic-scotland.gov.uk/orkney-management-plan-foundation.pdf

Historic Scotland. 2008c. http://www.historic-scotland.gov.uk/index/places/propertyresults/propertyoverview.htm?PropID=PL_244&PropName=Skara%20Brae%20Prehistoric%20Village

Historic Scotland. 2009. *Commercial Review of 2008-2009.* http://www.historic-scotland.gov.uk/hsb-commercial-review-june09.pdf

Johnston I. 2003. Damage fears may force heritage body to slash visitor numbers to Skara Brae, *Scotland on Sunday,* 31 August 2003.

Shackley M. (ed.) 2006. *Visitor Management: Case Studies from World Heritage Sites,* Oxford: Butterworth-Heinemann.

Shackley M. 2006. Visitor management at World Heritage Sites. In Leask A, Fyall A. (eds). *Managing World Heritage Sites*. Oxford: Elsevier; 83-93.

UNESCO. 2008. http://whc.unesco.org/en/list/514

VisitScotland. 2008. *Visitor Attraction Monitor 2007* www.scotexchange.net/vam2007-2.pdf

VisitScotland. 2010. Visitor Attraction Monitor 2009 www.visitscotland.org/pdf/visitor-attraction-monitor-2009.pdf

Ancillary Student Material

Further reading

Feilden B, Jokilehto J. 1998. *Management Guidelines for World Cultural Heritage Sites*, 2nd Edition. Rome: ICCROM.

ICOMOS. 1993. *Tourism at World Cultural Heritage Sites: The Site Manager's Handbook*. Madrid: WTO.

Leask A, Fyall A. 2007. Special Issue: Managing World Heritage Sites. *Journal of Heritage Tourism* **2** (3): 131-238.

Leask A, Fyall A. 2001. World Heritage Site designation: Future implications from a UK perspective. *Tourism Recreation Research* **26** (1): 55-63.

Leask A. 2006. World Heritage Site designation. In Leask A, Fyall, A (eds). *Managing World Heritage Sites*. Oxford: Elsevier; 1-19.

Related websites and audio-visual material

The following websites offer background information on the Skara Brae site, the Heart of Neolithic Orkney WHS and Orkney in general. In addition there is a range of sources for further material on WHS designation. The key resources also include those listed in the reference section of the case study.

Historic Scotland www.historic-scotland.gov.uk

Orkney Tourism Group http://www.orkneytourism.co.uk/

UNESCO (2008) http://whc.unesco.org/

VisitOrkney http://www.visitorkney.com/

Self-test questions

Try to answer the following questions to test your knowledge and understanding. If you are not sure of the answers then please refer to the suggested references and further reading sources.

1   Who manages Skara Brae Prehistoric Village and what does this mean for the management approach taken onsite?

2   Who are the key partners involved in the management of Skara Brae?

3   What forms of interpretation are used at Skara Brae and how do these contribute to the visitor experience?

Key themes and theories

The key themes raised in the case study relate to the following areas:

♦   Heritage site management

♦   World Heritage Site designation

♦   Visitor management

♦   Partnerships in visitor attractions management

The key theories relate to:

♦   Effective management of heritage visitor attractions

♦   World Heritage Site designation as a management tool

♦   Visitor management and interpretation

♦   Issues associated with the implications of public agency ownership

♦   Collaborative working in visitor attraction and destination management

If you need to source further information on any of the above themes and theories, then these headings could be used as key words to search for materials and case studies.

   Scan here to get the hyperlinks for this chapter.

5

Tourism, Climate Change and Carbon Management:

Three Case Studies

Stefan Gössling and Brian Garrod

Introduction

The tourism sector is highly dependent on the use of fossil fuels and is a substantial contributor to global emissions of greenhouse gases (GHGs) as a result. Cross-sector comparisons demonstrate that tourism is one of the most energy-intensive sectors of the world economy (e.g. Patterson and McDonald, 2004; Perch-Nielsen, Sesartic and Stucki, 2010). Tourism is estimated to account for around 5% of global emissions of CO_2, the most important GHG in terms of its overall contribution to global warming (UNWTO, UNEP and WMO, 2008). If emissions of other GHGs (such as nitrous oxides) and the radiative forcing associated with emissions of water vapour by jet aircraft[1] are included in the calculation, tourism's estimated contribution to global warming increases to between 5.2% and 12.5% (in 2005; see Scott, Peeters and Gössling, 2010). Aviation is the most significant tourism sub-sector in terms of its contribution to climate change, accounting for 40% of tourism's overall CO_2 emissions. This is followed by motor cars, accounting for another 32%, accommodation (21%), tourism activities (4%) and other transport including cruise ships (1.5%) (UNWTO, UNEP and WMO, 2008).

Tourism's 5% share in world CO_2 emissions has been termed 'non-negligible' by prominent global organisations (UNWTO, UNEP and WMO, 2008). At the same time, other organisations, notably some the world's major airlines, have argued that the share of GHG emissions attributable to aviation is actually comparatively small in global terms. Regardless of the perspective

---

[1] The emission of water vapour from jet engines leads to the formation of linear contrails and aviation-induced clouds (AICs). The range in the above estimate is attributed primarily to uncertainties regarding the role of AIC in trapping heat (Lee, Fahey, Forster, Newton, Wit, Lim, Owen and Sausen, 2009).

one takes, however, one thing that is widely agreed upon is that the importance of the tourism and transport sector is likely to grow considerably in the future. Based on a business-as-usual scenario for 2035, which considers changes in travel frequency, length of stay, travel distance and technological efficiency gains, UNWTO, UNEP and WMO (2008) estimate that CO_2 emissions from tourism will increase by 130% compared to 2005. Even higher figures have been presented by the World Economic Forum (WEF, 2009). Aviation will remain the most important contributor, with emissions expected to grow by a factor of two to three. This growth becomes even more relevant given the global climate policy goal of seeking to achieve emission reductions the order of 50% of 1990 emission levels by 2050, corresponding to the target of not overshooting 2°C global average warming by 2100 (UNFCCC, 2010). Figure 1 highlights the conflict between CO_2 emissions growth from tourism on the one hand and emission reductions as envisaged under global climate policy on the other. Including aviation's non-CO_2 contribution to global warming would heighten this conflict even further.

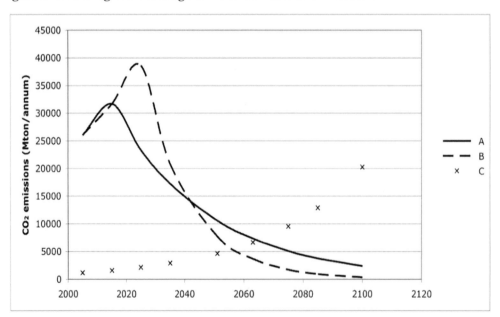

Figure 1: Global CO2 emission pathways versus unrestricted tourism emissions growth. *Source:* Scott *et al.* (2010)

Lines A and B represent emission pathways for the global economy under a -3% per year (A) and -6% per year (B) emission reduction scenario, with emissions peaking in 2015 and 2025 respectively. Both scenarios are based on the objective of avoiding a +2°C warming threshold by 2100 (for details see Scott *et al.*, 2010). A business-as-usual scenario in tourism, taking into account current trends in energy efficiency gains, would lead to rapid growth in emissions from the sector (C). By about 2060 the tourism sector would account for emissions exceeding the emissions budget for the entire global economy (intersection of line C with line A or B).

Achieving emission reductions in tourism in line with global climate policy will consequently require considerable changes in the tourism system, with reductions in overall energy use and a switch to renewable energy sources (e.g. UNEP, OU, UNWTO and WMO, 2008). However, as outlined by Gössling (2010), there is also a range of alternative arguments that support a rapid transition towards low-carbon tourism systems, including: (i) the ethical dimensions of tourism's contribution to climate change, i.e. global warming-related deaths and loss of biodiversity; (ii) the tourism sector's vulnerability to climate change in terms of loss of physical assets and other detrimental changes in the environment and socio-economic systems; (iii) increasing energy costs associated with 'peak oil' or, put another way, the current energy inefficiency of the sector and its potential to save energy, thereby reducing operational costs; (iv) growing customer expectations towards greener operations; and (v) the increasingly evident need for long-term strategic planning, where climate change will ultimately make it necessary to re-think business models irrespective of the mitigation[2] pathways chosen.

Failure to take action on saving energy and reducing emissions is therefore not a viable option for tourism businesses. Carbon management, i.e. efforts to reduce energy use and emissions, will have to be supported through technology change, management, policy, behavioural change, education and research (Gössling, 2010). Given the unwillingness of large parts of the tourism industry to act, government policy, including regulation, taxes and incentives will probably be the most important of these measures, and there is evidence that politicians are ready to move forward in this direction in many parts of the world (OECD and UNEP, 2011). An adaptive strategy for industry would adopt a pre-emptive approach to policy developments and seek to take advantage of the benefits associated with carbon management.

The following sections outline examples of business approaches to carbon management that have reduced energy use and GHG emissions while simultaneously leading either to significant economic savings or to other financial

---

2   The term 'mitigation' refers in this context to actions taken to reduce GHG emissions. It can also involve increasing the capacity of 'carbon sinks' (which are natural resources that are able to sequester carbon). Mitigation strategies are commonly contrasted with 'adaptation' strategies, which involve society taking measures to cope better with the effects of climate change as they become increasingly apparent.

and non-financial benefits (such as greater customer or employee loyalty). Ideally, the case examples included here would consider aviation, which is by far the most important component of tourism in terms of GHG emissions. Currently, however, there appear to be no airlines that are pro-actively engaging in carbon management. Arguably, therefore, the environmental credentials currently communicated by some airlines should be viewed as discursive strategies to forestall governmental action and convince customers that technological solutions are actively being developed (Gössling and Peeters, 2007). Considerable opportunities also exist to address the GHG emissions of tourism's second most energy-intensive sub-sector, motor cars. The manner in which cars are used in tourism is, however, potentially more relevant than technological progress; there is evidence, for instance, that buyers of cars using less fuel tend to drive more (Gilbert and Perl, 2008). Consequently, cars are only indirectly covered in the following case studies (in terms of modal shift[3]). What follows therefore focuses on other parts of the tourism sector where carbon management can be considered to be a realistic strategy. We begin with a discussion of the potential of carbon footprinting in the accommodation sector.

Six Senses: Carbon audits to reduce emissions

Six Senses is a management and development company operating under the brand names 'Soneva', 'Six Senses', 'Six Senses Sanctuary' and 'Evason', as well as 'Six Senses Spas' and 'Six Senses Private Residences'. Its spas and resorts are located in six countries: the Maldives, Thailand, Vietnam, Oman, Jordan and Spain. In 2009, the company operated 26 resorts and 41 spas with a total of 1,200 rooms and 3,700 employees (Six Senses, 2010). Six Senses has the corporate ambition of having a net-zero carbon footprint in 2010 and to become a net sink of emissions by 2020.

Six Senses began to pursue this goal by first undertaking a carbon audit. This ultimately resulted in the development an online carbon calculator that can be adapted to each of the chain's resorts or spas, enabling them to calculate their own carbon footprint at a particular point in time. In addition to CO_2 emissions, the calculator also covers emissions of methane (CH_4) and nitrogen oxide (N_2O). It weights CO_2 from aviation with a factor 1.9 to account for additional radiative forcing from this component of the customer's trip. The Six Senses' carbon footprint inventory covers the following 'scopes':

---

3   This term refers to the switching by travellers from one mode of transport to another, for example from cars to public transport.

- ◆ Scope 1: Direct carbon emissions from sources that are owned by the resort or spa.

- ◆ Scope 2: Indirect carbon emissions from the generation of purchased electricity.

- ◆ Scope 3: Indirect carbon emissions that occur as a result of the activities of the resort or spa, but from sources not owned or controlled by that resort or spa.

The results of the inventories of nine resorts show that the largest share of emissions is associated with production and consumption outside the resort/spa, particularly air travel, which accounted for a minimum of 76.4% of carbon emissions (Six Senses, 2009). In the case of the Evason Phuket resort, with its 260 rooms, air travel actually accounted for 93.8% of all emissions, corresponding to 67,112 tonnes of CO_2-eq[4]. Most of the remaining emissions (4.5%) were the result of electricity generation.

As an innovative strategy, Six Senses also used resort-specific data for benchmarking purposes, comparing emissions by scope, by revenue and by guest night. The results were also compared with benchmarks from other companies that publish their emission records, including Marriott International, Scandic Hotels and Whitbread. Through these comparisons, considerable differences in emissions were identified, varying for instance between 0.46 tonnes CO_2-eq and 1.66 tonnes CO_2-eq per guest night within the Six Senses resorts. On a revenue basis, even greater differences were identified. Measured as the emissions implied in generating US$1 million in revenue, the range was from 93 tonnes CO_2-eq to 490 tonnes CO_2-eq per US$1 million (see Table 1).

The carbon footprint data were also used to identify energy avoidance, substitution and efficiency measures, with return of investment times ranging between six months and ten years (see Table 2). While these results indicate a huge potential for retro-fitting, even greater potential savings can be realised when low-energy management is made a priority before a hotel is constructed. For instance, if diesel-driven generators (see Figure 2) can be avoided, a standard 150-room hotel in the tropics could avoid fuel use in the order of 5,000 litres per day, along with concomitant reductions in emissions. Overall, the case study has shown that the accommodation sector has potential to achieve significant emission reductions, often at negligible or even negative cost (see also Bohdanowicz, 2009; Gössling, 2010).

---

4   GHGs vary in their potential to cause global warming but tend to be emitted in combination with each other. The carbon dioxide equivalent (CO_2-eq) of a GHG is calculated by multiplying the weight of emissions of the gas in question by its global-warming potential relative to that of CO_2.

Table 1: Carbon footprints of nine Six Senses properties

Property	Revenue (US$ million)	CO_2-eq per US$ million, Scope 1-2	Guest nights	CO_2-eq per guest night. Scope 1-2	CO_2-eq per guest night. Scope 1-2
Soneva Fushi	23.3	177	37,458	0.11	0.66
Soneva Gili	16.9	191	24,632	0.13	0.82
Six Senses Samui	8.5	252	26,913	0.08	0.69
Six Senses Yao Noi	5.9	325	17,427	0.11	1.66
Six Senses Ninh Van Bay	7.5	274	22,884	0.09	1.47
Six Senses Zighy Bay	14.5	490	31,474	0.23	1.36
Evason & Six Senses Hua Hin	9.3	454	113,636	0.04	0.46
Evason Ana Mandara Nha	7.2	93	48,504	0.01	0.79
Evason Phuket	10.8	326	109,365	0.03	0.61

Source: Six Senses (2009)

Table 2: Return on energy-efficiency investments by Six Senses Evason Phuket

Project	Investment Cost (US$)	Annual Savings (US$)	Payback period
Energy monitoring system	4,500	10% energy costs	-
Mini chiller system	130,000	45,000	2.8 years
Heat recovery system	9,000	7,500	1.2 years
Laundry hot water system	27,000	17,000	1.6 years
Energy-efficient lighting system	8,500	16,000	< 6 months*
Water reservoir	36,000	330,000	< 1 month
Biomass absorption chiller	120,000	43,000	2.8 years
Medium-voltage electricity cables	300,000	-	10 years**

  *   Not including the longer lifespan of the light bulbs

  **   Other benefits include less radiation, less power fluctuation, reduced fire risk and im-
       proved aesthetics

Source: Six Senses (2009)

Figure 2: Diesel-driven generator to produce electricity (Seychelles). Photo credit: Stefan Gössling

Fritidsresor, Sweden: Transport modal shifts

Tour operators are key actors in the development of sustainable tourism because they have considerable influence on the destinations chosen, as well as the average length of stay of tourists. Both are key factors in average per-tourist, per-trip emissions. As outlined by various authors, the engagement of tour operators in contributing to low-carbon tourism has so far remained limited. It has further been suggested that tour operators are, in fact, responsible for the observed growth in travel distances by marketing cheap mass holidays based on air travel (e.g. Timothy and Ioannides, 2002). Swedish company Fritidsresor, part of the Touristik Union International (TUI) group, is no exception in this regard. For instance, the group heavily marketed the Maldives in Sweden in 2008 based on the slogan "the dream is just nine hours away". At roughly the same time, however, Fritidsresor also launched its 'Blue Train', which took travellers from Sweden all the way to Lake Garda or Cinque Terre in northern Italy, involving journeys of more than 20 hours by train, covering distances of up to 1,500 km.

Initially, there was great interest in the Blue Train among Swedish holiday-makers. In 2007, the company offered just 80 tickets for sale as an experiment, expecting no great demand, but received sufficient interest to increase the number of tickets available to 800. These sold out within a few days. In the following year around 5,000 passengers travelled from Sweden to Italy on the Blue Train. However, in 2009 traveller numbers fell to only 2,500. The company attributed this to the increasing number of direct-flight connections available in Sweden, particularly by the low-cost carriers, which offered prices that were hard to compete with.

The experience of the Blue Train does, however, demonstrate that if only travellers could be persuaded to use trains rather than air transport, and to take short-distance holidays rather than travelling to long-haul destinations, then there would be considerable reductions in GHG emissions. As a rough calculation, a journey by the Blue Train from Stockholm to northern Italy would lead to emissions in the order of 73 kg of CO_2 per return trip per traveller. The same trip by air would imply emissions of 346 kg of CO_2, thereby involving more than four times the CO_2 emissions per traveller. A return trip to the Maldives, meanwhile, would cause about 1,780 kg CO_2 per traveller, implying an emissions a factor more than five times greater than the trip from Sweden to northern Italy by air on a per-trip basis and nearly 25 times greater than the journey by the Blue Train. Given that Fritidsresor sells more than half a million package holidays involving air travel each year, any strategic management approach that focused on closer destinations that could be reached by train or car would make a considerable difference in overall emissions. This highlights the critical role that tour operators have to play in carbon management.

The initial demand for the Blue Train also shows that it is actually possible to achieve significant modal shifts in tourist transport. Train travel over distances of up to 2,000 km may actually be a realistic alternative to air travel. There is plenty of room for manoeuvre to achieve this in many countries. For example, the market share of train passenger transport in Switzerland and Japan is around 20%, while in the USA it is only about 0.3% (UNWTO, UNEP and WMO, 2008). Convincing tourists to use trains and other public transport to travel to their destination will nevertheless require considerable changes in the way these transport systems are currently managed. For instance, complicated booking procedures, particularly when travelling between countries, high prices in comparison to air travel, often considerable delays, the need to change connections frequently, capacity constraints and the low service orientation of most public transport providers (Figure 3) remain major obstacles to significant modal shifts. Passengers on the Blue Train had to change trains twice on their outbound journey: once in Malmö or Lund in Sweden and then again in Munich in Germany. Travellers may also require special amenities, such as compartments with shower and toilet facilities and play areas for children and – on top of all of this – they will also want to be charged competitive prices. This, however, may rather mean that direct and indirect subsidies to airlines need to be reconsidered by policy makers, as these are the root cause for the comparably low cost of air transport.

Figure 3: Travellers waiting in line to buy train tickets. Photo credit: Stefan Gössling

Carbon 'Foodprints': Carbon management in the foodservice sector

Food production and consumption are key issues in climate change because agriculture accounts for more than 10% of anthropogenic[5] GHG emissions (Smith, Martino, Cai, Gwary, Janzen, Kumar, McCarl, Ogle, O'Mara, Rice, Scholes and Sirotenko, 2009). In addition to this are impacts associated with the processing, packing, transportation, retail and preparation of food. Tourism is an important component of food consumption because it is estimated that some 200 million meals per day are prepared and consumed by tourists (Gössling, Garrod, Aall, Hille and Peeters, 2011). This, in turn, implies that foodservice providers[6] operating in the tourism sector have a significant potential to mitigate climate change through the use of carbon management practices. A wide range of foodservice providers operate in the tourism sector, including hotels, restaurants, cafés, bars, diners, aircraft, trains, cruise ships, ferries, fast-food outlets and street stalls. These operations are all very

---

5   The term 'anthropogenic' refers here to GHG emissions that are directly the effect of human activity.

6   This case study focuses on carbon management decisions on the part of foodservice providers. Many meals are, of course, prepared by tourists themselves in self-catering accommodation.

different, so carbon management strategies will need to be tailored to particular enterprises. However, for all foodservice providers it is possible to divide carbon management strategies into three groups: those that relate to the purchasing of foodstuffs, those that relate to the preparation of food and those that relate to how the food is presented to customers.

Purchasing

Food purchasing strategies have a significant potential to reduce the GHG emissions associated with food in tourism. If it is possible to select only ingredients that have a relatively small carbon footprint as they enter the foodservice provider's establishment, then clearly the carbon footprint of any meals that are prepared from such ingredients will automatically be reduced. However, while there have been a number of studies that have attempted to estimate the carbon footprint of various foodstuffs, these do not provide simple selection criteria for foodservice providers because they tend not to be calculated on an equivalent basis (Gössling *et al.*, 2011). Making food purchasing decisions on the basis of these figures is thus fraught with difficulty and mistakes can easily be made, resulting in foodstuffs with a relatively large carbon footprint being purchased in error. There are also a number of important complications in comparing the carbon footprints of various foodstuffs, including the mode of transport that is used to deliver them and seasonality considerations. Box 1 demonstrates these complications with respect to the purchase of tomatoes.

Box 1: Tomato tales: Why buying locally doesn't always make sense

Imagine a hypothetical tourism foodservice provider based in Sweden, a hotel perhaps. Imagine further that the purchasing manager could buy tomatoes grown in unheated greenhouses in Spain or tomatoes grown in heated greenhouses locally in Sweden. Table 3, which is based on carbon footprinting studies that have been conducted in various countries, shows that tomatoes grown in Spain have the lower carbon footprint per kilo of tomatoes; much lower than that associated with tomatoes grown in Sweden.

The GHG intensity of foodstuffs of course depends on a number of factors other than whether they are grown in heated or unheated greenhouses, including other features of the production method used (such as the use of fertiliser and pesticides), soil productivity or even the farmer's farming expertise. This at least partly explains why the GHG intensity of tomatoes grown in heated greenhouses varies according to whether they are grown in Sweden, the UK and Denmark[7]. However, it would be difficult to imagine that these factors alone could make up the considerable difference in the figures shown in Table 3. The heating of greenhouses clearly has a major effect on the footprint of the tomatoes and buying tomatoes grown in unheated greenhouses is the best purchase decision in terms of the impact of climate change.

Table 3: GHG intensity of tomatoes, production on farms

Country of origin	kg CO_2-eq/kg tomatoes
Spain (unheated)	0.456
Sweden	7.20
UK	33.00
Denmark	19.10

Source: Gössling et al. (2011)

Introducing transportation into the calculation can, however, complicate matters considerably. This is because the GHG emissions of transport will vary according to the mode of transport used. If, for example, the tomatoes were to be flown by aircraft from Spain to Sweden, it would be quite possible that the additional GHG emissions associated with the transport method could raise the GHG intensity of tomatoes grown in unheated greenhouses in Spain to above the GHG intensity of tomatoes grown in heated greenhouses in Sweden. This would reverse the situation, making locally grown tomatoes the best purchase in terms of their contribution to global warming, even if they are grown in heated greenhouses.

Table 4 demonstrates, however, this is not the case in our example. The GHG emissions associated with flying tomatoes from Spain to Sweden is only 1.77 kg CO_2-eq per kg of tomatoes. Adding this to the GHG emissions involved in producing the tomatoes, the total is still less than that associated with growing tomatoes locally in Sweden in heated greenhouses. Moreover, if the tomatoes are transported by overland methods, then the logic of importing tomatoes grown in unheated greenhouses from Spain is even stronger. Table 4 shows the GHG emissions involved in transporting tomatoes from Spain to Sweden. Adding these to the GHG intensity of producing the tomatoes on the farm (shown in Table 3) clearly finds in favour of the Spanish tomatoes rather than tomatoes grown locally in Sweden.

---

7   While every effort has been made to ensure that the figures are comparable, for example by standardising the system boundaries used, there is undoubtedly also some measurement error implied in the figures, which may also account for some of the difference.

Table 4: GHG emissions involved in transporting tomatoes from Spain to Sweden

Transport method	km shortest route Madrid to Stockholm	kg CO_2-eq/kg tomatoes
Aircraft	2,446	1.77
Truck	3,137	0.98
Train	Approx. 3,100	0.047

Source: Adapted from Gössling et al. (2011)

Much also depends on local transport patterns. If, for example, the tomatoes are grown in Sweden on a large number of small, widely distributed farms, then taken to a central warehouse and then redistributed to a large number of widely dispersed foodservice providers, then the transport-related GHG intensity of those tomatoes will be accordingly greater. Under such circumstances it might even make it optimal to import tomatoes from Denmark or even the UK that have been mass produced on a single, larger farm and then exported directly to the foodservice provider's premises in Sweden.

Figure 4: Buying directly from the farm makes sense when the food products are in season. Photo credit: Stefan Gössling

Introducing seasonality into the calculations complicated matters still further. The above calculation only applies when tomatoes are in season in Spain. In terms of the GHG emissions involved, it usually makes better sense to buy vegetables and fruit locally when it is in season (see Figure 4). At times of the year when the food is out of season, however, the decision is more complex. Tomatoes grown out of season in Spain need to be grown in heated greenhouses, just as they are in Sweden. Such tomatoes will tend to be more GHG intensive because of the energy required to heat the greenhouses they are grown in, and the difference in their GHG intensity compared with tomatoes grown in Sweden using under the same conditions will narrow as a result. When we add in the GHG implications of transporting the tomatoes from Spain, even by train rather than by truck, this could increase the GHG intensity of Spanish tomatoes higher still, perhaps resulting in them being more GHG-intensive than tomatoes grown locally in Sweden out of season when the additional GHG impacts of transporting them are also factored in to the calculation. In these circumstances it would make more sense to purchase the tomatoes locally.

This example is only hypothetical. The situation today is that tomatoes are rarely grown in Sweden any more, since heating greenhouses leads to uncompetitive price levels. On the other hand, there has been considerable progress in greenhouse technology, with plastic foils rather than glass being used for better insulation. This, in turn, could help to extend the season for growth of tomatoes in unheated greenhouses. The example does show, however, that purchase decisions can be complicated. Errors are easily made.

While purchasing decisions can be made on the basis of GHG intensity, it is often hard to determine the best purchasing choice due to complications associated with the transport mode used to deliver the food and seasonality considerations. Further complications arise when the preparation and presentation stages enter in to the equation, as these may make a significant contribution to the carbon footprint of the meal that is ultimately served to the tourist. The choice of ingredients for a meal may therefore not be as critical as decisions about how it is prepared and presented to the guest. It is also likely that the foodservice provider has more control over these stages of the foodservice provision process. The foodservice provider may therefore be better advised to focus on these considerations when attempting to reduce their carbon footprint.

Preparation

The most important considerations in terms of the preparation of meals relate to the choice of components and the management of waste. A good first step for foodservice providers is for them to examine the different components used in making each of the dishes on their menu and to identify which of those have the greatest GHG intensity. These components can then either be replaced in the dish by others that have a lower GHG intensity or the dish can be removed entirely from the menu and replaced by another which does not use the GHG-intensive component. In this way, the consumer's choice is shaped by what is available for them to choose from the menu: a process sometimes known as 'choice editing'. An example of this is the decision by Scandic, a major European hotel chain, to remove prawns entirely from their menu. Prawns are a highly GHG-intensive food, mainly because of the use of large amounts of fuel by the vessels used to catch them. Prawns are also increasingly being farmed and this has led to the destruction of large areas of mangrove to make way for aquaculture developments. This, in turn, has led to GHG emissions as the mangrove forests are no longer available to serve as carbon sinks (Gössling, 2010). Scandic has made the decision to serve crayfish in the place of prawns. Crayfish has a lower GHG intensity and does not involve the destruction of mangrove forests. Scandic reports that it has seen no negative impact on its business as a result.

Waste during the preparation process can also be a major factor in determining the carbon footprint of a tourist's meal. Substantial amounts of food waste are created in the kitchens of foodservice establishments, implying that good food – perhaps even purchased because of its low GHG intensity – is being thrown away. Often this is completely unnecessary, for example waste may occur in the form of food trimmings or supplies that have not been used and have either physically perished or simply gone past their use-by date. A good first step for foodservice providers to reduce this waste, and hence their overall carbon footprint, is to plan their purchases more carefully by collecting statistics on customer numbers and the amounts of different kinds of food served to different types of guests. For example, if it is known that the party arriving for dinner comprises pensioners rather than a teenage sports team, then the kitchen staff could be made aware of this fact and asked to prepare meals according to their expected preferences. It would, of course, be better not to prepare food in advance at all but only as it is ordered. However, this is not possible in the busy kitchens of many foodservice establishments. Purchasing high-quality food can also help to increase its shelf life, making it less likely that the food will be thrown away by the kitchen staff on quality grounds.

Presentation

Presentation refers to the way in which the food is served to the establishment's guests. The presentation of food has major implications for the purchasing choices and the preparation of meals, so this may actually be a very good place for the foodservice establishment to start in attempting to reduce its carbon footprint.

An example of the complexity involved in the presentation of food is the use of buffets rather than table service. Buffets are a popular way of presenting meals to guests, especially breakfasts, because they tend to be less labour-intensive. Guests also often like buffets because they have a wide range of choice (see Figure 5) and they have a chance to see what the food looks like before they choose it. However, observational evidence suggests that serving meals buffet-style may encourage guests to fill their plates with more food than they want to eat, resulting in more left-over food. There is also evidence that buffet guests also tend choose more GHG-intensive and otherwise environmentally problematic food items than they would normally eat at home, notably meats, shellfish, milk products and fruit juices, while the overall amount of food eaten is larger than at home.

Figure 5: A standard hotel buffet offers about a 100 components. Photo credit: Stefan Gössling

There are a number of techniques that could, however, be used to reduce the carbon footprint of buffets, perhaps even making them more GHG efficient than table service. Box 2 illustrates the practices adopted by the Maritim proArte Hotel in Berlin in this respect.

Box 2: Reducing the footprint of the hotel buffet

The Maritim proArte Hotel, Berlin, serves around 140,000 breakfast guests and another 300,000 lunch, dinner and banquet guests per year. The restaurant offers two breakfast buffets side by side: a 'conventional four-star' buffet with around 100 food items and an alternative 'organic' breakfast buffet with only 52 items on it, identified by the German 'Bio' label for organic food. The 'organic breakfast' is hence implicitly marketed as a healthier, more environmentally friendly and higher-quality breakfast for guests to choose. While organic food is not necessarily more climate-friendly than conventional foodstuffs, there are a number of additional benefits associated with organic produc-tion, including less use of pesticides and improved working conditions for growers (see Gössling et al., 2011). Furthermore, the organic buffet uses only foods that are in season: for example, it only uses strawberries from late April to the end of June, even though strawberries could easily be imported for use throughout the year.

The hotel also seeks to reduce wastage from both of its buffets by using smaller plates, with a diameter of only 26 cm. Meanwhile, the serving dishes set out on the table only have a capacity of only around 10 portions. This helps to avoid guests 'overloading' their plates with food. Guests can always go back to the buffet table a second time if they want more of the dish in question and members of staff are trained to monitor the serving dishes and refill them regularly. All items of food are served in small portions, again with the aim of avoiding leftovers.

A number of technical problems were encountered in establishing the organic buffet, including the tendency for organic food suppliers to trade in units much smaller than those needed by a hotel the size of the Maritim proArte. The lack of reliability of organic supply chains was also sometimes been a problem, resulting in certain organic foods not being available for a period of time. A further problem was that the price of some organic food components proved to be very high in comparison with conventional alternatives. For example, purchasing organic poultry cost the hotel three times more than conventional poultry. The price of organic food was, on average, some 10% to 15% more expensive than the conventional equivalents. These additional costs could not be passed on the guests for fear of negative price increase perceptions.

The hotel used a number of strategies to address these implementation problems. First, the organic element of the buffet was introduced not immediately, but gradually over time, in order to avoid a sudden increase in purchase costs. Secondly, dishes were cho-sen that used moderately more expensive organic ingredients, rather than those with a high price differential such as poultry. When organic poultry was bought, it was used in combination with much cheaper ingredients, such as to complement salads. This kind of strategic planning helps to spread the cost burden of purchasing organic food.

Despite these implementation difficulties, it was apparent that customers appreci-ated the organic buffet, perceiving it to represent a significant 'add on' to the product offer, matching their demands for a healthier lifestyle and a lighter footprint on the planet. Very few negative comments have been received by the hotel management. The reduced profit margin on organic foods might therefore be expected to be at least partly offset by the additional business that the hotel receives as its reputation as a pro-environmental establishment continues to grow.

Figure 6: Lower emissions? A B&B standard-served breakfast: Less food will be consumed, but potentially more thrown away.
Photo credit: Stefan Gössling

Conclusions

Most tourism organisations do not seem to perceive their energy use or level of GHG emissions to be important issues in their strategic management. Yet, as we have seen, there are many good reasons to engage with energy use and GHG emissions as key business issues.

♦ First, there are potential financial savings to be made through carbon management. The case study of Six Senses, for example, demonstrates that there may be considerable 'low-hanging fruit' available for tourism organisations to harvest as regards cost savings. The case study shows that a number of energy-efficiency investments in just one of their resorts – Six Senses Evason Phuket – had payback periods of mere days and months, rather than years or even decades, as would normally be the case with business investments. Indeed, if these energy-efficiency projects had been located within the conventional realm of business decision making, it is likely that they would have long ago been identified and already undertaken. This highlights the importance of bringing carbon management into the mainstream strategic remit of the tourism organisation.

♦ Second, it is clear that there are also a wide range of non-financial benefits to be captured through the application of carbon management strategies. While the decision to introduce an organic buffet by the Maritim proArte hotel in Berlin implied increased costs (the cost of Bio-labelled organic foodstuffs being typically 10% to 15% higher than conventional alternatives), the management of the hotel considered these additional costs to be acceptable in view of the extra business that the enhanced reputation of the hotel was likely to bring. Embracing carbon management could also lead to benefits such as greater customer loyalty, lower insurance costs, favourable conditions on bank loans or new opportunities for co-operation in sustainable business networks.

♦ Third, it is clear that the downside for actors not engaging in energy management will take the form of rising operating costs as world prices of fossil fuels continue to rise. Such organisations will find it increasingly difficult to compete effectively in the global market place. They will also face a rising burden of compliance with climate policy, which will only become more demanding in years to come. As the policy context becomes increasingly characterised by climate-change-based regulations, taxes and incentives, organisations that minimise their carbon footprints will also be limiting their exposure to such pressures.

♦ Fourth, and perhaps most significantly, consumer preferences are changing. While consumers may not be willing to pay a supplement to purchase a low-carbon alternative to their product – indeed many will not even understand what this is – consumers increasingly expect the products they buy to be 'environmentally friendly'. Organisations which catch this particular wave of consumer expectations are more likely to capture and retain market share. Arguably, then, effective carbon management strategies need to be seen not an optional 'add on' for today's tourism organisation but as an indispensable component of its business strategy.

The case studies also show that changing consumer behaviour is by no means an impossible task. The case study of Fritidsresor's 'Blue Train', for example, suggests that it is possible to achieve a substantial shift in tourists' travel-mode choices, provided that the incentives can be made right. The present policy context makes it very difficult for overland transport to compete with air transport but such barriers are not insurmountable. If the pattern of incentives faced by tourists is modified, then there seems to be a latent demand among tourists for low-carbon travel alternatives. Changes to the policy context would reveal this demand and enable it to be met.

References

Bohdanowicz, P. 2009. Theory and practice of environmental management and monitoring in hotel chains. In Gössling S, Hall CM, Weaver D. (eds) *Sustainable Tourism Futures: Perspectives on Systems, Restructuring and Innovations*. London: Routledge; 102–130.

Gilbert R, Perl A. 2008. *Transport Revolutions: Moving People and Freight without Oil*. Earthscan: London.

Gössling S. 2010. *Carbon Management in Tourism: Mitigating the Impacts on Climate Change*. Routledge: London.

Gössling S, Garrod B, Aall C, Hille J, Peeters P. 2011. Food management in tourism: Reducing tourism's carbon 'foodprint'. *Tourism Management* **32** (3): 534-543.

Gössling S, Peeters P. 2007. "It does not harm the environment!" An analysis of discourses on tourism, air travel and the environment. *Journal of Sustainable Tourism* **15** (4): 402-417.

Lee DS, Fahey DW, Forster PM, Newton PJ, Wit RCN, Lim LL, Owen B, Sausen R. 2009. Aviation and global climate change in the 21st century. *Atmospheric Environment* **43** (22-23): 3520-3537.

OECD, UNEP (Organisation for Economic Co-operation and Development, United Nations Environment Programme). *2011. Sustainable Tourism Development and Climate Change: Issues and Policies*. Organisation for Economic Co-operation and Development and United Nations Environment Programme (UNEP). OECD: Paris.

Patterson M, McDonald G. 2004. How clean and green is New Zealand tourism? Lifecycle and future environmentmal impacts. *Landcare Research Science Series* 24. Lincoln, Canterbury, New Zealand.

Perch-Nielsen S, Sesartic A, Stucki M. 2010. The greenhouse gas intensity of the tourism sector: The case of Switzerland. *Environmental Science & Policy* **13** (2): 131-140.

Scott D, Peeters P, Gössling S. 2010. Can tourism deliver its 'aspirational' greenhouse gas emission reduction targets? *Journal of Sustainable Tourism* **18** (3): 393-408.

Six Senses. 2009. *Carbon Inventory Report*. Evason Phuket 2008-2009. Six Senses Resorts & Spas, Bangkok, Thailand.

Six Senses. 2010. About us. www.sixsenses.com/corporate/document/company_profile.pdf

Smith P, Martino DI, Cai Z, Gwary D, Janzen H, Kumar P, McCarl B, Ogle S, O'Mara F, Rice C, Scholes B, Sirotenko O. 2009. *Agriculture*. In Metz B, Davidson OR,

Bosch PR, Dave R, Meyer LA. (eds) *Climate Change 2007: Mitigation*. Contribution of Working Group III to the Fourth Assessment Report of the Intergovernmental Panel on Climate Change, Cambridge and New York: Cambridge University Press; n.p.

Timothy DJ, Ioannides D. 2002. Tour operator hegemony: dependency and oligopoly in insular destinations. In Apostolopoulos Y, Gayle D.J. (eds) *Island Tourism and Sustainable Development: Caribbean, Pacific, and Mediterranean Experiences*, Westport: Praeger.

UNEP, OU, UNWTO, WMO (United Nations Environment Programme, Oxford University, United Nations World Tourism Organization, World Meteorological Organization). 2008. *Climate Change Adaptation and Mitigation in the Tourism Sector: Frameworks, Tools and Practice*. UNEP, Oxford University, UNWTO, WMO, Paris: UNEP.

UNWTO, UNEP, WMO (United Nations World Tourism Organization, United Nations Environment Programme, World Meteorological Organization). 2008. *Climate Change and Tourism: Responding to Global Challenges*, Madrid: UNWTO. www.unep.fr/shared/publications/pdf/WEBx0142xPA-ClimateChangeandTourism-GlobalChallenges.pdf

UNFCCC (United Nations Framework Convention on Climate Change). 2010. Report of the Conference of the Parties on its fifteenth session, held in Copenhagen from 7 to 19 December 2009. http://unfccc.int/resource/docs/2009/cop15/eng/11a01.pdf

World Economic Forum. 2009. *Climate Policies: From Kyoto to Copenhagen*

Ancillary Student Material

Further reading

Becken S. 2004. Harmonising climate change adaptation and mitigation: The case of tourist resorts in Fiji. *Global Environmental Change Part A* **15** (4): 381-393.

Becken S, Hay J.E. 2007. *Tourism and Climate Change: Risks and Opportunities*, Channel View: Clevedon.

Gössling S, Borgström Hansson C, Hörstmeier O, Saggel S. 2002. Ecological footprint analysis as a tool to assess tourism sustainability. *Ecological Economics* **43** (2-3): 199-211.

Gössling S. Peeters P, Ceron J-P, Dubois G, Patterson T, Richardson R.B. 2005. The eco-efficiency of tourism. *Ecological Economics* **54** (4): 417-434.

Hall CM, Higham J. (eds) 2005. *Tourism, Recreation and Climate Change*, Channel View: Clevedon.

Hunter C, Shaw J. (2007). The ecological footprint as a key indicator of sustainable tourism. *Tourism Management* **28** (1): 46-57.

Patterson T, Bastianoni S, Simpson M. 2006. Tourism and climate change: Two-way street, or vicious/virtuous circle? *Journal of Sustainable Tourism* **14** (4): 339-348.

Peeters P. (ed.) 2007. *Tourism and Climate Change Mitigation: Methods, Greenhouse Gas Reductions and Policies*. Breda: Colofon.

Yeoman I, McMahon-Beattie U. 2006. Understanding the impact of climate change on Scottish tourism. *Journal of Vacation Marketing* **12** (4): 371-379.

Related websites and audio-visual materials

United Nations Environment Programme (UNEP). Climate Neural Network: Hospitality and Tourism:
http://www.unep.org/climateneutral/Topics/TourismandHospitality/tabid/151/Default.aspx

United Nations World Tourism Organization (UNWTO) Climate Change and Tourism:
http://www.unwto.org/climate/index.php

World Meteorological Organisation (WMO) Tourism Sector:
http://www.wmo.int/pages/themes/climate/applications_tourism.php

Self-test questions

Try to answer the following questions to test your knowledge and understanding. If you are not sure of the answers the please refer to the suggested references and further reading sources.

1   Why is tourism an important issue for global warming? Why is global warming an important issue for tourism?

2   In addressing tourism's impact on climate change, what is the fundamental difference between mitigation strategies and adaptation strategies? Which strategy is the better one to adopt?

3   Given that aviation contributes such a large share of tourism's greenhouse gas emissions, why should we bother developing mitigation strategies in other tourism sub-sectors such as accommodation?

4   What are the benefits to a tourism company of taking a proactive approach to reducing its greenhouse gas emissions?

5   What are the principal barriers to a tourism company successfully developing and selling a low-carbon variant of their product?

6   What is the best way for a tourism foodservice provider to minimise its carbon footprint?

Key themes and theories

The key themes raised in this case study relate to the following areas:

♦   Tourism's contribution to climate change.

♦   The rationale for adopting a proactive approach to addressing tourism's global-warming impact.

♦   Tools and techniques of carbon management in tourism.

♦   Challenges of implementing carbon management strategies in tourism organisations.

The key theories relate to:

♦   Causes and effects of global climate change.

♦   Measuring the carbon footprint of an organisation or activity.

♦   Using carbon auditing in organisational decision making.

♦   Travel modes and encouraging a modal shift in tourism transport.

♦   Food management strategies with respect to purchasing, preparation and presentation strategies.

♦   Benefits and challenges of carbon management in tourism.

If you need to course further information on any of the above themes and theories then these headings could be used as key words to search for materials and case studies.

Scan here to get the hyperlinks for this chapter.

6

Slow Travel:

European Cycle Tourism

Janet Dickinson and Les Lumsdon

Introduction

The last ten years have seen the emergence of the term 'slow travel'. Based partly on the philosophy of the 'slow' movement, the term has been used by the academic community, the media, tourism guidebooks, tour operators, web communities and tourists to describe a different approach to tourism. The basic premise of slow travel is to travel more slowly, engage more fully with the places visited and show greater concern for the environment. For example, Lumsdon (2010, p.6) describes it as follows:

> "[Slow Travel] does not fit neatly into the image that comes to mind when you skip through the pages of a glossy holiday brochure. It's a way of travel that demands a different approach. Slow travel frees you, so that you can see more, talk with people and see what's going on ... Most of all, it is about time. In its crudest sense, you are trading in distance for time. You might cover less ground but what you get is far richer. With slow travel there's no need to bag tourism trophies, no advantage in notching up mile after mile and no hard sell package to keep up with as the week passes by. It's just a matter of relaxing more and getting closer to culture and nature at the places you visit. That closeness brings a really satisfying feeling. It is also a desire to be released from constraints and those day to day responsibilities so as to be more responsive to what comes along".

As a new approach, however, the concept of slow travel is far from consistent in its application and in many respects slow travel is nothing new at all. After all, those who took part in pilgrimages or some form of 'Grand Tour' in past times were slow travellers, not only by necessity but also in their mindset. The key difference in the 21st century is the advancement in transport technology, enabling rapid movement between places. This is re-enforced by the tendency of tourism providers to market tourism on the basis of distance, speed of travel and fastness, which are promoted as the ideal way to consume time and tourism. Slow travel, rather like slow food, represents an antidote to these tourism offerings, many of which have grown in an era of cheap oil and heavy consumption of other resources.

In its various guises, slow travel has the potential to reduce the greenhouse gas (GHG) emissions of tourism through less dependence on air and car travel, not only for journeys to and from the destination but also for travel within the destination. This presents a significant opportunity for the tourism sector to contribute to addressing the global challenge of climate change. Given the immediacy of this challenge, the purpose of this case is to examine the potential for slow travel to make tourism practices more sustainable. The example of European cycle tourism is used to develop this argument, focusing particularly on EuroVelo, a network of long-distance cycle routes spanning Europe. These routes provide an opportunity for tourists from the major urban areas of Europe to take cycling holidays in destinations near to their homes. The EuroVelo network is coordinated by the European Cycling Federation and is currently still in the making. However, some parts of the network utilise long-standing routes, such as the Danube Cycle Route in Austria and Germany. Long-distance cycle routes attract hundreds of thousands of cycle tourists every year and illustrate to good effect the appeal of slow travel: the journey is the thing. This case will examine slow travel as a new form of sustainable tourism that addresses some of the issues raised by previous approaches and analytical frameworks, such as 'ecotourism'.

Slow travel

Slow travel is an idea that has emerged from user communities, be they individual tourists, communities embedded in the wider 'slow movement' or tour operators promoting a different travel experience. Drawing on the principles expounded by the slow movement, these communities aim to do things at a slower speed, adopt different attitudes towards time and the use of it, and emphasise quality over quantity (Peters, 2006). Most interpretations of slow travel, though by no means all, also include the desire to address the environmental externalities of travel.

There are thus two broad interpretations of slow travel. The first focuses on encouraging long stays in one location. This perspective is predominantly aligned with the slow food movement and focuses on tourists immersing themselves in the destination they are visiting, remaining in the vicinity of their accommodation base and staying for longer periods of time. This is a destination-based interpretation of slow travel that ignores the tourist's outward and return journeys to and from the destination. It is exemplified by several North American web communities and tour operators promoting rental accommodation in Europe (e.g. Slowtravel, 2011). There are various benefits of longer stays, including some overall reduction in GHG emissions per day of stay. However, this perspective largely ignores the environmental impacts of travel and, in the case of North American visitors to Europe, is often dependent on, and linked to the promotion of, long-haul flights.

As a strategy to address climate change by offering a sustainable tourism option that addresses the core element of transport, the second interpretation of slow travel focuses on the journey as well as the destination. It offers much potential as a means to sustainable tourism, with an emphasis on gaining rich travel experiences as well as avoiding resource-intensive flights at the core of its approach. For some proponents, this also includes avoiding car use, as the car is associated with significant environmental externalities, especially GHG emissions. This latter approach represents a more holistic interpretation of slow travel, in which travel is as integral to the tourist experience as is the destination-based experience: neither is superior or subordinate to the other.

Slow travel therefore represents a re-appraisal of tourism as the consumption of leisure. It is about taking time to enjoy the journey, to absorb places en route and to engage with other people and places. It also represents a re-appraisal of the environmental context of tourism. In the past, tourism impact analysis has tended to focus predominantly on the destination environment. Recent analysis of climate change has, however, re-evaluated where the major impacts lie. This indicates that travel is a key problem for the tourism industry, from which most of its GHG emissions are derived (Becken and Hay, 2007). Slow travel therefore provides the environmentally concerned traveller, tour operator or destination with a lower-carbon alternative, without the loss of demand that is typically associated with other proposed forms of sustainable tourism.

The slow travel concept has been explored in depth elsewhere and for further examination the work by Dickinson and Lumsdon (2010) is recommended. However, a useful summary is provided by a conceptual framework of slow travel as a whole tourist experience. The core explanation is cited as follows:

> "It is a holistic idea that embraces both destination-based and travel experiences. More than this, it especially resituates travel as a fundamental part of tourism. As such, it facilitates tourist engagement with multiple places en route, as well as at the destination, with a growing environmental consciousness. Slow travel also recognizes the essential

sociability of tourism. A re-evaluation of modal choice emerges from the core ingredients, but equally, as with a low-carbon outcome, modal choice might be the main motivation for some" (Dickinson and Lumsdon, 2010: 191).

Figure 1 considers the context, ingredients and outcome of slow travel. The context is the whole tourist experience that includes the travel to, back from and around the destination area. Thus, it is worth re-stating that both the destination experience and travel experience are integral to slow travel. There are thus four core features to slow travel:

1 Slowness – the art of taking time to engage with the experience is important in slow travel. It can include periods of inactivity. This is derived from the slow movement perspective that slowing down enhances quality of life.

2 The experience itself – tourists co-produce their experiences, involving their friends, family, strangers, places and tourism services, including travel. The 'travel glance', for example, is generated by a tourist when on the move and is more often than not enjoyed in the company of others. This conceptual element is an extension of Urry's tourist gaze (see Urry, 2002, for a full explanation) and refers to the tourist's moving view of places during travel.

3 Locality – this refers to the consumption of experiences more locally. It is a reaction against extensive destination-based travel. It requires a re-focusing on the more simple pleasures to be found by immersion in the local environment. Thus, a core idea of slow travel is that proximity counts: proximity to other people, to the landscape, to the ways in which local people go about their everyday lives.

4 Environmental consciousness – this represents environmental concerns and how they might be addressed through slow travel. Slow travellers, for whom environmental concerns are core, have been termed 'hard slow travellers'. Others, who may welcome the associated environmental benefits but choose slow travel for other reasons, have been referred to as 'soft slow travellers' (Dickinson and Lumsdon, 2010).

People travel in order to accomplish tourism and the travel mode is often an ancillary outcome constrained by the options available for the chosen destination. However, tourists can chose a particular travel mode for a tourist experience and thus travel mode can also be a driver of slow travel, as illustrated by the two-way arrow in Figure 1. In this context, hard slow travellers choose low-carbon modes in order to reduce their carbon footprint. Soft slow travellers are seemingly less committed to using more sustainable forms of transport. Nevertheless, low-carbon tourism is, in both cases, an outcome of slow travel. This is essential if slow travel is to fulfil a useful role as a new form of sustainable tourism.

Slow travel interfaces with a wide range of travel modes. Indicative examples of slow travel include: travel by rail or coach (long-distance bus in the US) to destinations, rather than by air; touring regions by coach, bus or train; overland travel mixing a variety of modes of transport; cycle touring; and long-distance walking tours. It might also involve water-borne travel, such as by canoe or kayak, or the use of animals such as horses, donkeys or horse-drawn camping trailers. Slow travel may be organised as a package or independently.

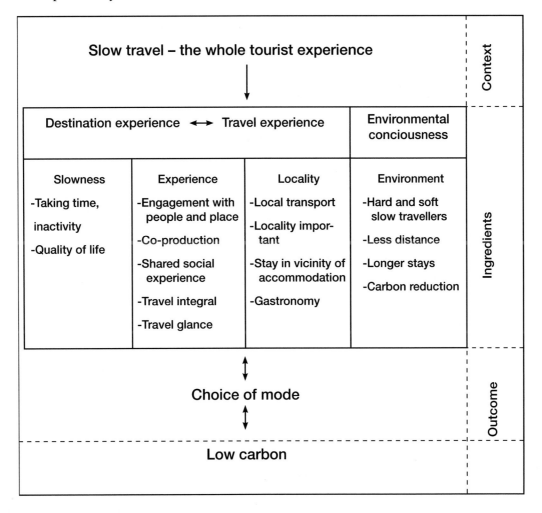

Figure 1: Conceptual diagram of slow travel. *Source*: Dickinson and Lumsdon (2010)

European cycle tourism

European cycle tourism provides a good example of slow travel, since it is very much about the travel experience but equally embraces a carbon-neutral travel mode. It is important to note that cycling can be both a means of transport and a tourist activity; it can be used as a method of travel to and from a destination but it also facilitates destination-based travel experiences such as casual day cycle rides, where tourists travel by other means to reach the destination. Cycle tourism can involve either of these patterns. The tourists may travel to the destination by other transport means, bringing their cycles with them or hiring them locally, or the holiday can begin and end at home.

Integration of multiple modes of travel is often an essential element of cycle tourism, yet it can be problematic. Given the paucity of literature on this topic, examining European cycle tourism provides an opportunity to explore such problems. Furthermore, because of the direct physical involvement of participants, and because they exert greater control over their holiday in comparison to other tourists, cycle tourists are necessarily co-producers of the holiday experience (Dickinson, Lumson and Robbins, 2011). Cycle tourism provides good experiential opportunities for participants to engage with people and places, and also takes participants away from the typical tourist sites, which in turn tends to spread visitor spending. It can be independently organised or undertaken as a package tour, either guided or self-guided.

EuroVelo

EuroVelo is a network of cycle routes spanning Europe. It has been in the making for 20 years and is, as yet, still incomplete. The map (Figure 2) shows the extent of the network and its potential as a slow travel experience across the continent.

The aim of EuroVelo is "to ensure that bicycle use achieves its fullest potential so as to bring about sustainable mobility and public well-being and economic development via sustainable tourism" (European Cyclists' Federation, 2011b, n.p.). It sets out to provide a Europe-wide network of high-quality cycle routes available to tourists. There are currently 12 long-distance cycle routes covering 66,000 km. A further route, the Iron Curtain Trail, stretches from the Barents Sea to the Black Sea and is soon to be added to the network. EuroVelo includes approximately 45,000 km of cycle routes that have already been developed. The remainder of the network is currently being upgraded to meet the standards set down for international cycle tourism, for example in relation to signage, route surfaces, continuity, comfort and safety. These long-distance routes not only generate tourist trips but also facilitate cycle use by the people living in the local communities through which they pass. Some of these will be local utility trips to schools or work as well as leisure outings.

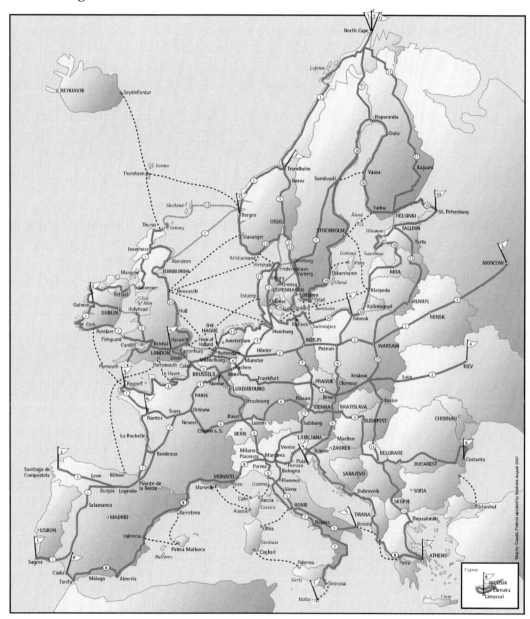

Figure 2: EuroVelo, the European Cycle Route Network. *Source*: European Cyclists' Federation (2011a).

Given the scale of the network, it is difficult to estimate total user numbers and revenues. The only current estimate is drawn from the 2009 study of EuroVelo, which estimated that the network generates €5 billion per annum: 12.5 million holidaymakers spending €4.4 billion and 33.3 million day trips adding €0.54 billion (European Parliament, 2009). The bulk of European cycle tourism is domestic (mirroring the wider tourism market) rather than international. The outbound cycle tourist markets are, however, known to be dominated by Germany and the UK. In contrast, Austria, Denmark and France are the main cycle tourist destinations (European Parliament, 2009).

In summary, the EuroVelo study estimated a total of 2,795 billion cycle tourism trips in Europe (domestic and international, including day trips), of which 25.6 million (3% of total trips generated by the EU) involved overnight stays (European Parliament, 2009). This estimate was generated by Breda University using a model which computed fractions of cycle tourism trips in relation to existing domestic and international tourism flows across the EU 27 countries plus Norway and Switzerland. Even small-scale domestic cycle routes can generate high user numbers, for example the Camel Trail in the South West of England generates over 250,000 cycle trips per annum, so the overall estimate seems plausible. Nevertheless, it should be borne in mind that the estimate is based on generalised data and thus more likely to provide a general indication rather than an accurate figure.

The slow travel experience

Slow travel does not make a clear distinction between travel and destination experiences, as the concept encompasses the whole holiday. This is applicable to cycle tourism, where cycling as a travel mode is an integral experiential element, while the destination experience incorporates travel. For cycle tourists there is often no single destination but multiple destination encounters: an important feature of slow travel. Given their intense physical involvement with the place visited and opportunities for encounters with other people en route, cycle tourists clearly demonstrate co-creation of experience (Binkhorst and Den Dekker, 2009). Co-creation refers to the growing recognition that leisure participants and leisure providers are jointly involved in the creation of experiences. The leisure provider provides the stage on which participants perform (Pine and Gilmore, 1999). Cyclists interact with the landscape through which they pass and achieve a sense of mastery over the environment. They are able to exert a high degree of control, allowing them to create unique individual experiences (Dickinson *et al.*, 2011).

Sociability is also a feature of slow travel. It is relatively rare for a tourist to be alone, most wishing to be with others in order to share a common experience. Cycle tourists may travel alone. However, most travel in small groups of family or friends. All share the route with other people passing along it. The market is dominated by independently organised holidays. However, there are packaged holidays available with a number of established operators in this area. These vary from highly structured, all-inclusive packages where tourists are accompanied by a tour guide, to more lightly packaged options where tourists cycle independently between accommodation establishments following a recommended itinerary. Packages typically offer luggage transfers, which minimises the weight cyclists need to carry with them during the day.

The slow pace of cycling enables tourists to take their time, providing an opportunity for them to recover from their everyday experiences and, in many cases, a faster pace of life. As contemporary tourism increasingly offers the opportunity to travel further, faster and more often, slow travel represents a "subversion of the dominance of speed" in our lives (Parkins, 2004, p.363). This reflects the idea that people are increasingly seeking out pauses and periods of inactivity, rather than a constant series of unforgettable experiences (Carù and Cova, 2003). A cycle tourist will cover less distance in comparison to motorised travellers. However, cycling allows participants to absorb rich experiences and to make the most of opportunities that arise unexpectedly, for example to sample local cuisine and culture: things that might otherwise be missed.

A key issue for slow travel is the journey to and back from the destination. Cycle tourists can utilise other modes of transport to reach a destination area, which they then tour by cycle. From a slow travel perspective, the travel from the tourist's place of origin to the destination area and back again is also embraced as an experiential opportunity. In the cycle tourism context, the extent to which tourists fit the pattern of slow travel depends on modal choice, level of engagement with the travel experience during the outward and return journeys, and the low-carbon outcome. Given various problems with modal integration, however, this journey may provide less than optimum conditions for the co-creation of slow travel. These problems are discussed shortly.

Low-carbon tourism opportunities

Climate change poses three issues for tourism. First, tourism is a climate-sensitive sector and will need to adapt to climate change. Second, the tourism sector is a generator of GHG emissions and there is a need for mitigation efforts to reduce emissions. Third, since the sector emits GHGs, it will be subject to policy measures and regulations aiming to mitigate impacts of climate change. Slow travel represents both an adaptation and mitigation strategy for the tourism sector.

In tourism, GHG emissions are attributed to transport, accommodation and activities. While studies vary in their estimates, there is a consensus that transport is the main contributor to GHG emissions. Peeters (2007) calculates that transport is responsible for 87% of emissions, accommodation 9% and activities 4%. From this it is apparent that transport should be the focus of climate change mitigation strategies to 'decarbonise' the tourism sector. For slow travel to provide a meaningful sustainable tourism strategy, it is evident that low carbon should be an integral concept and outcome. While some of the current interpretations of slow travel fail to grasp this, it is clear that a holistic interpretation of slow travel presents a significant opportunity for the tourism sector.

In the conceptual diagram (Figure 1), low carbon is an outcome of slow travel. Depending on the tourist motivation, low-carbon tourism may also be a core incentive for slow travel. Slow travel therefore provides a mitigation option for industry because it involves fewer GHG emissions. It also represents an adaptation strategy since is avoids fossil-fuel-intensive car and air transport that are increasingly subject to policy regulations that aim to address climate change impacts.

Cycling can be considered a carbon-neutral activity. Aside from the cyclist's increased physical activity, leading to higher food consumption, and a small carbon footprint associated with cycle manufacture and use, there is no fossil fuel use. Cycle tourism therefore provides a low-carbon tourism opportunity. Much, however, depends on how tourists access cycle tourism opportunities. If a German tourist flies from Berlin to Madrid in order to undertake a cycle tourism holiday, then the low-carbon benefit, an essential outcome of the second, more holistic interpretation of slow travel, is lost. It is unlikely, although by no means impossible, for a tourist to cycle all the way from Berlin to Madrid and back again. It is, however, feasible to travel overland by much less carbon-intensive modes than air travel, the most obvious option in this example being by train.

Therefore, while cycle tourism can be undertaken directly from home, it often depends on other modes of transport to access the destination. One of the reasons why cycle tourism is highly compatible with slow travel is that in comparison to other forms of tourism it is much less dependent on air and car travel for the origin to destination trip. There are little data available on European cycle tourists' integration with other modes or distance travelled. However, the analysis included in a European Parliament report (2009) suggests that cycle tourism generates fewer emissions compared to other forms of tourism as follows:

♦   In Germany, cycle tourists are more likely to use environmentally friendly transport modes and travel shorter distances: rail use is three times higher, car sharing to the destination is 30% lower and the air transport share is 75% lower. As a result, emissions per German cycle tourism holiday are 66% less than other holidays.

♦   In the Netherlands, data points to lower GHG emissions from cycle tourists: as much as 28% less CO_2 per holiday trip.

♦   Data from Austria and Switzerland also point towards cycling being a more sustainable form of tourist transport.

Furthermore, a study of the North Sea Cycle Route in the UK (part of the EuroVelo network), showed high levels of train and ferry use in comparison to other modes of travel to access the route (Lumsdon *et al.*, 2004).

Given that most cycle tourists will use other modes of transport, travel integration is a key concern. This is recognised by the EuroVelo network, which promotes interchange between cycling and other modes of transport (train, bus, ferry, tram) and works to improve physical interchange, fare integration and information integration (Dickinson and Lumsdon, 2010). An aspect of cycle tourism posing significant problems for integration is the carriage of cycles on public transport. Train travel with cycles has been contentious for some years. Train operators in different countries adopt different approaches and there are even differences among train operators within countries. Policy regarding booking, packaging of cycles and costs vary considerably. For example, in Germany most rail services have the capacity to accommodate cycles, but the high speed and long-distance Inter-City Express (ICE) trains, which are potentially useful for tourists, do not. The Swiss provide probably the best overall example of integrated transport provision and cycles can be carried on almost all trains. The European Third Railway Package 2007 (part of the strategy to rejuvenate the EU railways) aims to address these problems through improvements to provision for cycle carriage on trains. Long-distance coaches provide another alternative but the European network is currently relatively patchy and carriage of cycles subject to space and packaging.

There are many localised good practice examples of public transport and cycle integration. For example, in the Swiss and Italian Alps there are train carriages dedicated to cycles, which assist cycle tourists by enabling train rides with cycle carriage to valley heads, thereby avoiding steep climbs. Cycle hire at railway stations is also good practice for rail-cycle integration. However, while such destination-based examples have the capacity to improve the cycle tourist's destination-based experience, they fail to address the need to carry cycles on the origin-to-destination route.

Integration is also an issue for other modes of transport. There are widespread problems and a lack of linked-up networks, especially in rural areas. Integrated ticketing is limited and, in the EU at least, it is still not easy to book train trips that cross more than one international boundary. The Swiss provide the best example of integrated transport within Europe but elsewhere integration can be poor. Interchanges provide opportunities for slow travel experiences but much depends on the quality of opportunities available.

Given the high carbon footprint associated with tourist travel and the potential of slow travel to minimise environmental externalities, another essential consideration is distance travelled. Travel by any motorised form of transport leads to GHG emissions. For instance, coach travel is generally shown to be the most carbon efficient form of travel for tourists, in part due to high vehicle loadings (Dickinson and Lumsdon, 2010). However, as per other modes, over very long distances, the cumulative GHG emissions of coach travel inevitably become quite significant. Thus, if slow travel is to provide tourism with an opportunity to minimise GHG emissions it would need to embrace less distant travel. This suggests a need to re-appraise tourism markets and appropriate destinations. Such an adjustment is easy for the cycle tourist who, as a slow traveller, can re-consider destinations closer to home. Within a European context, it is also relatively easy for destinations and tour operators to target marketing to establish closer geographical connections between potential visitors and destinations. In other parts of the world, especially remote destinations and small islands, this strategy is not available. However, where good opportunities are available this is a sound strategy to reduce the carbon footprint of tourism. Research for the European Parliament (2009) showed that cycle tourists travel shorter distances compared to mainstream tourists (on average 1,146 km and 2,417 km respectively for a return trip).

The European Parliament study (2009, p.18-19) concludes that EuroVelo has the potential to:

♦   Enhance domestic tourism and to reduce long-distance tourist travel, thus helping greatly to curb CO_2 emissions.

◆ Encourage short-distance, cross-border tourism with minimal environmental impact and a low level of emissions.

◆ Encourage people to use public transport to travel to the destination, resulting in lower environmental impact than in the case of private cars or air transport.

◆ Re-use assets such as old railways, forest tracks and canal towpaths.

◆ Stimulate economic development in rural areas that are not prime tourist destinations.

◆ Bring about a diversification of land-based businesses to provide accommodation, attractions and food and beverage for local consumption.

◆ Offer local residents the opportunity to improve their quality of life by taking more physical exercise.

◆ Generate nearly zero CO_2 emissions by users on the route.

◆ Offer a form of slow travel which encourages interest in the richness of local gastronomy, heritage and community life across different countries and regions of the EU.

Other sustainable tourism issues

Aside from the climate change concerns relating to GHG emissions, tourism also raises a number of destination-based environmental concerns. These predominantly relate to physical impacts to natural or cultural resources. Slow travel, as per other forms of tourism, has potential to induce physical changes in the natural environment through physical presence of tourists, use of natural resources and waste. A number of studies have conducted impact analysis of cycling on specific routes or within natural areas. These studies conclude that physical impacts are generally minimal. However, cycling may be inappropriate for some sensitive environments, where even minimal disturbance can have long-lasting impacts, and should be subject to localised visitor management.

From an economic development perspective, slow travel, and especially walking and cycling, enables spending beyond the main tourism destinations. There is also less leakage (that is, loss of tourism income from local communities to international operators). Slow travellers also support local transport and may enable public transport routes to be maintained that might otherwise be financially unviable. From a social equity perspective, an essential part of sustainable development, Holden (2007) suggests more people should have access to transport resources and the ability to travel, but average travel distances should be shorter. Slow travel may go some way to addressing this dilemma in tourism.

Aligned to a further social issue, cyclists tend to be at least partly motivated by the health benefits that arise from physical activity. While most of the benefits from cycling would accrue from regular cycling for utility or leisure purposes, health is a strong motivation for cycle tourism (European Parliament, 2009). Health is high on the agenda of government priorities and while many forms of slow travel do not offer health benefits, those based on cycling and walking have some potential to contribute to national health promotion.

Conclusions

Slow travel, cycle tourism and the case of EuroVelo in particular illustrate the need for the tourism sector to take a holistic approach to the analysis of sustainable tourism. Slow travel is a relatively new idea, and the way it evolves and is implemented in practice will determine to a large extent the role it plays in sustainable tourism. The growing slow travel movement is advocating a new form of tourism but much remains to be seen regarding how this might develop. There is a pressing need for new forms of tourism that are less dependent on fossil fuel and it is inevitable that a transition will occur in the not too distant future as fuel prices increase in an era of resource scarcity.

Slow travel represents an opportunity for the tourism sector to mitigate climate change impacts while, at the same time, offer products which are appealing. In the longer term, it represents a climate change adaptation strategy, assuming that the costs of air and car travel rise in relation to those of other more sustainable forms of transport, and assuming that governments introduce other barriers to travel to reduce carbon consumption. Three possible scenarios have been suggested for slow travel during this transition (Dickinson and Lumsdon, 2010):

♦   Slow travel continues to grow as a niche market.

♦   Slow travel destinations emerge. In this scenario slow travel becomes more mainstream and destinations re-invent themselves using the slow travel 'brand'. The EuroVelo network includes destinations, such as the River Danube and Veloland Schweiz, which have considerable potential to embrace this strategy.

♦   Slow travel becomes a set of principles applied to all types of tourism.

This case study illustrates several key issues. First, there are currently competing interpretations of slow travel. This case study uses a holistic interpretation that embraces the travel to and from, as well as at the destination. There are, however, alternative interpretations that ignore the travel between origin and destination. These interpretations, while able to embrace sustainable tourism at a destination level, fail to address the global challenge of climate change since they overlook the tourism component responsible for the largest share of GHG emissions. This has been a criticism levelled at other forms of alternative tourism where the sustainable tourism development has taken a destination-centred approach, for example ecotourism developments in remote island locations. Much then depends on how the tourism sector responds to the concept of slow travel and how far its principles are embraced. If, as is the case with some operators, slow travel is seen as a means to promote cultural tours dependent on long-haul flights, then the concept will be of little value beyond being another form of 'greenwash', that is promising more than is delivered with respect to environmentally sustainable practices (Dief and Font, 2010), to sell tourism products. The conceptual framework presented has analysed a holistic perspective that considers the whole tourist experience in order to set out how slow travel might provide a new form of sustainable tourism.

The second key issue leads on from and concerns the significance of the travel from origin to destination. Currently, air and car travel represent a large share of international tourism. If tourism is to tackle the issues of global sustainability, then much of this travel needs to shift to less carbon-intensive modes. This presents a challenge to the industry to make overland travel attractive, pleasant and more feasible. Part of this challenge is improving the integration of modes and that includes making both cycling and walking tourism mainstream.

A third issue concerns how to reverse the current trend of travelling faster, further and more often. It is rarely questioned whether this is a good thing. Slow travel explicitly reflects a desire to slow down and this implies travelling shorter distances. It remains to be seen whether the tourism industry, with its remit to fulfil dreams to visit increasingly remote and exotic locations, can re-invent itself to provide fulfilling holidays closer to home. Cycle tourism and the EuroVelo network offers considerable potential to develop a wider market than currently is the case. That potential needs to be realised.

References

Becken S, Hay JE. 2007. *Tourism and Climate Change: Risks and Opportunities*, Clevedon: Channel View Publications.

Binkhorst E, Den Dekker T. 2009. Agenda for co-creation tourist experience research. *Journal of Hospitality, Marketing and Management* **18** (2&3): 311-327.

Carù A, Cova B. 2003. Revisiting consumption experience: A more humble but complete view of the concept. *Marketing Theory* **3** (2): 267-286.

Dickinson J, Lumsdon L. 2010. *Slow Travel and Tourism*, London: Earthscan.

Dickinson JE, Lumsdon L, Robbins D. 2011. Slow travel: Issues for tourism and climate change. *Journal of Sustainable Tourism* **19** (3): 281-300.

Dief ME, Font X. 2010. The determinants of hotels' marketing managers' green marketing behaviour. *Journal of Sustainable Tourism* **19** (2): 157-174.

European Cyclists' Federation. 2011a. *EuroVelo Map.* http://www.ecf.com/3188_1

European Cyclists' Federation. 2011b. *What is EuroVelo?* http://www.ecf.com/14_1

European Parliament. 2009. *The European Cycle Route Network EuroVelo.* Directorate-General for Internal Policies, Policy Department B Structural and Cohesion Policies. http://www.europarl.europa.eu/activities/committees/studies/download. do?language=en&file=26868

Holden E. 2007. *Achieving Sustainable Mobility: Everyday and Leisure-time Travel in the EU*, Aldershot: Ashgate.

Lumsdon L. 2010. *A Guide to Slow Travel in the Marches*, Logaston: Logaston Press.

Lumsdon L, Downward P, Cope A. 2004. Monitoring of cycle tourism on long distance trails: The North Sea Cycle Route. *Journal of Transport Geography,* **12** (1): 13-22.

Parkins W. 2004. Out of time: Fast subjects and slow living. *Time and Society* **13** (2-3): 363-382.

Peeters P. 2007. Mitigating tourism's contribution to climate change: An introduction'. In Peeters P. (ed.) *Tourism and Climate Change Mitigation: Methods, Greenhouse Gas Reductions and Policies.* Breda: Stichting NHTV Breda; 11-26.

Peters P. 2006. *Time, Innovation and Mobilities: Travel in Technological Cultures*, London: Taylor & Francis.

Pine BJ, Gilmore JH. 1999. *The Experience Economy*, Boston: Harvard Business School Press.

Slowtravel. 2011. *Slow Travel: Travel slowly, staying in vacation rentals (villas, farms, cottages, apartments).* http://www.slowtrav.com

Urry J. 2002. *The Tourist Gaze,* London: Sage.

Ancillary Student Material

Further reading

Dickinson JE, Robbins D. 2009. 'Other people, other times and special places': A social representations perspective of cycling in a tourism destination. *Tourism and Hospitality: Planning and Development* **6** (1): 69-85.

Dickinson JE, Robbins D, Lumsdon L. 2010. Holiday travel discourses and climate change. *Journal of Transport Geography* **18** (3): 482-489.

Downward P, Lumsdon L. 2001. The development of recreational cycle routes: An evaluation of user needs. *Managing Leisure* **6** (1): 50-60

Germann Molz JG. 2009. Representing pace in tourism mobilities: staycations, slow travel and The Amazing Race. *Journal of Tourism and Cultural Change* **7** (4): 270–286.

Gössling S, Upham P. 2009. *Climate Change and Aviation: Issues, Challenges and Solutions.* London: Earthscan.

Lumsdon L, McGrath P. 2011. Developing a conceptual framework for slow travel: A grounded theory approach. *Journal of Sustainable Tourism* **19** (3): 265-279.

Mintel. 2003. *Cycling Holidays in Europe.* London: Mintel.

Mintel. 2007. *Cycling Holidays UK.* London: Mintel.

Mintel. 2009. *Slow Travel Special Report.* London: Mintel.

Mintel. 2011. *The Evolution of Slow Travel.* London: Mintel.

Related websites and audio-visual material

Sustrans web site http://www.sustrans.org.uk/

European Cyclists' Federation http://www.ecf.com/

Eurovelo 6 http://www.eurovelo6.org/view?set_language=en

Self-test questions

Try to answer the following questions to test your knowledge and understanding. If you are not sure of the answers please re-read the case study and refer to the suggested references and further reading sources.

1   What are the core ingredients of slow travel?

2   How does European cycle tourism fit with the slow travel concept?

3   How does slow travel provide a climate change mitigation and adaptation strategy for tourism?

Key themes and theories

The key themes raised in the case study relate to the following areas:

- ◆   Carbon footprint
- ◆   The tourist experience
- ◆   Origin-to-destination travel
- ◆   Low-carbon tourism
- ◆   Cycle tourism
- ◆   Climate change mitigation and adaptation

The key theories relate to:

- ◆   Sustainable tourism
- ◆   Slow travel
- ◆   Tourist experience
- ◆   Carbon-footprint analysis

If you need to source further information on any of the above themes and theories then these headings could be used as key words to search for materials and case studies.

 Scan here to get the hyperlinks for this chapter.

NICHE

TOURISM

7

Diversification into Farm Tourism:

Case Studies from Wales

Brian Garrod

Introduction

Tourism has been a focus of diversification by farms in many countries for a considerable period of time. Indeed, Busby and Rendle (2000) note that farm-based tourism has been recognised as a distinct activity for more than a century in certain parts of Europe. Its growth has been particularly strong in the European countries (especially so in the countries of the 'New Europe'), but farm-based tourism is also increasingly evident in Canada, the USA and New Zealand (Busby and Rendle, 2000).

The growing popularity of farm-based tourism has been ascribed in large part to the changing policy context in which the farming sector of many developed countries finds itself (Walford, 2001). Agricultural policy has undergone a radical shift in emphasis over the past 50 years (Sharpley and Vass, 2006). Policies that encourage increased production, the intensification of farming and protection from market forces have been progressively replaced by those that encourage the protection of the natural environment, the use of extensive farming methods and increased exposure to the market. This has included the de-linking of farm incomes from production, as typified by the introduction of the system of single farm payments in the UK. Such major changes in policy emphasis have made it increasingly difficult for farming enterprises to survive on farming incomes alone. Recognising the danger that the countryside will become increasingly abandoned and rural landscapes neglected, governments have encouraged farm enterprises to develop a wider range of income streams. This has included, in many cases, the introduction of diversification grant schemes (Hjalager, 1996). Typically such schemes have provided a proportion of the capital costs of diversification. Pluriactivity[1] has thus become the watchword for the farming sectors of many developed countries.

---

1   Pluriactivity refers to the activity of farming in conjunction with other gainful activities, whether on-farm or off-farm.

At the same time, tourism has been viewed by governments in many developed countries as a means of addressing the problems being experienced in the countryside (Sharpley and Vass, 2006). Tourism offers a particularly attractive economic alternative for many rural areas, particularly those that are able to offer visitors the opportunity to engage in active forms of outdoor recreation such as walking, mountain biking or rock climbing, and those that possess distinctive landscapes reflecting people's perception of the rural idyll[2] (Roberts and Hall, 2001). The latter are typified by the networks of national parks and other protected areas that have been developed in many developed countries. Tourism has thus been recognised as one of the main activities into which farms can diversity.

Walford (2001) divides the factors motivating farm diversification into internal and external drivers. These forces interact to help determine the decision whether or not to diversify at any given point in time. Internal drivers could be said to include the degree of indebtedness in which the farm business presently finds itself, the age and educational status of the farmer and whether the family has children who wish to continue in the business of farming. External drivers include the general economic environment, the ease by which planning consent can be acquired, and the availability of grants and loans to assist in the diversification process.

Others have identified a wider range of factors influencing the diversification decision. Bowler, Clark, Crockett, Ilbery and Shaw (1996), for example, employ a system of 34 variables, divided into three major groups, in an empirical investigation of diversification motivations of farms in northern England. The first group, entitled 'farm business characteristics', includes variables such as farm size, land quality, tenure, livestock stocking density, farm debt, farm debt intensity (defined as farm debt per hectare), degree of dependency on hired labour and urban market access. The second group relates to the characteristics of the farmer, including age, formal education, skills and community leadership (whether the farmer holds a position in a community organisation). The third group, meanwhile, is entitled 'farm household characteristics' and includes variables such as the formal education and skills training of the farmer's spouse, community leadership by the spouse, the number of children and adults in the farm family, the amount of family labour not currently (or fully) employed and the number of institutional contacts the family have.

---

2   The 'rural idyll' is an idealised vision of the countryside based on characteristics, tangible or intangible, real or imagined, that differentiate such places from urban ones. These might include, for example, a sense of timelessness, the air of peace and tranquillity, and the maintenance of traditions and traditional values.

A further study by Ollenburg and Buckley (2007) used a questionnaire survey of farm tourism operators in Australia. Economic and social motivations were found to be of almost equal importance in explaining the diversification decision. Operators' motivations did tend to diverge, however, according to the stage of the family lifecycle the farming family was in. Thus, for some families the decision to diversify was based primarily on the desire to keep the current generation farming, while for others it was effectively a retirement strategy.

Nickerson, Black and McCool (2001), meanwhile, conduct a study of diversification into farm (and ranch) tourism in Montana. Eleven variables are identified in their study as being relevant to the diversification decision, namely: the degree of fluctuation in farming income, employment status of family members, amount of additional income, loss of government support, meeting a need in the recreation or vacation market, tax incentives, the desire to for companionship with guests, interests and hobbies related to the particular form of diversification chosen, the desire to make better use of the farm or ranch resources, degree of success in other farm or ranch enterprises, and the level of education of guests to the farm or ranch. A more recent study by McGehee and Kim (2004) tested these variables in Virginia, USA, and found them to be relevant in that context also.

Such factors do not, of course, go very far to explain what form of diversification is selected. Why should a farming enterprise choose tourism as its means of diversification? Indeed, Bowler *et al.* (1996) suggest that there are three broad responses to such stimuli: (i) scale enlargement, intensification or specialisation using conventional farm products or services; (ii) changing the production emphasis to focus on non-conventional farm products or services (such as growing flowers or energy crops), non-farm products or services (such as wind turbines or tourist accommodation) or one or more family members taking paid jobs off the farm; or (iii) winding down the farm by reducing it in scale or turning it into a 'hobby farm'. Ultimately, the latter of these options may mean retirement from farming altogether. Of course, a fourth possible response would simply be to do nothing, presumably in the hope that the current pressures will ease.

Walford (2001) argues that some farms are more likely to diversify into farm-based tourism than others. In particular, he suggests that for farm-based tourism to be attractive as a diversification strategy, the farm will need to be located either close to a large centre of population or near to a natural environment that provides attractive landscapes, a tranquil rural setting or plentiful outdoor recreational opportunities, i.e. areas that are rich in 'countryside capital'[3]. Walford (2001) then goes on to hypothesise that farm-based tourism tends to work best in locations that abound in all of these characteristics, such as national parks and other areas that are designated as having high scenic or heritage values. Indeed, his study of the spatial patterns of on-farm tourist accommodation in England and Wales finds evidence of a 'neighbourhood' effect in which such enterprises tend to be located in the buffer zones immediately surrounding these designated areas. Diversification into farm-based tourism in such areas is more prevalent because these locations are considered close enough to the designated areas to allow potential visitors easy access to them while at the same time being subject to fewer planning controls than they would be if they were actually located within the designated areas.

It might be said, however, that the preceding analysis is much more about the growth of 'tourism on farms' than it is about farm diversification into 'farm tourism' per se. Busby and Rendle (2000) distinguish between these two approaches, and indicate that many farms were making a transition from the former to the latter in the 1990s. This process has continued into the 2000s and is still relevant today. They go on to argue that the principal driver of this transition has been a shift in fundamental consumer motivation, in which the visitor increasingly recognises and anticipates the farming environment to be part of the overall tourism product. This has been accompanied on the supply-side by a reconsideration of the tourism product. Tourism on farms has almost entirely taken the form of on-farm accommodation, either in the farmhouse itself or in guest accommodation elsewhere on the farm. The approach has tended to be to provide accommodation that just happens to be on a farm. Farm tourism, meanwhile, explicitly recognises the farming context, involving a much wider range of tourism services (see Table 1), generally taking a more integrated approach to delivering them. Indeed, Busby and Rendle (2000) argue that farm tourism has often been adopted as a diversification strategy because of the potential it has to form a symbiotic relationship with farming. In such a relationship, both sides of the business stand to benefit from the presence of the other.

Busby and Rendle also argue that the incomes earned through tourism tend increasingly to outweigh those earned through farming in those farm enterprises that are in the process of transition. This, in turn, has led to increasing professionalisation of the farm tourism sector, the tourism side of the business no longer representing a source of 'pin money' for the household but an important income stream in its own right.

---

3   Countryside capital has been defined by the UK Countryside Agency as "the fabric of the countryside, its villages and its market towns". See also Garrod, Wornell and Youell (2006).

Table 1: Farm tourism elements

Attractions - permanent	Attractions - events
Farm visitor centres	Farm open days
Self-guided walks	Guided walks
Farm museums	Educational visits
Farm centres	Demonstrations
Conservation areas	**Activities**
Country parks	Horse-riding/trekking
Access	Fishing
Stile/gate maintenance	Shooting
Footpa ths/bridleways/tracks	Boating
Accommodation	**Amenities**
Bed and breakfast	Restaurants
Self-catering	Cafés/tea rooms
Camping and caravanning	Farm shops/roadside stalls
Bunkhouse barns	Pick your own
	Picnic sites

Source: Busby and Rendle (2000)

The following case studies examine the diversification strategies of two family farms in Wales: Aberhyddnant Farm near the village of Crai, and Upper Cantref Farm, which is located near to the town of Brecon. Both are located within the Brecon Beacons National Park (BBNP) and both have chosen activities that could broadly be classified as 'farm tourism' as their focus of diversification. However, their strategies are distinctly different. While the former has selected new income streams that are all linked closely to the operation of the farm and are those closely integrated with each other, the latter has adopted a strategy that is less farm-based and more loosely integrated. Both strategies have, however, been highly successful.

Aberhyddnant Farm

Aberhyddnant Farm is a family farm located near the village of Crai, just within the boundaries of the BBNP. The farm itself is some 92 hectares in size, ranging from 290 to 400m in altitude and receiving over 2.5m rainfall annually (Aberhyddnant Organic Farm, 2008). It was bought by the Matthews family in 1983. The land had been neglected by the previous owner, so the family's first priority was to bring the land back into production. In 1999 the family then began converting the farm to organic status[4]. This was achieved in 2001 with the Soil Association and certification has been maintained ever since. Recently, however, the farm has switched to the Welsh Organic Scheme. This was in recognition of the benefits of maintaining local links, being certified by an organisation that is in close touch with the needs both of farms and their customers. The farm also participates in the 'Tir Gofal' agri-environment scheme (see below). Furthermore, since 2004 the farm has operated as an organic demonstration farm, working closely with research staff from the Organic Centre Wales, which is based at Aberystwyth University.

The farm

The farm is stocked with 300 breeding ewes. This represents a considerable reduction in stock numbers compared to the time before the farm undertook organic conversion. The conversion to organic methods has made it necessary to stop turning the flock out onto common grazing land in the summer. This has implied the gradual substitution of the Brecknock Cheviot ewes with Texel crossbreeds, which respond better to such conditions. There are also 26 Murray Grey suckler cows, which calve in the spring. The calves are then sold at the local market in November and December. Since achieving organic status, the farm has adopted a small crop rotation comprising stubble turnips, whole-crop oats and red/white clover leys. These crops, together with silage and haylage grown on the farm, constitute the primary source of fodder for the livestock. This particular choice of crops not only increases the conservation value of the land, thus helping the farm to meet its commitments to the Tir Gofal scheme, but also helps to reduce worm problems in the livestock, particularly the lambs (Aberhyddnant Organic Farm, 2008).

Also on the farm is a flock of 250 laying hens and a small herd of pigs. The hens live in groups of around 50 with an organic rotation and are kept primarily to supply eggs for the farm and a local organic produce box scheme. While the pigs are ultimately on the farm for their meat, they are also used to assist in cultivation by being overwintered on land that has grown barley.

---

4   This requires the farm to be managed using methods that rely on crop rotation, natural manure, composting, mechanical cultivation and biological pest control, avoiding the use of feed additives, chemical fertilisers, synthetic pesticides and genetically modified materials. Farms in the UK must be certified with a valid certification organisation in order to sell their produce as organic. Compliance with organic standards is verified by regular on-farm inspections and there are grants available to assist with the conversion process.

There they act as natural ploughs as they root up the land, as well as enhancing soil fertility through their manure and helping to impede the growth of weeds (Aberhyddnant Organic Farm, 2008).

Nature conservation activities

The farm is part of Tir Gofal, the Welsh Assembly Government's flagship agri-environment scheme[5]. Membership has implied many changes for the way in which Aberhyddnant is managed as a farm. It has also opened up many opportunities. For example, the scheme has helped pay for the coppicing and filling of gaps in 1.5 km of hedgerows, as well as the establishment of two areas of woodland to serve as a 'shelter belt' for the farm. The family has also been able to restore two old ponds and introduce four more on the land. The scheme has also helped pay for an area of Japanese larch to be replanted with native trees, including oak, ash, alder, hazel and birch. The timber was used to build some new post-and-rail fencing for the farm, having been processed at a local timber yard, as well as providing some gateposts. Grassland on the farm is now managed sympathetically for wildlife, and rare lapwings now visit two sites on the farm. The number of hares on the farm has also increased noticeably (Aberhyddnant Organic Farm, 2008).

Diversification

While the farm remains the family's primary concern, consistent efforts have been made in recent years to diversify into educational visits, food retailing and tourist accommodation.

Educational visits

Despite being located in a rural part of Wales, where farming forms the backbone of the economy, the family found it surprising to discover how few

---

5   Tir Gofal means 'Land Care' in Welsh. There are currently over 3,000 farms in the scheme, covering over 300,000 hectares of land across Wales. The scheme offers payments to farmers who agree to put their land into the scheme for a minimum of 10 years and to manage it in ways that are beneficial to nature conservation. This includes promoting biodiversity through habitat conservation, preserving the rural character of the area by adopting appropriate land-management practices, protecting historic and archaeological features such as traditional farm buildings and field boundaries, and providing public access. Participants must take a 'whole-farm' approach by drawing up and implementing a farm-level environmental policy. Targeted capital grants and training opportunities are also provided through the scheme. From 2012, the five existing agri-environment schemes in Wales will be replaced by one overarching scheme, to be called 'Glastir'.

local children were familiar with farming practices or had ever spent time on a farm. The family therefore decided to encourage access to the farm, not only by local children but also by schools visiting the area and various adult groups. The existence of guest cottages on the farm assisted greatly in this process, insofar as there was no great capital expenditure necessary. Indeed, the guest cottages already included a large room which could be used as a meeting room, classroom or resource room, as well as toilet and hand-washing facilities. These could be used whenever the cottages were not occupied by holiday makers.

The farm's commitment to educational visits has taken on several dimensions. First, the farm took the 'education access' route within the Tir Gofal scheme, which allows the farm to specialise in managing its land for the benefit of visitors. This has resulted in visits by the local Brownie pack, visits by schools staying at study centres in the area, inclusion in the National Park's 'Guided Walks' programme and the occasional hosting of Tir Gofal training days.

The farm has also been actively working with local schools. This started by running an open evening for local school teachers to explain how the farm could be used as the basis for activities linked to various educational curricula. This had led to numerous local schools returning to look at different aspects of the farm, involving pupils from nursery age through to those studying for their 'A' levels. The farm has also hosted visits from University groups, including even a visit by a group from the University of the Third Age.

Food retailing

Since 2006, the farm has been involved in food retailing under the brand name of Crai Valley Produce. For many years prior to this, the family had sold food hampers to visitors staying in their guest cottages. Initially the food products were sourced locally but over time the family moved over to supplying the meat products and eggs themselves, while buying in most of the organic vegetables and fruit from a local vegetable box scheme. When possible, the hampers are supplemented by the addition of seasonal produce from the farm's small kitchen garden. Home-made organic preserves are also included in the hampers when possible.

This part of the business is also responsible for the organic egg production enterprise, which sells the free-range eggs to various local companies, including some of the best restaurants in the area. The family also runs a small farm shop and tea room in the nearby village of Trecastle. The village is situated on a busy road that runs along the edge of the National Park, so the shop is in a good position to pick up passing trade, both locals and tourists. The shop sells organic meat and eggs produced on the farm, as well as a selection of seasonal fruit and vegetables produced in the local area. The tea room also makes use of the farm's own meat and eggs, as well as selling Fairtrade tea and coffee.

Tourist accommodation

Two self-catering holiday cottages are available on the farm, which have both been sympathetically converted from existing farm buildings. This part of the business is known as Aberyddnant Farm Cottages. Nyth y Wennol (which means 'Swallow's Nest' in Welsh) was converted from the old dairy, where butter and cheese would have been made in the days when the farm had a dairy herd, and sleeps six adults and two infants (see Figure 1). Bryniau Pell (meaning 'Distant Hills') was converted from the cart shed and hay loft. It sleeps four adults and two infants and affords panoramic views across the National Park (see Figure 2). Groups booking both cottages also have access to Y Beudy (meaning 'The Byre' in Welsh), which provides a large space for guests to sit and eat together. There is an outside area for eating and cooking barbecues, as well as an outdoor children's play area.

Figure 1: Nyth y Wennol. Photo credit: Brian Garrod

Prices in 2011 started at £300 per week for Bryniau Pell and £345 for Nyth y Wennol in the low season, to £420 and £445 per week for the two cottages respectively in the high season. Y Beudy could be hired for £65 per week.

Figure 2: Bryniau Pell. Photo credit: Brian Garrod

The accommodation is accredited under the Green Dragon environmental standard. Accredited organisations are required to develop and implement a rigorous environmental strategy (see Box 1). Accredited organisations may then display the Green Dragon logo (see Figure 3) in order to communicate their achievement to potential customers. The drive for achieving Green Dragon accreditation has involved making a wide range of changes to the way in which the accommodation is run, including providing a range of receptacles for recycling various forms of household waste. Each cottage is also supplied with a variety of eco-friendly cleaning products. Recycled paper products are used in the cottages as a matter of course. Wherever possible, supplies are sourced locally in order to reduce the environmental impacts of their transport and to help support the local economy. Improved energy use is encouraged through the provision of wood-burning stoves in both cottages. The farm also now produces its own energy through the installation of a micro-hydroelectricity generator in the stream that runs through the farm. This provides electricity directly to the farm and surplus energy is sold back to the National Grid.

Figure 3: Green Dragon environmental standard logo

Box 1: Aberhyddnant Farm Cottages Environmental Policy

Aberhyddnant Farm Cottages form part of a working 220-acre (92 ha) organic hill farm in the Brecon Beacons National Park. The two cottages have been sympathetically converted from stone farm buildings and are managed with environmental issues in mind. The farm also has a Tir Gofal management plan which gives permissive access to paths through the farm as well as renewing hedgerows and providing streamside corridors. Visitors to the cottages are encouraged to make the most of these facilities in order to raise their awareness of the countryside and their possible impact on it.

The most important management considerations are as follows:

♦ Compliance with all relevant environmental legislation.

♦ Work towards the reduction of domestic waste by encouraging recycling and composting. Recycling facilities are provided for our guests and we would encourage our visitors to use them.

♦ Work towards the reduction of electricity consumption. Light bulbs are being changed to low energy alternatives, all radiators have individual controls and heating is on a timer.

♦ To increase awareness of the environment and the importance of farming to the countryside. Farm trails and quizzes are available for visitors and guests are most welcome to ask questions about our methods and organic farming in general.

♦ Encourage the use of local food products by visitors. Details on the availability of local and organic produce are made available prior to the guest's arrival. Continue with the Holiday Hampers scheme providing local food to visitors to the National Park. During 2008 we opened a farm shop and tea room to make it easier for locals and visitors to access local and organic food.

♦ Commitment to the prevention of pollution.

♦ Continual environmental improvement. An energy survey has been carried out and proposals made to introduce our own energy production by solar and micro-hydro systems. The micro-hydro system should be introduced during 2009.

The environmental policy will be updated annually and will be made available to all interested parties. Environmental legislation relevant to this business and our environmental improvement plan will be reviewed on a yearly basis. All appropriate documentation will be stored safely for five years.

Source: Aberhyddnant Organic Farm (2008)

Recently the farm has also implemented 'cyclists welcome' and 'walkers welcome' policies, which involve taking steps to ensure that the specialist needs of such guests are well catered for. In the case of walkers, for example, this includes the provision of a place to dry wet clothing, facilities to clean dirty walking boots, maps of the local area and public transport timetables (see Box 2). The farm even provides a luggage-delivery service, so that guests following an itinerary can have their luggage forwarded to their next destination. Comparable provisions are in place to meet the needs of cyclists (see Box 3). These provisions are similar to those included in the Walkers Welcome and Cyclists Welcome schemes currently operated by Visit Wales, the national tourism organisation in Wales.

Box 2: Aberhyddnant Walkers Welcome Statement

Aberhyddnant is pleased to welcome walkers of all abilities to stay on the farm for long or short breaks. Please find below a list of the amenities that are supplied for your use.

1   There are ample storage facilities for rucksacks etc when not being used.

2   Access to outside tap and hosepipe for washing boots etc.

3   Both cottages contain a complete first aid kit.

4   There is a pay phone for use by both cottages with numbers of emergency contacts and their location displayed above.

5   In the porch you will find a box file containing a selection of maps and reference material providing information on walking in the area.

6   The box also includes details of cycle hire shops and public transport in the area.

7   The porch/boiler room offers washing machines, a tumble drier, a boot drying area and a place to hang and dry wet coats etc.

8   Each cottage contains tea and coffee making facilities.

9   We have organic meat and vegetables for sale on the farm and we will gladly shop for you prior to your arrival for items you may require for evening meals or packed lunches.

10 We are able to take your luggage to your next location, up to 20 miles free of charge and 26p/mile thereafter. We may also arrange collection from and delivery to railway stations in the area.

11 Should you have any requirements not covered by the above, please do not hesitate to contact us.

Source: Aberhyddnant Organic Farm (2008)

Box 3: Aberhyddnant Cyclists Welcome Statement

Aberhyddnant is pleased to welcome cyclists of all kinds to stay on the farm for long or short breaks. Please find below a list of the amenities that are supplied for your use.

1   There is a lockable undercover area for safe storage of bicycles.

2   Access to outside tap and hosepipe for washing bikes.

3   An emergency repair kit is supplied for your use with items consumed being charged at cost.

4   Both cottages contain a complete first aid kit.

5   There is a pay phone for use by both cottages with numbers of emergency contacts and their location displayed above.

6   In the porch you will find a box file containing a selection of maps and reference material providing information on cycling in the area.

7   The box also includes details of cycle hire shops and public transport in the area.

8   The porch/boiler room offers washing machines, a tumble drier, a boot drying area and a place to hang and dry wet coats etc.

9   Each cottage contains tea and coffee making facilities.

10 We have organic meat and vegetables for sale on the farm and we will gladly shop for you prior to your arrival for items you may require for evening meals or packed lunches.

11 We are able to take your luggage to your next location, up to 20 miles free of charge and 26p/mile thereafter. We may also arrange collection from and delivery to railway stations in the area.

12 Should you have any requirements not covered by the above, please do not hesitate to contact us.

Source: Aberhyddnant Organic Farm (2008)

Woofers

The farm welcomes 'woofers', who are volunteers who spend time living on organic farms helping with various aspects of their work[6]. Woofers are especially welcome at lambing time, when extra pairs of hands are always

---

6   'Woofer' is the term used for people participating in WWOOF, a charity organisation which seeks to place short-term volunteers on organic farms. In the UK, WWOOF originally stood for Working Weekends on Organic Farms. It now stands for World Wide Opportunities on Organic Farms.

needed. The farm can be a particularly busy time on changeover day, when guests leave and arrive. This has recently been changed from a Saturday to a Friday, the former always being a busy day in the tea rooms and shop.

Integrated approach

One of the central features of the diversification strategy adopted at Aber-hyddnant Farm, which differentiates it from most others, is the highly integrated nature of the approach taken. The cottages were originally started as an entirely separate business but it soon became apparent that many guests were choosing the cottages specifically because they are located on a working organic farm. The family has therefore encouraged guests to explore all of the different parts of the farm. A way-marked farm trail has been developed to help guests to navigate around the land, but visitors are free to wander as they wish. Guests are also welcome to assist in various jobs around the farm, such as feeding the hens and collecting their eggs. Family members are always on hand to answer any questions visitors might have.

Indeed, the family's philosophy is that the three new business streams into which the farm has diversified – tourist accommodation, food and education – are intrinsically linked, not only to each other but also to the farming side of the business. For example, guests staying in the cottages are offered the opportunity to buy hampers containing organic meat, fruit and vegetables produced either on the farm or in the local area. This not only provides an additional market for the farm produce but it also links the cottages more effectively into the local economy and enables guests to sample various kinds of organic produce, perhaps for the first time. Guests may then be inclined to stock up with more organic food produce for the rest of the week.

Further integration is between the farm production and tourist accommodation elements of the business. Prior to 2006, when the herd of pigs was introduced to the farm, the family had been buying in bacon and sausages to sell on to the guests in the cottages. Part of the rationale for acquiring the herd was to provide more of the farm's own produce to guests, thereby keeping the production chain as short as possible. The overwhelming philosophy of the business is to achieve as great a degree of self-sufficiency as possible and the close integration of the farm's various diversification streams is a major way in which this goal is pursued. Guests are also allowed to pet the pigs, which is a popular activity for children.

Opening up the farm to school children for educational visits has also served to integrate the various business streams by generating future business for the holiday accommodation. Children will often try to persuade their parents to book a holiday in the cottages at a later date, especially if they have really enjoyed their time on the farm.

Another link between the business streams is that guests at the cottages are offered the opportunity to fish in four of the ponds that are located on the farm. These contain naturally regenerating stocks of brown trout, weighing up to 5lb. The ponds are located in some of the most tranquil parts of the farm, and are abundant in wildlife and wild flowers, providing a place of quiet contemplation not just for anglers but for guests in general. The ponds thus serve not only as part of the farm's commitment to the Tir Gofal scheme but also as a recreational resource for visitors.

As mentioned above, links have also been made between the guest accommodation and educational visits diversification streams. The cottages provide a ready-made resource for educational activities, including the provision of a large meeting room, toilet facilities and a place for people to wash their hands after touching the farm animals. The cottages are also available for overnight stays, so that the farm is able to cater for residential groups as well as day visits.

Upper Cantref Farm

Like Aberhyddnant farm, Upper Cantref Farm is a small family-run farm located in the BBNP. While the farm has maintained its conventional farming practices, it has also undertaken substantial diversification in recent times. This includes the development of a visitor attraction themed loosely around farming life and outdoor fun (see Figure 4), as well as converting a barn to bunkhouse-style accommodation and continuing the development of a riding centre that was already part of the family business.

Cantref Adventure Farm

The adventure farm side of the business comprises both indoor and outdoor activities, aimed mainly at children of primary school age. Having a mix of outdoor and indoor activities is important in the strategy of the adventure farm. Visitors need to have something exciting to do in both good and bad weather. The weather in Wales is famously unpredictable and may change from fine to foul in minutes. Cantref Adventure Farm therefore has a number of more extensive, outdoor activities for when the weather is fine. In poor weather, visitors can take refuge indoors and still be well entertained.

Figure 4: Cantref Adventure Farm and Riding Centre. Photo credit: Brian Garrod

Indoor activities include an indoor soft-play area with various climbing obstacles, ball pits and slides (see Figure 5). Adults as well as children are permitted in the soft play area, and there is a special reservation for smaller children. Some of the entertainments have a farming theme, for example there are ride-on tractors for smaller children to play on. There are also sheep-shearing demonstrations at appropriate times of the year. However, most of the activities have little or no substantial connection with farming. For example, the indoor play area also includes ball canons, worked by compressed air, and a pet-handling area. In the main visitor season there are pantomimes featuring the farm's mascot, a pantomime horse named 'Mr Ev' after the owner of the farm. Children also get an opportunity to bottle-feed lambs.

Outdoor attractions include a sledge ride, which is open to both children and adults and is billed as Europe's longest (see Figure 6), hand-propelled paddle boats and a new 'swamp ride', in which the whole family can propel themselves around a specially dug canal system using only one paddle and a series of ropes. There is outdoor play equipment for children of all ages, including trampolines and a sand pit with ride-on mechanical diggers. Soccer skills activities are also available. Again, while many activities do not have a farming theme, there are some that do. For example, there are tractor-and-trailer rides offered throughout the day, which take visitors around the farm to show them the livestock in the fields. Attendants are on duty to provide information to visitors about the animals they meet. Visitors are also invited on an early evening walking tour around the farm to help the farm staff feed them and ensure that they are safe for the night.

Figure 5: Indoor play area at Cantref Adventure Farm. Photo credit: Brian Garrod

Figure 6: The Mega-Sledge Ride at Cantref Adventure Farm. Photo credit: Brian Garrod

Another popular outdoor activity is the daily pig races, where visitors are encouraged to cheer for their favourite pig as the animals race each other around a purpose-built track. There are also special events from time to time, such as sheep-dog trials.

Visitors pay for entry to the adventure farm on a pay-one-price (POP) basis: once they have paid at the entry gate, all of the activities on the farm are free of charge. Entry prices in 2011 were £6.50 for children, £7.50 for adults and £6.50 for seniors. Discounts for families and groups were also available.

During the main tourist season, the adventure farm is open every day from Easter to the end of the autumn half-term school holidays. Out of season, opening is restricted to weekends. Throughout the month of December there is a special Christmas grotto, where visitors get a chance to meet Santa personally. There is also a mini-pantomime for guests to enjoy.

Inside the adventure farm area is a café offering a range of hot and cold food, including various home-made dishes. The cafeteria also hosts children's birthday parties. Guests at such parties are also entitled to use the indoor soft play area and pet barn free of charge. Next to the cafeteria is a small gift shop.

Cantref Adventure Farm also welcomes school groups throughout the year. Programmes of activity can be tailored specifically to the curriculum requirements of the visiting students.

Riding Centre

Cantref Riding Centre was established over 40 years ago and is an increasingly important part of the farm business. As well as offering horse-riding lessons for children and adults, the centre offers visitors the chance to go pony trekking in the spectacular landscape of the national park. Prices start at £7.50 for a 20-minute ride and rise to £50 for a full day's trekking. The centre offers treks of different levels of challenge for those with various degrees of riding experience. Rides are led by instructors and basic instruction is given before leaving the centre for those requiring it.

In the last 10 years, the centre has also begun to develop longer trail rides, lasting from three to five days in total. These are for more experienced riders and use the centre's own native horses, which are mainly Welsh cobs. Overnight accommodation is provided as part of the package, which starts at £285 per person for a two-day ride. Riders' luggage is transferred each day to the next stop. A guide accompanies each party on a variety of routes recommended by the centre.

Accommodation

The farm has also diversified into providing basic tourist accommodation (see Figure 7). Two bunkhouses have been converted from disused farm buildings, one of which can sleep up to 24 people and the other up to ten. The bunkhouses are both self-catering, although guests are encouraged to make good use of the nearby adventure farm café. The larger bunkhouse has a large room which can be used by groups as a common room or classroom.

Figure 7: Bunkhouse accommodation at Upper Cantref Farm. Photo credit: Brian Garrod

The bunkhouses are particularly popular with groups, including schools and youth organisations, which often book out one or both of the bunkhouses. However, the bunkhouses have separate bedrooms which can be booked by individuals or families. Prices in 2009 were £14 per person per night. The farm also offers camping, priced at £3.50 per person per night in 2009. Facilities are quite basic, comprising toilets, hand-wash basins and a mains water tap.

While the promotion of the bunkhouse accommodation makes it clear that it is located on a farm, guests are not invited to explore the farm or given the expectation that they can participate in particular tasks around the farm. Nor is much emphasis placed on the opportunities guests would have to visit the adventure farm or use the services of the riding centre. Rather, the main focus is on promoting the qualities of the National Park and the outdoor activities on offer, such as walking and cycling.

Overall strategic approach

The overall strategic approach to diversification taken by Upper Cantref Farm is rather different to that adopted by Aberhyddnant Farm. While Aberhyddnant has undergone conversion to organic farming, Upper Cantref continues to use conventional methods. As such, Upper Cantref Farm has not tended to encourage visitor access to the farm and, until quite recently, has not provided visitors with the opportunity to look around and explore. Access to different parts of the farm has been limited mainly to the tractor-and-trailer rides, although visitors to the adventure farm are now invited to accompany the farm staff on their evening rounds.

Recently, however, the family have also developed a walking trail around the farm. The walk takes visitors through the farm's wildflower meadow, into arable fields with wildlife habitats, and into the woodlands to see the stream and badger setts. The trail takes approximately 30 minutes to one hour to complete. While this development does begin to open up access to the farm, it contrasts sharply with that of Aberhyddnant Farm, where visitor access is a central feature of the strategy that has been taken.

Otherwise, there are surprisingly few links between the farming and adventure farm sides of the business. Indeed, few of the activities provided to tourists have a genuine link to farming, the main exception perhaps being the sheep-shearing demonstrations, the tractor-and-trailer rides and the animal-feeding sessions. It would be hard to argue that the pig racing is linked to farming, other than to concede that pigs are farm animals.

Links between the riding centre and the adventure farm are also quite limited. While the riding school is involved in providing short pony rides for children in the adventure farm at various times of the day, the adventure farm and riding centre operate essentially as separate businesses.

Links between the farm and the café are also limited. While the cafeteria offers homemade food, this does not imply that the ingredients have been sourced locally. The farm does not currently use the gift shop as a direct sales outlet for its produce. While the gift shop does sell farm-themed gifts, such as toy animals and model tractors, a considerable proportion of the stock is made up by general souvenirs of Wales.

One of the implications of the different strategies that have been taken by the two farms is the Aberhyddnant continues to operate very much as a family farm, with little need for employing staff from outside of the family. A concession to this is the use of woofers at lambing time, when the family tends to be very stretched. The changeover day for the guest cottages was changed in order to avoid the overstretching of staff and allow the operations to remain family based. Upper Cantref Farm, on the other hand, has to employ a rather larger complement of staff, which must be drawn from outside of the immediate family. This is partly because Upper Cantref operates at a larger scale than Aberhyddnant, even though they are both relatively small family farms, but mainly because the approach to diversification has been so different.

Conclusions

While Aberhyddnant Farm and Upper Cantref Farm have both chosen to diversify into farm tourism, broadly defined, the two farm enterprises have clearly adopted different strategies. Upper Cantref Farm has pursued a strategy that is not strongly based around the operation of the farm. Until recently, visitors to the adventure farm have not been encouraged to walk around the farm or to participate in the activities of the farm, such as feeding livestock. The same is true of those staying in the overnight accommodation, which is bunkhouse-style and aimed very much at attracting people who are interested in visiting the nearby National Park, rather than experiencing the farm itself. Similarly, while the riding centre does provide pony rides for visitors to the adventure farm, there are few links with the farm itself. Indeed, the focus is an outward one, as exemplified by the recent introduction of trekking and longer trail rides into the BBNP. The farming side of the business is now a relatively minor source of farm income, while the adventure farm, riding centre and accommodation have all grown in importance, enabling the farm to remain in existence. The farm now depends on the wider diversification streams much more than the diversification streams rely on the ongoing operation of the farm.

Aberhyddnant Farm, meanwhile, has developed a portfolio of activities that are more closely related to the operation of the farm, including the provision of visitor access, encouraging guests in the tourist accommodation to experience life on an organic farm, and the sale of food produce to both guests on the farm and tourists in the local area through their tea room and farm shop. Whilst the farm initially followed what Busby and Rendle (2000) would consider be a 'tourism on a farm' approach, their approach is now very much a 'farm tourism' one. The strategy has been to develop income streams that are highly dependent on one another. The diversification streams rely entirely upon the ongoing successful operation of the farm, and the farm relies heavily on the diversification streams to keep it going.

It would be a mistake, however, to suppose that the more integrated approach is necessarily more successful than the less integrated one. Indeed, both farms can be considered to have made a successful transition from 'tourism on the farm' to 'farm tourism'.

References

Aberhyddnant Organic Farm. 2008. Information pack for guests.

Bowler I, Clarke G, Crockett A, Ilbery B, Shaw A. 1996. The development of alternative farm enterprises: A study of family labour farms in the Northern Pennines of England. *Journal of Rural Studies* **12** (3): 285-295.

Busby G, Rendle S. 2000. The transition from tourism on farms to farm tourism. *Tourism Management* **21** (6): 635-642.

Garrod B, Wornell R, Youell R. 2006. Re-conceptualising rural resources as countryside capital: The case of rural tourism. *Journal of Rural Studies* **22** (1): 117-128.

Hjalager A-M. 1996. Agricultural diversification into tourism: Evidence of a European Community development programme. *Tourism Management* **17** (2), 103-111.

McGehee NG, Kim K. 2004. Motivations for agri-tourism entrepreneurship. *Journal of Travel Research* **43** (2): 161-170.

Nickerson NP, Black RJ, McCool SF. 2001. Agritourism: Motivations behind farm/ranch diversification. *Journal of Travel Research* **40** (1): 19-26.

Ollenburg C, Buckley R. 2007. Stated economic and social motivations of farm tourism operators. *Journal of Travel Research* **45** (3), 444-453.

Roberts L, Hall D (eds). 2001. *Rural Tourism and Recreation: Principles to Practice*, Wallingford: CABI.

Sharpley T, Vass A. 2006. Tourism, farming and diversification: An attitudinal study. *Tourism Management* **27** (5): *1040-1052.*

Walford N. 2001. Patterns of development in tourist accommodation enterprises on farms in England and Wales. *Applied Geography* **21** (4): 331-345.

Ancillary Student Material

Further reading

Arnold J. 2004. Why rural tourism is not picnic. http://news.bbc.co.uk/1/hi/business/3683742.stm

Clarke, J. 1999. Marketing strategies for farm tourism: Beyond the individual provider of rural tourism. *Journal of Sustainable Tourism* **7** (1): 26-47.

Farmers Guardian. 2008. Two sisters, two farms and two successful farming-linked diversification ventures. http://www.farmersguardian.com/two-sisters-two-farms-and-two-successful-farming-linked-diversification-ventures/15505.article

McNally S. 2001. Farm diversification in England and Wales: What can we learn from the farm business survey? *Journal of Rural Studies* **17** (2): 247-257.

Nilsson, PÅ. 2002. Staying on farms: An ideological background. *Annals of Tourism Research* **29** (1): 7-24.

Page SJ, Getz D. 1997. *The Business of Rural Tourism: International Perspectives*. London: International Thomson Business Press.

Weaver DB, Fennell DA. 1997. The vacation farm sector in Saskatchewan: A profile of operations. *Tourism Management* **18** (6): 357-365.

Wilson, L-A. 2007. The family farm business? Insights into family, business and ownership dimensions of open-farms. *Leisure Studies* **26** (3), 357-374.

Related websites and audio-visual materials

Defra (Department for Environment, Farming and Rural Affairs, UK) Farm Diversification Benchmarking Study:
http://archive.defra.gov.uk/evidence/economics/foodfarm/reports/farmdiv/

Farm and Diversification. Biz/ed:
http://www.bized.co.uk/current/mind/2004_5/ 251004.htm

Welsh Assembly Government: Farm Diversification in Wales 2006/07:
http://wales.gov.uk/topics/statistics/headlines/agric2008/hdw200806242/?lang=en

Self-test questions

Try to answer the following questions to test your knowledge and understanding. If you are not sure of the answers then please refer to the suggested references and further reading sources:

1   What factors encourage farmers to diversify their business activities?

2   What is 'farm tourism' and how is this different to 'tourism on a farm'?

3   What are the benefits of choosing a more integrated approach to on-farm diversification, such as that adopted by Aberhyddnant farm? What are the risks inherent to such an approach?

4   Which of the two farms you think provides the most 'authentic' experience? Do you think that it is important that farm tourism providers offer authentic experiences?

5   Is it necessary for the farm to remain in economic operation in order for its tourism provision to be considered farm tourism?

6   Would farm tourism be a suitable diversification choice for any farm?

Key themes and theories

The key themes raised in this case study relate to the following areas:

♦   Impact of policy changes on farming and rural areas more generally.

♦   Motives for farm diversification.

♦   Implementing a diversification strategy based on farm tourism.

♦   Potentials and problems of farm tourism.

The key theories relate to:

♦   Forces driving the adoption of farm diversification strategies.

♦   Factors promoting the adoption of farm-based tourism as a focus for diversification.

♦   The transition from 'tourism in farms' to 'farm tourism'.

♦   Integrated and non-integrated farm tourism diversification approaches.

♦   Benefits and risks of different approaches to diversification into farm tourism.

 Scan here to get the hyperlinks for this chapter.

8

Bumps for Boomers:

Marketing Sport Tourism to the Aging Tourist

Simon Hudson

Introduction

In today's business environment, companies devise their marketing strategies based on the concept of market segmentation. When a market is segmented, it is divided into smaller homogenous markets or segments based on common needs or characteristics (Dickson and Ginter, 1987). The core advantage of segmentation is that customers will be more satisfied with the services provided because they have been designed with their needs in mind. One common criterion used by tourism and hospitality suppliers to segment the market is through demographics using the primary variables of age, gender, family life cycle, and ethnicity. The most significant implication of demographic change in this century is the ageing of the world's population. The world median age is projected to rise from 26 years in 2000 to 44 years by 2100. The senior travel market is both lucrative and unique because it is less tied to seasonal travel, involves longer trips and is not wedded to midweek or weekend travel, so it can boost occupancy rates for business and leisure travel opportunities. One particular cohort targeted by an increasing number of tourism businesses is the 'baby boomers': those born between 1946 and 1964. One such business is called 'Bumps for Boomers'.

Bumps for Boomers

"The program is going very well and is into its eighth year, but I am looking to the future", said Joe Nevin, who was talking to a journalist who had joined a skiing course in Aspen Colorado called 'Bumps for Boomers', the brainchild of the former Apple executive. "I am thinking about expanding the program but I am not sure how. I could expand to include other types of terrain other than moguls – 'Groomers for Boomers' for example, or 'Powder for Boomers'? Or I could franchise out Bumps for Boomers around the world but I'm not sure how. I am also wondering if I should be using other types of media apart from the Internet".

Nevin, founder and coach for Bumps for Boomers, had been teaching baby boomers (46 to 64 age range) in both bumps and powder[1] for the past eight years, with a focus on longevity and safety. Nevin first got the idea when a research study revealed that baby boomer skiers were primarily interested in skiing longevity. His tagline is now "Ski for Life". "Boomers are slowing down and concerned about injury. They are also worried about skiing on overcrowded runs where they could get knocked down", said Nevin. While working in California for Apple, Nevin also taught skiing at Alpine Meadows. He then retired and moved to Aspen. "I worked for Apple computers for 12 years where the DNA is all about making complexity simple so what I started with was integrating the short boards with teaching progressions. First from the mogul perspective and second how to moderate that based on demographics. Most mogul programs are fast, follow me? Our first thing is to find where the brakes are and give techniques for skiing longevity". When he set up Bumps for Boomers in 2003 he was backed by Rich Berkeley, who was ski school director at Aspen at the time. Berkeley is now Vice President of mountain operations.

Bumps for Boomers is one of the most popular specialised instruction programmes offered by the Aspen Skiing Company (ASC), with skiers flying in from around the country weekly, from the middle of December through to March. Three- and four-day clinics have been joined by a new 'MBA – Master of Bumps Academy' (see Box 1) featuring a different mountain for each of the three days of mogul ski lessons taking participants to Aspen Highlands, Snowmass and Aspen Mountain. Throwing away all pre-conceived notions about how to teach off-piste skiing, Nevin makes older skiers feel safer in bumps and powder than on groomed slopes where 80% of skiers congregate and the chance of a collision is highest. "The single biggest differentiator is teaching people to ski moguls without the need for fast reflexes", he explains.

---

1   Moguls or bumps are a series of undulations on a trail formed when skiers push the snow into mounds or piles as they execute short-radius turns. Powder skiing is the act of skiing in freshly fallen, un-compacted snow.

Box1 : Press Release about MBA: Master of Bumps Academy

Baby Boomers Get New MBA Degree on Slopes of Aspen Colorado at BUMPS FOR BOOMERS ® Master of Bumps Academy

Aspen, CO (PRWEB) August 3, 2010

BUMPS FOR BOOMERS, an innovative ski instruction program for Baby Boomers, announces the expansion of its clinic offerings for the 2010/2011 ski season. The New "MBA – Master of Bumps Academy" features a different mountain for each of the three days of mogul ski lessons taking participants to Aspen Highlands, Snowmass and Aspen Mountain. Since 2003, BUMPS FOR BOOMERS has successfully taught hundreds of Boomers how to ski moguls safely and effortlessly.

BUMPS FOR BOOMERS unique approach is designed to accommodate slowing reflexes and hips and knees that can no longer pound a path down a mogul field. Techniques emphasize control, efficiency and safety. Joe Nevin, founder of BUMPS FOR BOOMERS says, "We want to help people ski for life, and not just on the groomed runs they've skied for decades. Safety doesn't have to equal boring. We're having the time of our life effortlessly floating down every mogul field we can find."

The Baby Boom generation continues to be the largest demographic for the North American skiing industry and BUMPS FOR BOOMERS is the only mogul and powder skiing program in North America that is designed by Baby Boomers, for Boomers and taught by Boomers. Nevin says, "We have clients who have taken our program multiple times and we wanted to offer them some new challenges and expand their learning."

According to national Baby Boomer marketing expert, John W. Martin, co-author of "Boomer Consumer" and CEO of the Boomer Project, more companies are tapping into the 76 million Baby Boomer market by aligning themselves with Baby Boomer's core generational values – being in control, feeling entitled, realizing personal gratification from hard work, challenging the status quo, etc. Martin says, "The BUMPS FOR BOOMERS MBA program is a great example of tapping into these values." Martin explains, "The BUMPS FOR BOOMERS MBA program puts conquering what may initially seem like a difficult hill or age-inappropriate ski run within Boomers' easy reach by giving them what they crave – a way to be in control and experience immediate rewards – personal gratification – for their work. Throw in the benefit of challenging the status quo – the traditional mindset of skiing is for the youth, and it's no wonder more and more Boomers are turning skiing into an ageless pursuit."

Another coveted MBA degree? Nevin says, "So many of us Boomers worked hard in our 20's to get our MBA so we could succeed at our careers. Now it's time to put that same energy into something we really love - an MBA in skiing. I have the greatest job in the world," states Nevin. "Every day clients tell me that our program changed their lives. Sure it's about the skiing, but it's about so much more."

BUMPS FOR BOOMERS MBA clinics will be offered twice during the 2010/11 ski season. The cost for the three-day clinic is $897 (not including lift tickets unless a combined clinic and lift ticket package is purchased). In addition to the MBA program, three and four-day clinics are offered from November 2010 through March 2011. In addition to the ski program, BUMPS FOR BOOMERS offer ski enthusiasts complimentary weekly skiing tips, and an online ski fitness training program developed by Bill Fabrocini, a world-class Aspen, Colorado physical therapist and personal trainer. For more details visit the Aspen mogul ski lesson website or call 970-989-2529

BUMPS FOR BOOMERS ®, based in Aspen, Colorado and founded by Joe Nevin, a former Apple Computer executive, is an nationally renowned, accelerated ski lesson program that enables intermediate-level Baby Boomer and senior skiers to ski for life by teaching techniques to confidently ski moguls and powder. It is an adult specialty program of the Ski and Snowboard Schools of Aspen. BUMPS FOR BOOMERS facilitates Boomers' ability to reach peak performance and extends the longevity of their skiing years. Visit http://www.bumpsforboomers.com for information on clinics or to view complimentary weekly skiing tips and fitness video training series.

For the first two days of the four-day course, skiers use 95 cm-long ski boards: sometimes known as 'blades' (see Figure 1). The truncated boards challenge auto-movement patterns and help define and eradicate bad habits on traditional skis. "I take skiers outside the box and put them on equipment they've never seen before. They become the most attentive students and are able to break the old connection between the brain and the feet. They go on to learn new skills very quickly", says Nevin. Within the first hour students figure out their new centre of balance and two hours into the first lesson are skiing slowly on bumps with control. The philosophy behind the short-ski method is that they are a 'truth serum', revealing every microscopic error. Their small sweet spot precludes old habits and compels perfect technique. "Training on these skiboards accelerates learning due to forcing better balance, minimizing the consequences of generating too much speed resulting from too much edge angle when you are learning and breaking the connection between brain and feet which takes you out of your comfort zone and facilitates (accelerated) learning", says Nevin. After two days, skiers then go back to their own skis through a 'coached transition'.

Figure 1: Ski boards, or 'blades'

Nevin only employs instructors who are boomers themselves so that they can identify with their clients. "You can't take a 30-year-old instructor and expect them to know what it's like to be 50, 60, 70 or even 80." On this particular day, his group included the journalist, who was writing for a Canadian newspaper, and three Americans. Dennis Levine (62) and his wife, Elke (52) from Utah had met their Californian ski buddy, Art Reiss (62), in Aspen so that they could do the clinic together and all progress apace. "They don't have a bumps clinic like this with short skis at Park City", Elke explained. "I did Ski College there and all the good skiers recommended the Bumps for Boomers course as I have never skied bumps before". The four days had cost them US$1,196 per person.

Around 75% of Bumps for Boomers students are 50 or older, 73% are male, and 88% come to Aspen specifically for the programme, having seen it online through the website or social media. In fact, this is the only way Nevin advertises his programme. His website (see Figure 2) is 300 pages deep and packed with information, including a downloadable brochure (see Figure 3) and a ski fitness training series developed by Aspen physical therapist and personal trainer, Bill Fabrocini. "The average person spends eight minutes on our website and it is updated regularly", he says.

Figure 2: Front page of 'Bumps for Boomers' website

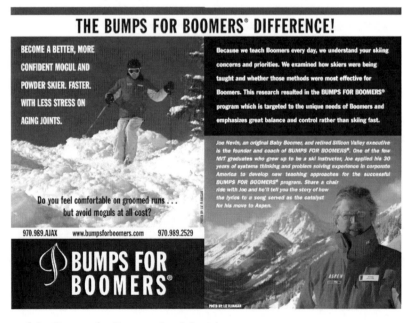

Figure 3: First page of the 'Bumps for Boomers' web brochure

Nevin is a great believer in the value of giving away information for free in order to increase his reputation. "I believe in giving out information, so you can go to my website and read about all my techniques, fitness instruction, demographics, weekly tips, all for free", he said. He was influenced by Chris Anderson's books – The Long Tail and Free. Anderson suggested that if you give information away for free you will benefit in the long term. So by giving away ski tips every week to subscribers, Nevin believes some of them will eventually convert to customers.

The company is involved with the major social media sites; Facebook, You-Tube and Twitter. The company has 2,300 Facebook followers, and 3,000 subscribers have signed up to receive skiing tips plus insider perspectives on Aspen and Aspen skiing (see Figure 4). Nevin speaks knowledgeably on subjects such as search engine optimisation, database management and anchor texting. He has even produced a summary of how he uses technology for marketing (see Figure 5).

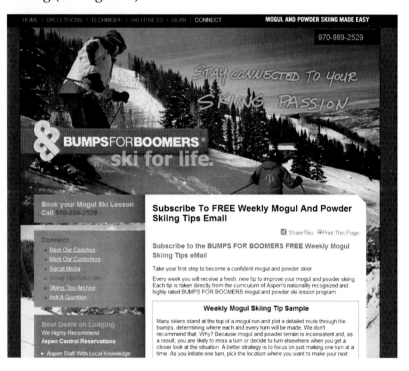

Figure 4: Website page for signing up to skiing tips

Nevin also collects customers' email addresses and then follows up after the course with a survey to gain feedback on perceptions of the programme (see Box 2).

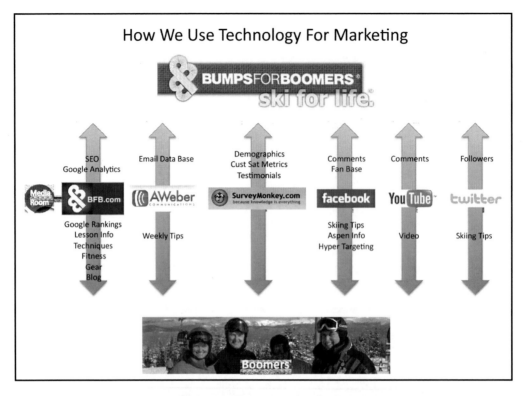

Figure 5: Summary of the use of technology for marketing by Bumps for Boomers

Box 2: Customer satisfaction survey sent out by Bumps for Boomers

Thank you for participating in the BUMPS FOR BOOMERS® program this season in Aspen. Our coaching staff prides itself on customer satisfaction, which is why we are taking this opportunity to ask you for feedback about your experience.

Please help us strengthen our program by answering the following short list of questions. Just click the "submit" button when you are done. Thank you in advance for completing this survey.

From The BUMPS FOR BOOMERS Coaching Staff:
Joe Nevin, Larry Feher, Alan Bush, Sam Green, Bob Mattice and Walter Hanselmann

1. Rate your overall BUMPS FOR BOOMERS® experience (select one)

☐ Exceeded My Expectations

☐ Met My Expectations

☐ Did Not Meet My Expectations

2. In comparison to other ski lesson programs you have taken, how would you rate BUMPS FOR BOOMERS® ? (select one)

☐ Significantly Better   ☐ Somewhat Better   ☐ Equal   ☐ Somewhat Worse   ☐ Significantly Worse

3. Describe how you felt about your participation in the BUMPS FOR BOOMERS® program. Any comments about the program design, coaching quality, knowledge you gained, new skills you learned and/or the degree to which we achieved your personal goals would be appreciated. (Type a brief one or two sentence response in the text box below)

4. On a scale of zero to 10 (low to high), how likely is it that you would recommend BUMPS FOR BOOMERS® to your friends or colleagues?

☐ 0   ☐ 1   ☐ 2   ☐ 3   ☐ 4   ☐ 5   ☐ 6   ☐ 7   ☐ 8   ☐ 9   ☐ 10

5. You Are: (select one)
☐ Male
☐ Female

6. Your Age Is: (select one)
☐ age 49 or under
☐ age 50 - 59
☐ age 60 - 69
☐ age 70 or beyond

7. Indicate which BUMPS FOR BOOMERS® program you participated in: (select one)
☐ 3 Day BUMPS FOR BOOMERS Clinic
☐ Private Lesson (One Or More Days)
☐ Combination Of A Clinic And One Or More Private Lessons

8. Who was your "primary" BUMPS FOR BOOMERS ® coach? If you skied with two different coaches please select the coach who you believe had the biggest influence on your skiing and/or who you spent the most time with (select one name).
☐ Alan   ☐ Joe   ☐ Larry   ☐ Sam   ☐ Bob   ☐ Walter

9. Was attending the BUMPS FOR BOOMERS® program your primary reason for traveling to Aspen? (select one)
☐ Yes
☐ No

10. Was this your first time skiing in Aspen? (select one)
☐ Yes
☐ No

**11. If there was one thing we could do to strengthen the BUMPS FOR BOOMERS®
program ... what would it be? (type your response in text box below)**

Nevin is media savvy, having hosted a number of journalists to take part in
the programme. He has a media room accessible via the website. His greatest
success came when an article on Bumps for Boomers was published in the
New York Times (see Box 3). He saw an immediate spike in website hits having tracked the response through Google, which resulted in an increase in
business. However, he does acknowledge that he tends to wait for journalists
to contact him, rather than actively seeking media coverage.

Box 3: New York Times article

December 21, 2007

Ski Report
Smoothing Bumps for Boomers

By Bill Pennington

IT was at the top of a trail called Hanging Tree that the fear set in. And at the crest of
a steep, mogul-filled and tree-strewn trail, it's all about the fear, isn't it? This was near
the top of Aspen Mountain last winter, and at moments like these — surveying a no-
nonsense double-black-diamond run — the mind will race.

Here was my central thought: Who names a trail Hanging Tree? O.K., so that noose
playfully dangling from a tree near the trail entrance might be a tip-off, but what exactly are they trying to tell me here? For a large sector of the skiing public, the message
is clear: Go away, you don't belong. And people listen. It's not about one Aspen trail, it's
about a disquieting reality at any major ski resort — 80 percent of the skiers use only
20 percent of the mountain. The blue-square groomers are packed, while the mogul
and tree runs are empty. There are a few reasons for this, including the advent of terrain parks and halfpipes that have lured away a lot of young talent.

But there is a bigger factor. The baby boom generation, which created the American
ski craze of the 1960s and '70s, has grown averse to risk. Resorts ought to rename
every intermediate cruising trail in the country the 401(k). Because the more you have
invested in a retirement account, the more likely that's the trail you'll be on.

Joe Nevin, a 61-year-old Aspen ski instructor, knows the story. He's heard it over and over on Aspen's lifts, talking with middle-age skiers. "It's kind of the forgotten society of skiing," he said. "They look in the ski magazines, and the stories and pictures are about cliff jumping. They don't want to fly in the air. They don't want to end up in physical therapy. And if they see somebody in the moguls, it's always some 20-year-old banging through the course with his knees in his face. They know that's not for them, either. "So they stay where they think they belong. People told me they would love to get off the groomers, but there's a fear factor."

There's that word again. Baby boomers nationwide have bought snow-country second homes and want to be able to continue to ski on the tougher parts of the mountain with their children, or grandchildren. But for many, fear is keeping them away.

Five years ago, Mr. Nevin decided to do something with all the information he had acquired during those chair-lift rides. He devised a pioneering instruction program aimed at those born between 1946 and 1964 called Bumps for Boomers. In three days of lessons, Mr. Nevin erases the fear and, without demanding young, quick reflexes or extraordinary agility, teaches his students to confidently ski black-diamond, even double-black-diamond, mogul runs. And it works. Mr. Nevin's program, which costs $840 for a three-day session, has turned hundreds of former boomer-groomers into mogul and glade skiers. It is now one of the most popular specialized instruction programs offered by the Aspen Skiing Company, with students flying in from around the country weekly from the middle of December through March. Reservations are required (970-989-2529; www.bumpsforboomers.com).

Nevin has been helped in his marketing efforts by a Virginia-based company called BCF, a brand communications firm that specialises in marketing products and experiences to baby boomers. Although Bumps for Boomers enjoyed moderate participation from the day of its inception, the programme lacked consistent branding. In March 2009, BCF conducted several in-depth interviews in Aspen with participants and staff. BCF identified the heart and soul of Bumps for Boomers and created a brand identity that would emotionally connect with its target audience. The result was a comprehensive brand campaign, 'Ski for Life', which is intended to bring the exhilaration of skiing powder and moguls to life. Since the re-launch of the website in October 2009, average pages viewed per visit have increased, and average time spent on the site has increased. Two clinic participants in January 2010 cited the new web design as the reason why they signed up for the course. Participants noted that they had been looking at the former site for four years, and the new video features and design convinced them to enrol.

Figure 6: Map of Aspen Mountain

Nevin's relationship with the Aspen Ski Company, which operates the skiing in Aspen, is a good one. "Nearly 90% of people on the program are coming to Aspen specifically for Bumps for Boomers, so we are bringing incremental business to the Aspen Ski Company", he says. Jeff Hanle, Director of Public Relations at ASC agrees. "Bumps for Boomers is a wonderful program for extending the skiing lifespan of some of our guests. With a 70% return customer rate, one of the highest in the industry, it is great to keep these long-time guests on the hill. They are now able to continue to ski with multiple generations of their families and pass on the tradition of skiing at Aspen/ Snowmass. It is important for us to deliver products to our guests that appeal to all ages and all abilities. This is our future, and our past".

A History of skiing in Aspen

The City of Aspen was founded as a mining camp in the Colorado Silver Boom of the late 19th century and named because of the abundance of aspen trees in the area. The city is now primarily known as an upscale ski resort and is operated by the ASC. The company owns four ski resorts: Aspen Mountain, Aspen Highlands, Buttermilk Mountain and Snowmass, all of which are located within a short distance of its headquarters. These four resorts, together referred to as 'Aspen', form one of the world's most famous and popular ski areas (see Figure 6).

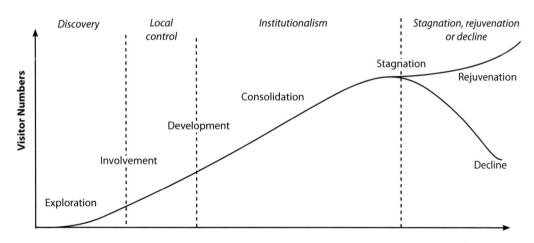

Figure 7: The destination life cycle. *Source*: Adapted from Butler (1980)

As Aspen has moved along the destination life cycle (see Figure 7), visitor numbers have increased. In the 2009-10 season, ASC recorded 1,338,210 skier visits at its four ski areas. The company is currently under the control of the Crown family of Chicago.

The foundations for the ASC were laid in the 1930s, when interest in the sport was growing in the US, despite the Great Depression. The Winter Olympics were held in Lake Placid, New York, in 1932, and in 1936 a group of investors opened Sun Valley, a ski resort in Idaho, with surprising success. The first attempt at developing a resort at Aspen came in 1936, when three men (T.J. Flynn, Ted Ryan, and Billy Fiske) formed the Highland Bavarian Corporation. Flynn, the only local of the three businessmen, remembered Scandinavian miners racing down the mountains for recreation. After announcing their resort plans to the Aspen Lions Club, the town enthusiastically backed the project. Although only one lodge had been constructed, the resort opened in December 1936. The lift, not built until the following year, would be called the 'boat tow'. It was made of an old car motor, two mine hoists, and two ten-person sleds. Aggressive advertising through brochures, films and ski races brought attention to Aspen, and the Federal Government, through the Works Project Administration[2], helped construct a new warming hut, jumping hill and clubhouse.

World War II interrupted the resort's development but the popularity of Aspen grew considerably in the 1960s, in part because of broader developments in the ski industry. The 1960 Winter Olympics in Squaw Valley, California, brought greater visibility to skiing in the US, and the industry benefited from improved equipment, significant growth in airline traffic and a desire for second-home ownership in the mountains. In the 1970s and 1980s there were further changes in the ski industry as skiers began to shun small, basic ski areas for those that provided the largest number of trails, the most and fastest lifts, and the best facilities. The ASC, like other ski resort companies, responded by providing additional services and constructing more luxurious accommodation. More trails were cut, slopes were groomed frequently for ease of skiing and more lifts were built to reduce lift lines.

In 2011, ASC's four resorts undoubtedly form one of North America's premier ski areas, along with such 'mega-resorts' as Vail Mountain in Colorado and Whistler/Blackcomb in British Columbia. Aspen Mountain, Aspen Highlands, Buttermilk and Snowmass together have 5,300 acres of skiable terrain, 43 lifts, and 15 on-mountain restaurants. A single lift ticket gives access to all four resorts, which are advertised together as one ski area. Equally importantly, it has the advantage of owning a ski area with universal

2   The Work Projects Administration (WPA) was established in 1935 by executive order of President Franklin Delano Roosevelt as the Works Progress Administration. Created when unemployment was widespread, the WPA – headed by Harry L. Hopkins until 1938 – was designed to increase the purchasing power of persons on relief by employing them on useful projects.

name recognition among skiers: 'Aspen'. Aspen has become legendary in the history of skiing.

Building on this rich history and embracing its past, Aspen continues to rewrite its story every day. From the classic tradition of World Cup ski racing, which continues on Aspen Mountain's slopes today, comes the ESPN Winter X Games held on Buttermilk, a winter action sports event featuring athletes from across the globe competing for medals and prize money in the sports of ski, snowboard and snowmobile. With over US$138 million invested in on-mountain improvements between 2004 and 2011, Aspen is aiming to provide guests the most seamless skiing/riding experience in the industry. Improvements over that period have seen the introduction of 11 new lifts including two gondolas, the industry-leading Treehouse Kids' Adventure Center, three new restaurants, additional terrain plus the new Snowmass Base Village. The Aspen Skiing Company has received several awards over the years including the Colorado Ethics in Business Award for overall business ethics in areas such as corporate guiding principles, environmental responsibility and employee programmes. Mountain Sports Media has honoured the company for environmental excellence in the ski industry with the prestigious Golden Eagle Award and the Snowmass Club has received the American Hotel and Lodging Association's Enviro-Management Award.

The ski industry today

The ski industry has experienced remarkable growth in the last 50 years. It is estimated that there are about 115 million skiers worldwide and around 2,000 ski resorts in 70 countries catering to this growing market (Vanat, 2010). New resorts in Asia and Eastern Europe are competing for these visitors, with established destinations in North America, New Zealand and Australia, Japan and Western Europe. There are also a number of lesser-known ski destinations spread around the globe, including Algeria, Cyprus, Greece, India, Iran, Israel, Lebanon, Morocco, Pakistan, South Africa and Turkey (see Figure 8).

In the US, for the 2009/10 season winter sports visits were 59.7 million, the second-highest on record, despite a weak economy, lower snowfall and a shorter season. Tables 1 and 2 show the skiing and snowboarding participation rates between 2000 and 2009, which show that the trend in the total number of participants has been largely flat for the past decade. The primarily white audience is getting older and it is projected to grow very little in the next 40 years, while the Hispanic and Asian population will rise by 200%. There are some signs that the industry can attract these populations; in the

15 to 35 age group, between 15 and 20% of current guests are non-white. To maintain the winter sports population, many resorts believe they must continue to focus on level one beginner lessons and to target minority populations. The growing ethnic population poses a challenge for most winter resorts, which have not traditionally appealed to minority markets and "don't much know how"' (Kahl, 2004, p.40).

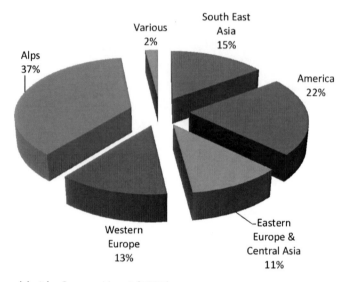

Figure 8: Ski resorts worldwide. Source: Vanat (2010)

Table 1: US downhill skiing participation 2000-09

DOWNHILL SKI PARTICIPATION									
Seven years of age and older, more than once, calendar year									
	2009	**2008**	**2007**	**2006**	**2005**	**2004**	**2003**	**2002**	**2001**	**2000**
Total (in millions)	7.0	6.5	6.4	6.4	6.9	5.9	6.8	7.4	7.7	7.4
Percent of U. S. Population	2.6%	2.4%	2.4%	2.4%	2.6%	2.3%	2.6%	2.9%	3.0%	3.0%
Average Number of Days	7.6	6.7	6.2	12.9	8.0	10.0	6.6	9.1	8.3	9.1
Male	62.7%	62.3%	60.7%	63.0%	50.6%	55.6%	57.4%	60.7%	60.2%	58.9%
Female	37.3%	37.7%	39.3%	37.0%	49.4%	44.4%	42.6%	39.3%	39.8%	41.1%
HH Income of $100,000+	46.1%	49.8%	45.1%	37.5%	40.5%	23.8%	na	na	na	na
HH Income of $50,000+	77.2%	83.7%	78.0%	78.6%	87.3%	74.7%	78.7%	83.4%	72.7%	73.0%
HH Income of $35-50,000	7.1%	8.4%	14.5%	7.4%	5.4%	12.9%	11.9%	6.7%	13.2%	12.5%
Mean Age -- Male	33.6	29.3	33.5	31.8	32.4	32.2	33.0	30.2	30.7	
Mean Age -- Female	35.7	30.4	35.8	32.6	27.7	29.9	30.3	29.2	28.7	
Age 25 or Older	66.3%	53.2%	64.2%	62.4%	53.5%	60.6%	63.7%	71.7%	57.6%	60.8%
HH with Children under 18	56.1%	57.8%	59.9%	49.4%	62.0%	60.6%	57.3%	56.2%	58.2%	59.2%
Frequent (10+ Days)*	25.9%	21.0%	24.8%	8.3%	11.9%	18.2%	6.6%	15.6%	13.4%	15.3%
Occasional (4-9 Days)*	36.3%	36.2%	27.6%	55.5%	41.7%	39.1%	40.4%	31.3%	41.3%	36.9%
Infrequent (2-3 Days)*	37.8%	42.8%	47.6%	36.2%	46.5%	42.7%	53.1%	53.2%	45.3%	47.8%
Skier Visits (in millions) **	59.7	57.1	60.1	55.1	58.9	57.1	57.6	54.4	57.3	52.2

* Frequency definition changed beginning in 2007. Prevously, 20+ Days, 5-19 Days & 2-4 Days.
** 2009 reflects 2009-10 ski season, etc.; source: National Ski Areas Association. All other data reflects calendar year.
Source: NATIONAL SKI & SNOWBOARD RETAILERS ASSOCIATION, Mt. Prospect IL 60056 Tel: 847.391.9825 Fax: 847.391.9827 info@nssra.com

Table 2: US snowboarding participation 2000-09

	2009	2008	2007	2006	2005	2004	2003	2002	2001	2000
SNOWBOARDING PARTICIPATION* Seven years of age and older, more than once, calendar year										
Total (in millions)	6.2	5.8	5.1	5.2	6.0	6.3	6.3	5.9	5.3	4.3
Percent of U. S. Population	2.3%	2.2%	2.0%	2.0%	2.3%	2.5%	2.5%	2.2%	2.1%	1.7%
Average Number of Days	8.2	7.8	10.0	9.1	9.0	8.8	8.3	8.9	7.2	7.7
Male	69.7%	71.9%	73.5%	72.9%	74.2%	73.4%	65.7%	77.0%	72.4%	74.1%
Female	30.3%	28.1%	26.5%	27.1%	25.8%	26.6%	34.3%	23.0%	27.6%	25.9%
HH Income of $100,000+	28.5%	36.2%	32.4%							
HH Income of $50,000+	73.3%	75.8%	70.6%	66.7%	62.7%	66.3%	64.1%	65.1%	58.5%	54.6%
HH Income of $35-50,000	9.4%	13.8%	13.8%	15.8%	13.4%	14.6%	14.8%	15.4%	16.4%	17.0%
Mean Age -- Male	23.4	21.0	21.6	20.3	21.3	21.3	19.4	22.0	20.1	
Mean Age -- Female	25.6	26.1	18.8	22.7	23.0	26.2	19.6	23.5	22.1	
Age 24 or Younger	59.3%	69.1%	79.7%	75.7%	73.0%	77.3%	80.4%	67.6%	75.1%	80.8%
Frequent (10+ Days)**	31.0%	23.6%	32.0%	30.6%	41.2%	39.6%	38.2%	36.4%	30.5%	34.6%
Occasional (3-9 Days)**	53.0%	55.7%	48.7%	49.6%	37.2%	60.4%	61.8%	63.6%	69.5%	65.4%
Infrequent (2 Days)**	16.0%	20.7%	19.3%	19.8%	21.6%					
Percent who Alpine Skied	11.5%	20.0%	13.9%	9.8%	13.0%	10.5%	12.3%	11.5%	na	8.2%

* Net of Snowboarding at resort and Snowboarding not at resort
** Frequency definition changed beginning in 2005. Prevously, 20+ Days & 2-9 Days.

Source: NATIONAL SKI & SNOWBOARD RETAILERS ASSOCIATION, Mt. Prospect IL 60056 Tel: 847.391.9825 Fax: 847.391.9827

However, National Ski Areas Association (NSAA) president Michael Berry notes that there has been a 9% decline in beginner conversion between 2006 and 2010. Without an increase in these numbers, the NSAA Model for Growth predicts that the current volume of business will be the industry's peak for the foreseeable (15-year) future (see Figure 9).

The conversion and retention rate for both new and existing skiers and snowboarders remains a worrisome issue for Berry. As baby boomers increasingly retreat from the sport, the Model for Growth is predicting a 2.5% decline in ski and snowboard visits every season from now until the year 2021 unless the industry improves its conversion rates. Add in the fact that only 10% of participants who try snowsports are actually 'converted' to continuing participation and there is a long-term scenario where, as the boomer exodus accelerates, 'Millennials' and 'Gen X'ers' are not stepping up to the snow in significant enough numbers to replace them.

RRC Associates believes that core baby boomers will inevitably drop out of the sport as they reach their 60s (RRC Associates, 2006). The rate of age-related dropout they say is a combination of physiology and sociology. While physiology may be beyond the control of the industry, they think the industry might be able to influence some of the sociological factors. For example, some of the factors influencing the high dropout rate of female boomers are a lack of a peer group to ski/snowboard with, safety concerns, an increasing desire to visit warm-weather destinations, all combined with the perception that a skiing/snowboarding trip is not going to be a relaxing one. Highlighting safety, the strong family bonding element of the sport, and reducing hassle factors for older female skiers and riders, including the availability of newer and much improved equipment, would likely go a long way towards reducing the dropout rate for this group according to RRC.

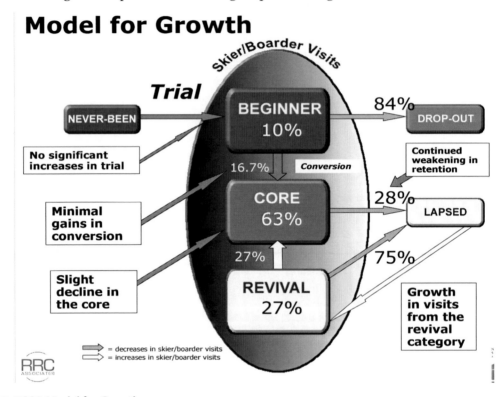

Figure 9: NSSA Model for Growth

Baby boomers and travel

Nevin was well aware of these trends in the skiing industry and had done his homework on the travelling boomers. He was browsing a new journal article on the subject written in *Marketing Intelligence & Planning* by Hudson (2010). Sometimes called Zoomers – 'baby boomers with zip' – this generation, born between 1946 and 1964, is very different from the stereotype of mature travellers of past eras, who tended to seek more passive travel experiences and activities. Boomers have no intention of leaving their youthful pursuits behind as they get older, and are looking for more active travel pursuits in which health and fitness play prominent roles. What is more, this market just gets bigger and bigger. With life expectancy over 80, there will be 115 million people 50 or older in the US by 2020, 50% more than now (see Figure 10).

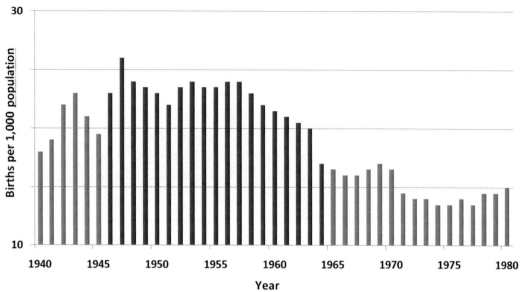

Figure 10: US birth rate, 1940-1980.

Source: Halbert (2006). The baby boomer generation is in black

According to the University of South Carolina professor's article (Hudson, 2010), attempts by marketers to reach boomers have been miserably unsuccessful. "The key to securing and retaining this growing lucrative segment is better understanding of how they behave, their buying motivations and their needs as they get older", he says. "Many advertisers still cling to the concept that 18-49-year-olds – the demographic still used as a standard in the advertising business – are the most desirable age group to court. The stereotype persists that once people reach the age of 50 years, they have fewer needs, are unwilling to try new products and have little buying power. But remember, this is a generation that has always defied existing values, attitudes and preferences. If tourism marketers ignore baby boomers, they are missing out on a profitable market segment" (Hudson, 2010, p.458).

The older adult segment has drawn increased attention from researchers in the last decade with the growing recognition that they place tourism high in their priorities. Such research has included the study of their tourism motivations, tourism behaviour, factors influencing decision making and constraints to tourism. There have also been a number of attempts to segment the mature travelling market in general. Few studies have, however, focused specifically on the travelling baby boomers cohort. Sociologists typically divide boomers into two segments: leading-edge and trailing-edge, each carrying a different portfolio of attitudes and interests. Leading-edge boomers (or classic baby boomers as they are sometimes referred to) were born between 1946 and 1955, while trailing-edge boomers were born between 1956 and 1964. For the leading-edge boomers, travel takes a central role in post-retirement reality. In fact, research has shown that a decline in the frequency of travel does not occur until people reach their late 70s and 80s. Trailing-edge boomers have been offered a plethora of credit cards all their lives and hence have accumulated enormous consumer debt. They have therefore been among the hardest hit by recent economic struggles and have curtailed their travel habits somewhat compared to leading-edge boomers. However, for both groups, travel remains a very important component in their lives, and over the last decade some clear behavioural trends have emerged that are beginning to have a significant impact on the travel industry.

Hudson's (2010) article discusses how baby boomers, who represent 27% of the US population, are completely reshaping and redefining the travel landscape. His article highlights the consumer trends relating to this genera-tion by identifying the key psychographic nuances of the travelling boomer: one that is looking for a memorable experience rather than a holiday, seek-ing authenticity, spiritual and mental enlightenment, nostalgia, convenience and spontaneity, all packaged in a safe, customised, healthy, green wrap-ping and delivered with great customer service. These boomer trends can be seen in Figure 11.

Figure 11: Psychographic nuances of the travelling boomer

Hudson suggests, however, that understanding the behaviour of this cohort is merely the first stage in tapping into this lucrative market. Tourism marketers must connect with boomers by producing relevant marketing communications. The second part of his article therefore outlines how marketers in the travel industry can reach boomers using effective communications. An analysis of the research and best practice case studies suggests that marketers should implement the tactics illustrated in Figure 12. Emphasising boomers' continued youthfulness and showing how to improve their lives is one strategy. "Marketers targeting boomers should avoid stressing their declining years", says Hudson. "Not only because it can be frustrating in general, but because boomers do not associate themselves with old age – in fact, boomers on average feel 7-12 years younger than they actually are!" (Hudson, 2010, pp.452).

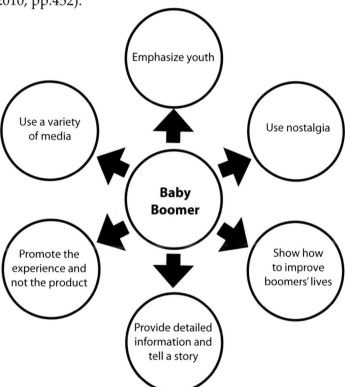

Figure 12: Communication tactics to connect with boomers

Hudson suggests that tourism marketers should also use nostalgia, emotions and stories, and promote experiences rather than products and services. "As people mature, cognition patterns become more right-brain oriented which has a critical impact on marketing, as the right brain is where emotions and memories reside", Hudson says. "So destinations like Las Vegas, Australia and Canada have begun to focus on promoting experiences as opposed to products and service" (Hudson, 2010, pp.455). Hotels, too, are promoting the experience of staying in their properties as opposed to physical attributes. Hilton Hotels, for example, in its 'Travel Should Take You Places' advertising campaign, attempts to engage guests at an emotional level, instead of trying to entice guests through rational product attributes, winning their hearts rather than their heads.

The future for Bumps for Boomers

Nevin's day with the Canadian journalist and the three Americans was coming to an end. On the last ride up the mountain, Nevin contemplated the future. Despite the success of his venture, Nevin was interested in developing the business. He had read the night before a tourism text book (Holloway and Plant, 1992) that suggested different alternatives for new product development (see Figure 13). The book provided a useful matrix to illustrate the permutations of market/product interaction that are possible and the product moves that might be suitable for each. According to the model, a company has four alternatives: market penetration (modifying an existing product for the current market), market development (identifying and developing new markets for current products), product development (developing a genuinely new product to be sold to existing customers) and diversification (seeking opportunities outside the present business).

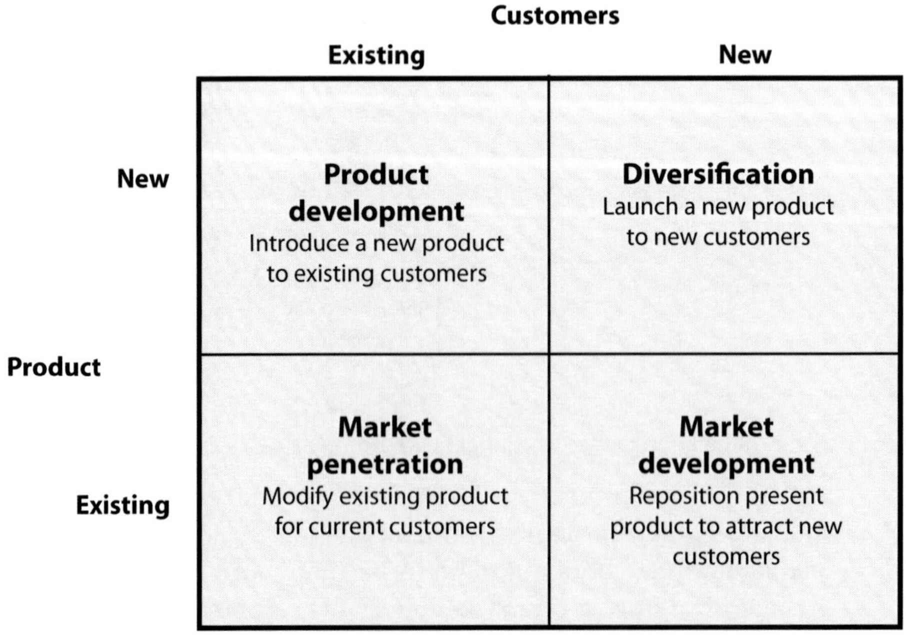

	Customers	
	Existing	**New**
New	**Product development** Introduce a new product to existing customers	**Diversification** Launch a new product to new customers
Existing	**Market penetration** Modify existing product for current customers	**Market development** Reposition present product to attract new customers

(Product axis label: **Product** — New / Existing on the left side)

Figure 13: New product development matrix. *Source*: Adapted from Holloway and Plant (1992)

All these options were certainly giving Nevin food for thought. He did not know a great deal about franchising but he was interested in the idea of franchising Bumps for Boomers. Ski resorts around the world might be interested. Was it worth having a stand at the upcoming Snowsports Industries America Snow Show in Denver to promote his idea to the industry? Or would he be better off growing the programme organically by providing variations on the existing programme to attract different demographics? Or should he stick with boomers and try to attract those who would like to ski powder or groomed runs as well as bumps? He was also concerned about keeping on top of the rapidly changing world of social media. Was he doing enough to leverage the power of the Internet? He was aware that tourism marketers need to do a better job of connecting with boomers by producing relevant marketing communications. Did he have a good enough understanding of the services and strategies most appealing to older consumers?

Throwing those thoughts aside, he turned his mind to more pressing matters. Where could he find the best snow for the next ski down?

References

Butler RW. 1980. The concept of a tourism area life cycle of evolution: Implications for management of resources. *The Canadian Geographer* **24** (1): 5-12.

Dickson PR, Ginter JL. 1987. Market segmentation, product differentiation, and marketing strategy. *Journal of Marketing* **51** (2): 1-10.

Halbert GD. 2006. Will the baby boomers wreck the market? *Forecasts & Trends E-letter*, August 15. http://www.profutures.com

Holloway JC, Plant RV. 1992. *Marketing for Tourism*. London: Pitman.

Hudson S. 2010. Wooing zoomers: Marketing tourism to the mature traveler. *Marketing Intelligence & Planning* **28** (4): 444-461.

Kahl R. (2004). Minority report: Different approaches to diversity. *Ski Area Management* **43** (6): 40.

RRC Associates. 2006. *Projected Demand and Visitation for U.S. Ski Areas*. July.

Vanat L. 2010. *2010 International Report on Mountain Tourism*. Geneva. http://vanat.ch

Ancillary Student Material

Further Reading

Anderson C. 2006. *The Long Tail: Why the Future of Business is Selling Less of More.* New York: Hyperion.

Anderson C. 2009. *Free.* New York: Hyperion.

FundingUniverse 2011. *Aspen Skiing Company.* http://www.fundinguniverse.com/company-histories/Aspen-Skiing-Company-Company-History.html

Hudson S. 2000. *Snow Business: A Study of the International Ski Industry.* London: Continuum.

Hudson S. 2004. Winter sport tourism in North America. In Ritchie B, Adair, D (eds.) *Sport Tourism: Interrelationships, Impacts and Issues.* Clevedon: Channel View; 77-100.

Hudson S. 2006. Creating memorable Alpine winter experiences. In Weiermair K, Brunner-Sperdin A (eds) *Erlebnisinszenierung im Tourismus.* Berlin: Erich Schmidt Verlag; 137-152.

Hudson S. 2006. Ski Resorts. Enjoyment vs. environmental responsibility: Does there have to be a choice. In Herremans I (ed.) *Sustainable Tourism Cases: An Experimental Approach to Making Decisions.* Binghampton, NY: The Haworth Press; 123-139.

Hudson S, Cross P. 2005. Winter sports destinations: Dealing with seasonality. In Higham J, Hinch, T (eds) *Sport Tourism Destinations: Issues, Opportunities and Analysis.* Oxford: Butterworth Heinemann; 188-204.

Hudson S, Hinch T, Walker GJ, Simpson B. 2010. Constraints to sport tourism: A cross-cultural analysis. *Journal of Sport Tourism* **15** (1): 71-88.

Additional Websites

Aspen Chamber of Commerce: http://www.aspenchamber.org/

Aspen Ski Company: http://www.aspensnowmass.com/

BCF: Boom Your Brand communications company: http://www.boomyour-brand.com/

Bumps for Boomers: http://www.bumpsforboomers.com/

ESPN Winter X Games in Aspen: http://www.stayaspensnowmass.com/p-winter-x-games.php

National Ski Areas Association: http://www.nsaa.org/nsaa/home/

RRC Associates, ski industry analysts: http://rrcinfo.com/rrcassoc2/

Travel website for baby boomers: http://www.boomeropia.com/

Travel portal for baby boomers: http://www.babyboomertrips.com/

Website and television show for baby boomers: http://www.boomeradventurestv.com/

Self-test questions

1   How are demographic changes impacting participation rates in the ski industry?

2   How is Joe Nevin using social media to attract baby boomers to his programme?

3   Explain the key psychographic nuances of the travelling baby boomer

4   What tactics can marketers in the travel industry use to communicate effectively with boomers?

5   How did Aspen become one of the world's most famous and popular ski areas?

6   What is the resort doing to avoid stagnation?

7   What options does Nevin have for growing his business?

Key themes and sub-themes

- ◆ The ski industry in America
  - ◇ Demographic challenges facing the industry
  - ◇ Aspen resort and the Aspen Ski Company
  - ◇ Retention of boomers in the skiing market
- ◆ Baby boomers and travel
  - ◇ Baby boomer psychographics
  - ◇ Communicating to boomers
- ◆ The use of social media in marketing
- ◆ Strategies for new product development
- ◆ The destination lifecycle

Scan here to get the hyperlinks for this chapter.

9

Community Involvement in Trekking Tourism:

The Rinjani Trek Ecotourism Programme, Lombok, Indonesia

Carl Cater

Introduction

This case study examines community involvement in trekking tourism in Lombok, Indonesia. The project used participatory techniques in the management of tourism development, particularly in regard to developing mutually advantageous relationships between managers of the Gunung Rinjani National Park (GRNP) and poor communities situated around the park boundaries. Ecotourism associated with trekking in the park was envisaged as the engine-room of an integrated programme of conservation and community development. The New Zealand Government-funded Rinjani Trek Ecotourism Programme (RTEP) focuses on three sectors: park management, tourism and community development. The participatory approach focused on a community mapping exercise and the cataloguing of local heritage. A network of local stakeholder committees and co-operatives was formed to manage the trekking revenue. Under the Rinjani Trek Management Board (RTMB) umbrella, village stakeholder committees ensure decisions are made locally and carried through, and that tourism revenue brings benefits to the village in return for park protection. This case demonstrates two key areas of community empowerment through tourism as defined by Timothy (2002): public participation in decision making and involvement in the benefits of tourism.

Background

> "Rinjani is the heart of Lombok… it must be protected… if we don't, we say goodbye to our heart". Moelyo Nugroho. Orisa Tours and Travel Operations Manager, Mataram

Rising to over 3700m, Mount Rinjani is the second highest volcano in Indonesia, lying on the 'ring of fire' that encircles the Pacific Ocean. The volcano dominates the island of Lombok, which lies east of Bali (Figure 1). The island stretches about 80 km from north to south and more or less 70 km from east to west. Now largely inactive, the peak is on the edge of a crater rim, which itself is filled with a number of more recent volcanic cones and a large lake. The flanks of the volcano are a mixture of primary rainforest in the north and grassland savannah to the east. The region has a rich biodiversity, lying within the major transition zone called Wallaceae, where the flora and fauna of South-East Asia meets Australasia. The three-day Rinjani Trek route from Senaru to the crater rim, down to the crater-lake then on to Sembalun La-wang (Figure 2), is considered one of the best treks in South-East Asia.

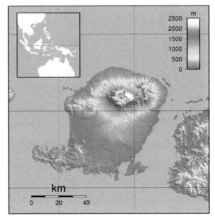

Figure 1: Location and topography of Lombok.
Source: Wikipedia commons

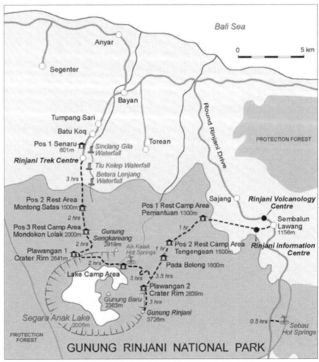

Figure 2: The trekking route.
Source: Rinjani Trek Management
Board

The volcano is also very important to the people of Lombok, both as a spiritual focus and as a source of most of the island's fresh water. Approximately 70% of the island's population (approximately 3 million people) relies on Rinjani's streams to provide water for drinking and agriculture, especially rice cultivation. The Sasak population of Lombok are mostly Muslim and the island is known as the 'island of a thousand mosques', although the local people incorporate many of their former animist beliefs into their religion. There are also a number of Balinese, who follow Hinduism. For the people of Lombok, Sasak and Balinese alike, the volcano is revered as a sacred place and the abode of deities. Its crater lake is the destination of thousands of pilgrims who place offerings in the water and bathe away ailments in the hot springs.

Tourism in Lombok

Lombok has a well-established tourism industry, with resorts being established on the north-west coast and offshore in the Gili islands in the early 1990s (Hampton, 2005). This was in response to the Indonesian government seeking to alter the dominance of Bali in the national tourism picture. However, international tourism to Indonesia has fluctuated greatly over the past 20 years as a result of political crises, terrorism and natural disasters (Hampton, 2005). From 26,000 foreign arrivals in 1967, visitors increased to around 400,000 per year in the mid-70s, passing 2.17 million in 1990 and peaking at 5.6 million in 1996. However, the fall of long-term political dictator Suharto in 1997 saw international arrivals dip to 5.2 million, while the Asian Financial Crisis of 1998 led to arrivals falling further to an estimated 3.8 million in 1998 (Hampton, 2005). A brief recovery was reversed with the Bali terrorist bombings[1] of October 2002 and the Boxing Day tsunami[2] of 2004, which negatively impacted on international tourism flows. International arrivals to Indonesia only recovered to their former level by the end of the decade. While Balinese tourism recovered quite quickly, Lombok took much longer to do so, as the origin of the Bali bombers was from that island. Low international arrivals have been a challenge for all tourism operators in Indonesia over the last decade, especially those seeking a sustainable future and to achieve community involvement. However, Lombok is pursuing international tourism

---

1   On 12th October 2002 an extremist Islamic group carried out terrorist bombings in nightclubs in the tourist resort of Kuta, Bali, killing 202 people.

2   On 26th December 2004 a large earthquake caused a Tsunami that killed over 130,000 people in Indonesia alone. However, these were mainly in Aceh province on Sumatra and Lombok was not directly affected.

growth with the development of the southern Kuta region for resort development and a new international airport.

Figure 3: Seasonal trekking. Photo credit: Carl Cater

Despite these challenges, the GRNP has been popular since the 1980s with more adventurous international tourists, who typically trek over three or four days between the major trailheads, Senaru in the north and Sembalun in the east, visiting the rim, lake and summit in between (Figure 2). The first guesthouse or losmen was built in 1982. Since then, many small businesses have emerged to serve this market, hiring out camping equipment, arranging guides and porters or organising logistics in the form of simple trekking packages (Schellhorn, 2010). Trekking is highly seasonal, as heavy rains between December and March make treks both dangerous and pointless, as most of the summit is persistently engulfed in cloud. During this time the trekking routes are closed to international tourists (Figure 3).

Gunung Rinjani National Park

The GRNP was established in 1997 to protect the ecosystem surrounding the volcano. Rinjani Conservation Area (RCA) consists of 125,740 ha of forest cover, which represents 26.5% of the surface area and 86% of the total forest cover of the island. The forests of Gunung Rinjani have been classified into a number of different protection zones, those being 'National Park' (41,330 ha), 'Protection Forest' (48,345 ha), 'Production Forest' (22,975 ha), 'Limited Production Forest' (9,935 ha) and 'Botanical Park' (3,155 ha) (Astawa, 2004). Animal species include: deer-rusa (Cervus timorensis); kijang (Muntiacus muntjak); wild boar (Sus scrofa), long-tailed macaque (Macaca fascicularis), lutung (Presbytis cristata), and a number of bird species such as the helmeted friarbird (Philemon buceroides), the rainbow Lorikeet (Trichoglossus haematodus) and the scaly-crowned honeyeater (Lichmera lombokia) (Beudels and Hardi, 1981). Research conducted by the World Wildlife Foundation Indonesia, Nusa Tenggara Programme, in 2002, estimated that the RCA produces economic and ecosystem service benefits from the sale of agricultural produce, bottled mineral water and tourism.

At the same time, half a million people reside in over 80 village communities surrounding the park, more than half of which directly share a border with the national park (Astawa, 2004). Consequently, a number of social, economic, cultural, political and environmental problems threaten the integrity of the RCA. These include illegal logging, population pressure, abandonment of women and young children, low educational status and conflicts over the management of the natural resources. Astawa (2004) also points to problems related to governmental structures in Indonesia, which tend to favour a top-down approach, a piecemeal approach to conservation and development, a lack of coordination among development agencies, a strong sectoral focus and a short-term orientation to development. "These policy orientations often lead to further debates about development objectives, competition among stakeholders, lack of sharing of information, and the lack of overall coordination" (Astawa, 2004, p.6). These problems have been compounded by visitor impacts, which include littering, insensitive village visits, pollution of the hot springs, poaching of flora and fauna, and erosion along the trekking trail (McKinnon and Suwan, 2000).

Rinjani trek

Following a 1996 feasibility study, in 1999 the New Zealand Official Development Assistance (NZODA) Programme[3] made a commitment to sustainable tourism and community development in the Rinjani area. From 1999 to 2002, the Gunung Rinjani National Park Project (GRNPP) focused on improving park management, fostering community development and developing responsible park tourism (Schellhorn, 2010). A second project phase, from 2002

---

3   Now superseded by the New Zealand Aid Programme (NZAID).

to 2005, known as the Rinjani Trek Ecotourism Programme (RTEP), concentrated on social, economic and conservation management benefits for local communities living adjacent to the park (Tourism Resource Consultants, 2005). Between 1999 and 2005, New Zealand provided over US$2.4 million in funding to these programmes (Scheyvens, 2007).

Many trekking-based destinations in developing countries have built on the experience of the Annapurna Conservation Area Project (ACAP) in Nepal. ACAP took a people-oriented approach to protected-area management that is somewhat different from traditional park management systems. Historically, protected area management was solely concerned with the protection of wildlife and biological species, with limited regard for the welfare or the role of indigenous people. The ACAP project was one of the first to recognise that local people have a crucial role to play in conservation and sustainable development, and that they must be regarded as being both the executors and beneficiaries of the conservation area. ACAP has been guided by three principles: ensuring people's participation, facilitating a catalyst approach and promoting sustainability (Gurung, 2002). The latter is particularly important, as many developments that rely on foreign aid fail because no provision is made for sustaining them once the donor agencies leave. At that moment, the newly completed projects can neither be maintained nor managed by the local people or the government. If the project is terminated it would often result in all the money, time and effort that had been invested in the project being lost. Often the only practical way to maintain financial viability is through the imposition of a trekking levy to be paid by tourists to the management authority. As such, tourism often becomes the paymaster of park conservation.

Using this approach, the RTMB was formed under the authority of the Governor of West Nusa Tenggara as a partnership between the national park, the tourism industry and the local communities. The RTMB is an example of a non-governmental organisation (NGO) involved in developing community tourism. Its activities focus on enabling and encouraging the formally registered community cooperative trek centres to work with the park managers. These are the Rinjani Trek Centre (RTC), Senaru and the Rinjani Information Centre (RIC), Sembalun Lawang. Under the direction of the RTMB, each centre has a cooperative, a roster system for trekking and porters, village tour activities, trek-trail maintenance and handicraft sales. The executive functions of the Board are carried out by a small staff based in Mataram, the only sizeable town on Lombok, who undertake regular field consultations.

RTMB is responsible for the collection of a trekking fee, which was introduced in 2003. In 2008 this was increased from $6 to $17 for international tourists, although it is much lower for domestic tourists. Pilgrims using the trails to access those parts of the park considered to be sacred do not currently pay fees. The majority of the fee revenue is allocated to the local community cooperatives, with 25% of the fee going toward administration of the RTMB and 12.5% toward national park operating costs. NZAID funding expired in late 2008, but the new fee structure is designed to provide self-sufficiency in current RTMB operations. A number of strategic initiatives, such as product diversification, have been earmarked for possible future donor funding. Revenue from tourism activities and entry fees collected at the park centres is used for conservation, training and management of the Rinjani Trek, thus ensuring long-term viability. In 2007 there were 4,032 international tourists who completed the trek and 1,997 domestic tourists (this does not include pilgrims using the trails). Data from ticket sales suggest, however, that trekker numbers have still failed to recover to the level of the early 1990s (see Table 1).

Table 1: Rinjani trek foreign users (1991–2008).

Year	No. of foreign trekker tickets issued	Change on previous year (%)
1991	7,297 (est.)	
2002	2,451	
2003	1,486	−39.4
2004	1,877	+26.3
2005	2,802	+49.3
2006	3,222	+15.0
2007	4,032	+25.1
2008	5,626	+39.5

Source: Schellhorn (2010)

Once established, the RTMB was encouraged to broaden its vision to include not only the trek but also other community and park partnerships, fostering tourism and recreation-related income-generating opportunities for communities. RTMB adopted a 'three circles' approach, recognising that park management and sustainable tourism relies on community development and empowerment. According to Timothy (2002), there are two key areas of community empowerment: public participation in decision making and involvement in benefits of tourism, both of which are well demonstrated by the RTMB. The following sections look at these in respect of the efforts of the RTMB.

Public participation in decision making

The RTMB has implemented and fostered a wide variety of initiatives that required long discussions and participation with community members to determine appropriate solutions. RTMB took a grassroots approach based on participatory rural appraisal (PRA). PRA is not necessarily 'rural' in focus, but it is often implemented in a rural context because of its small scale and community focus. Furthermore, many of its methods draw from the implementation of rural development initiatives in Africa and India in the late 1980s. PRA methods are context-dependent, as PRA seeks to work with a spirit of inventiveness and improvisation, helping people in different parts of the world to develop their own varieties of approach and method (Scheyvens, 1999). PRA is also sometimes referred to as participatory rapid appraisal, as it seeks a rapid assessment of development goals. However, this term may be considered inappropriate, as significant timescales are the hallmark of effective community engagement. Indeed, PRA "goals are not achieved overnight" (Cater and Cater, 2007, p.128). Examples from the Philippines (Calumpong, 2000) illustrate that community-based resource management is a long and never-ending undertaking, requiring sustained commitment by all stakeholders.

The principal method for public participation used in Rinjani was a community mapping exercise. This was carried out in 2000/01 in the two main gateway communities, the purpose being to identify the views of major stakeholders. Sketch maps are a useful tool for getting community stakeholders to express their understanding of place and are often used in tourism planning. Different mental maps of the Rinjani region were developed with farmers, village residents, national park representatives and tourism operators, as well as with different gender groups. These maps reflected the beliefs, interests and issues of most concern to these different sectors, and were developed in focus groups and workshops. For example, indigenous female residents were most interested in where their crops and water sources were located, whereas park authority representatives took a much more scientific approach to the landscape (see Figures 4 and 5). These sketches were then combined to create a regional map that would act as the focal point for tourist information (Figure 6). The evolution of this map, from community to publication, now forms an exhibit in the Visitor Centre at Senaru.

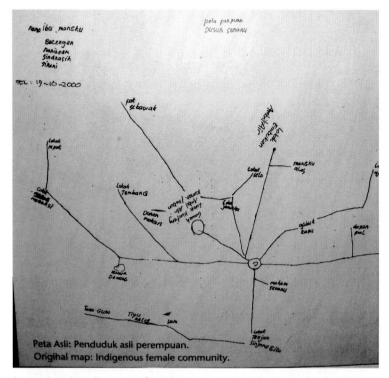

Figure 4: Map derived with indigenous female community. Photo credit: Carl Cater

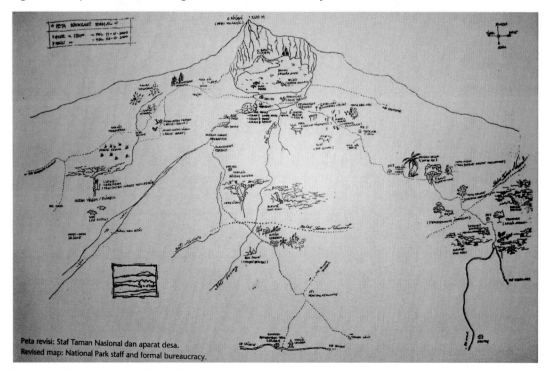

Figure 5: Map derived with park managers. Photo credit: Carl Cater

Figure 6: Tourist map. Photo credit: Carl Cater

Trek guiding and village interpretation products were developed with local leaders to highlight the deep cultural traditions of the Sasak and Balinese people. Traditional medical practices are maintained through the importance of a local healer, although this is in conjunction with regular visiting clinics from medical personnel. Stories from the verbal tradition collected during the PRA phase have been recorded in bilingual booklets, which catalogue the stories and beliefs of the Rinjani area. Useful as a resource by local guides to enrich their interpretation skills, it also promotes cultural pride and enriches the visitor experience (see Figure 7). Centre displays make a major feature of local culture and traditions. Trekkers may also engage in a traditional blessing ceremony prior to their trek to ensure good fortune on their hike.

Figure 7: Local cultural interpretation in 'Rinjani Mountain Stories' booklet. Photo credit: Carl Cater

RTMB is also involved with cooperative strategic planning for the future and continue to hold planning workshops. Two more Rinjani communities are to be involved in the RTMB programme in the future. One of these already benefits from fee contributions to the local cooperative. Undoubtedly, the Rinjani project faces some challenges in the future, as indeed it has in the past. However, the participatory approach has created structures that are well suited to meeting these threats and ensure maximum positive benefits and minimum impacts. At present, the use of green technology such as power generation or waste treatment is low, but it is important that implementation of these has not taken precedence over creating sustainable community livelihoods first and foremost. With this foundation, the successful introduction of such initiatives will have a greater chance of success.

Involvement in the benefits of tourism

RTMB has also fostered the development of the community-based cooperatives, which aim to ensure that the benefits of tourism are spread beyond the tourism industry. Slightly higher numbers of tourists travel from Sembalun to Senaru than vice versa. However, the higher contributions to the community cooperative in Sembalun are offset by the greater numbers of homestays and other tourist products in Senaru, which provide increased multiplier[4] effects. In Senaru, tourist contributions have enabled the cooperative to provide low-interest credit to farmers and small traders. In Sembalun, increased profits from tourism in 2007 enabled the purchase of an additional five cattle for the cooperative (Figure 8). These cooperatives have outlasted previous cooperative efforts in these communities because of their organisation and financial oversight from RTMB.

Figure 8: Cattle in the community cooperative at Sembalun. Photo credit: Carl Cater

The human capital[5] of the host communities has been increased through workshops and training programmes. Courses for guides and porters provide education on park awareness, conservation, visitor interpretation, service standards, cooking and hygiene, equipment handling, the English and Indonesian languages, mountain lore, wildlife, Sasak culture, first aid, safety and rescue procedures, and radio handling. By 2008, RTMB had provided

---

4   The multiplier effect is concerned with the way that expenditure on tourism filters through the economy, stimulating other sectors as it does so. Income earned by tourism is spent in other sectors such as agriculture, multiplying the effect of the initial expenditure.

5   Human capital includes skills, knowledge, ability to labour and good health. These are important to be able to pursue different livelihood strategies

training on these topics to 49 trek guides and 180 porters from the total of 312 porters based in village communities. Role plays have assisted in the development of these skills. Another course on monitoring and evaluation assists with the collection of baseline data to monitor tourist impacts. A travel cooperative was established with 15 local trek organisers to become a licensed Indonesian travel agency, thus regularising community-based trek operations. A roster system of guides and porters ensures that equal opportunities are provided for all those who wish to participate.

In order to spread the benefits of tourism in the communities, and so as to appeal to a wider cross-section of the market, RTMB has also pursued a product development strategy. A number of trekking agencies now offer a 'deluxe' version of the trek, with a toilet tent and better food, providing higher margins for local operators. A recent development of geotourism[6] is carried out in partnership with the West Nusa Tenggara Mining and Energy Office, and intended to appeal to those interested in the geological history of the caldera. A range of shorter walks in and around the villages allow for visits to waterfalls and enable a more in-depth understanding of village life. The traditional village at Senaru is an attraction to visitors, as are basket makers and weavers at Sembalun (Figure 9). In addition, RTMB is currently developing a range of volunteer and interactive programmes to cater to the special interest market. It is felt that the harvesting and preparation of a number of cash crops[7], such as cocoa and coffee, would be of particular interest. To appeal to the more adventurous market, an adventure race took place in partnership with Visit Indonesia's 2008 promotion.

The RTMB has also fostered gender equality through the involvement of female residents in the tourism programmes. Women are frequently overlooked in tourist development processes, with "scant, if any regard" to their position in society (Scheyvens, 2002, p.122). In Indonesia there is a cultural issue, whereby guiding is often seen as an inappropriate activity for women. Some studies even suggest that this is viewed by villagers as an activity equivalent to prostitution (Wilkinson and Pratiwi, 1995). In Rinjani, it would widely be considered as inappropriate for females to be involved with overnight trekking on a multi-day trek. However, the development of shorter village and waterfall tours has provided opportunities for a number of female guides, who frequently take tourists on these walks.

---

6   Geotourism is the travel to and appreciation of natural landscapes and geological phenomena, such as volcanic or fluvial features.

7   Cash crops are high value crops, often grown for export rather than subsistence or domestic agricultural production.

Figure 9: Basketweavers at Sembalun. Photo credit: Carl Cater

For those that do not participate directly in tourism, there have also been opportunities to share in indirect benefits. RTMB has arranged training for seven small-business groups with the aim of encouraging local people to produce food, handicrafts, weaving, bamboo craft, organic farming and cattle-raising. It has also providing credit to about 100 more small traders as start-up capital. Interestingly, most of these have been women, demonstrating the further gender-empowerment potential of such microcredit[8] schemes.

Conservation of the park itself is still at the core of the RTMB programme, given its importance as a watershed for the majority of Lombok. The national park staff members work closely with the RTMB and surrounding communities to try to ensure that this goal is met. This creates a philosophy of a shared resource for conservation and recreational use that is evident in many of the operating procedures. Litter clean-up campaigns initiated by the park authority are funded by RTMB and take place every two weeks during the trekking season. Since domestic visitors are at present responsible for much of the litter, partnerships have been formed with religious organisations in

---

8   Microcredit is a small amount of money loaned to a client by a bank or other institution. The clients of microfinance are generally poor and low-income people.

Lombok and Bali to educate appropriate behaviour. In 2008, RTMB trialled a financial deposit scheme for the 'pack-in, pack-out' approach to waste. Closure of the park during the wet season ensures that the park is given time to recover from tourist use. Expectations of increased future visitation are high and RTMB and the national park authority carried out a carrying capacity assessment in 2009 to determine appropriate levels.

Tourist benefits

The tourists themselves have also benefitted from the greater organisation of trekking. The visitor centres also assist guides, as it creates an image of respectability for the operators and improves their position of power in relation to guests. Tourist education is a cornerstone of the RTMB approach, facilitated through interpretative material, visitor centres and accredited guides. The community-managed centres (the RTC and the RIC) are designed to educate tourists about the park and to give in-depth information about the natural and cultural environment, so that visitors can feel comfortable and enjoy their visit. Designed as a tourism focus for both trekkers and non-trekking visitors, displays have been developed in partnership with the local people. They include sections on:

♦   Sasak cultural traditions and local village life

♦   Significance of the mountain in Sasak and Balinese culture

♦   Environmental and cultural do's and don'ts

♦   Safety codes on the mountain and how to organise a Rinjani Trek

♦   Flora and fauna of the GRNP

♦   Volcanology.

Local stories which communicate a strong sense of place are also evident. Tourist codes of conduct are also communicated, with the aim of to reducing inappropriate behaviour by visitors. The codes particular focus is on encouraging visitors not to make certain displays of affection, while also promoting sexual abstinence by trek participants.

For a volcanic peak that is often underestimated because of its tropical location, rising to a height that would be a serious proposition at higher latitudes, safety management is also paramount. Indeed, the mountain has claimed more than its fair share of people's lives over the years, mostly as a result of excess bravado and a failure to respect local knowledge. However, the RTMB have not overlooked this issue and have put procedures in place to minimise such risks. An evacuation plan developed in partnership with park rangers and the loan of radios to trekking groups reduces risk. The closure of the park during the wet season, when conditions are highly changeable, is an important part of the risk management strategy. Each year 7% of the entry fee is set aside to cover search-and-rescue operation costs in the event of an accident. Trekkers are strongly encouraged to pay for a guide or at the very least a porter on their trip, so that they can rely on local knowledge of the conditions in the park.

Continuing challenges

In the dynamic tourism setting described in this case, there are a number of on-going issues that the communities of Rinjani face. Some of these correspond to community development barriers described by Timothy (2002). These include power, socio-political traditions, gender and ethnicity, information accessibility, lack of awareness, economic issues, lack of cooperation and partnerships and peripherality.

Pilgrimage

Apart from international tourists, approximately 10,000 domestic pilgrims visit the volcano annually in order to engage in religious rituals and worship. Large numbers of Balinese pilgrims in particular visit the lakeshore in order to engage in catharsis of all sorts of ailments, often leaving offerings, trinkets and clothing at the site. This has presented a management challenge for park authorities, especially as arrivals tend to be highly concentrated (sometimes several thousand at a time), and they have differing conceptions of natural value and park infrastructure. Some benches and shelters have been dismantled for use as firewood by these pilgrims in the past. As Cochrane (2006, p.979) acknowledges, users of national parks in Indonesia often have differing "cognitive interpretations of nature" to international tourists, and this is an ongoing management challenge.

Indigenous benefits

A second challenge related to the success of the RTMB and trekking tourism has been ensuring indigenous benefits in the face of migration into the region. In the 1970s, Suharto encouraged transmigration within Lombok, which has meant that over half of the residents of Senaru village have settled since this time (Schellhorn, 2010). There are significant cultural and social differences between these 'newcomers' and the original wetu telu inhabitants, for example the integration of traditional beliefs with Islamic ones (Schellhorn, 2010). Schellhorn shows how the long-term residents of the village are less well-equipped to deal with the business of tourism and find themselves isolated from the cash economy. This leads to uneven distribution of opportunity within the communities, largely as the 16 trekking businesses currently in Senaru are owned by newcomers and they control the brokering of the trekking with the tourists. In 2011, there were also reports that a travel agency based on Bali was selling trekking packages and falsely claiming to be affiliated with RTMB.

There are suggestions that the shorter women's tours have been hijacked by copycat entrepreneurs and that in total "native employees represent less than 5% of the entire workforce in Senaru's hospitality sector" (Schellhorn, 2010, p.122). Indeed, there is a suggestion that the later stages of tourism product development were less inclusive of women than the earlier capacity-building phases (Scheyvens, 2007). This poses a legitimate question about whose heritage is being sold as a tourism product and the degree of ownership (and consequent benefit) that the original residents have over this heritage. Schellhorn suggests that "while the Sasak wetu telu supply their adat tradition and lifestyle as free attractions, it is outsiders and migrants who control the business of tourism" (Schellhorn, 2010, p.122). The indigenous residents have a number of distinct barriers to greater involvement in decision making and benefit sharing, which are suggested to be a lack of education, a lack of understanding of tourism, high levels of competition and the spatial distribution of traditional settlements relative to tourist access routes. Consequently:

> "To date, the wetu telu peasants continue to play a rather passive role in the process of tourism production. The fact that an aid project has not managed to fundamentally change this situation is indicative of the institutional challenges that disadvantaged minorities face within donor-funded ecotourism programmes. These challenges are additional to the more obvious barriers resulting from the conditions of culture, education, ethnicity, gender, politics, history, location, mobility, socio-economy, tourism skills and knowledge"(Schellhorn, 2010, p.124)

Recognition

Despite these challenges, RTMB is an exemplary model for sustainable tourism planning in developing countries. It is an example of new tourism thinking that puts community participation and empowerment at the centre of the tourism-environment nexus. RTMB was one of the winners of a National Geographic Legacy award in 2004 and a finalist in the Tourism for Tomorrow Awards in 2005. The latter award seeks to recognise best practice in sustainable tourism within the travel and tourism industry worldwide. RTMB was invited to apply for the Tourism for Tomorrow awards again in 2008, in the destination stewardship category, and was once again a finalist. Destinations in this category must demonstrate sustainable tourism planning and policies that enhance the natural, historic and cultural assets unique to a destination (WTTC, 2011). This includes minimum negative impacts to the environment; protection of the destination's natural and cultural heritage, promotion of sense of place and authenticity, direct economic and social benefits to the host community, and educating visitors on the sustainable tourism efforts of the destination. International recognition has provided RTMB with a show-case to promote the project to other destinations and, perhaps more impor-tantly, foreign tourists.

Conclusions

This case study demonstrates some of the methods used to involve com-munities in planning and development of trekking tourism products in a protected area. The research by Schellhorn (2010) shows that ensuring the complete involvement of all members of the community in both decision making and benefit sharing is far from easy. However, RTMB has taken a number of innovative approaches with the broad spectrum of stakeholders to try to achieve community empowerment. The community mapping ex-ercise involving the collection of local beliefs and practices can be consid-ered to be a good example of sustainable stakeholder involvement. Local community concerns are considered to be an integral part of the success of the Rinjani Trek. Initially, local issues were systematically recorded and as-sessed in participatory rural appraisals. Involvement continues with routine monitoring and on-going representation within the management system of a wide spectrum of local groups, including the role of women in them.

RTMB has also been active in thinking outside of the tourism 'box' in aug-menting the human capital of residents. A wide range of training courses have enabled many people from the communities to have the opportunity to become involved in tourism, and have also increased the professional-ism of the tourism offering, thereby increasing tourist satisfaction. Outside of tourism, the trekking fees have enabled the establishment of community cooperatives and microcredit schemes which have increased the livelihood options for residents of the Rinjani area.

Another issue that is clear in sustainable tourism development is the im-portance of thinking on long-term timescales. Perhaps the concerns about indigenous benefits that Schellhorn (2010) has identified will only be met as the various initiatives put in place by RTMB filter down to all members of the various communities involved. There is a degree of external dependence here, as many tourism-based developments in Indonesia have been particularly vulnerable in a decade of instability. Indeed, local people are responding to the opportunities presented by tourism, despite relatively low visitor numbers. A growing understanding of the importance of preserving natural and cultural attractions is demonstrated by the communities with corresponding reforestation initiatives, trek maintenance and declines in poaching. When visitor numbers recover, particularly higher-yield trekkers, mechanisms are now in place to more effectively benefit local people.

References

Astawa B. 2004. Finding common ground in Rinjani, Lombok, Indonesia: Towards improved governance, conflict resolution, and institutional reform. Paper presented at *The Commons in an Age of Global Transition: Challenges, Risks and Opportunities, the Tenth Biennial Conference of the International Association for the Study of Common Property* Oaxaca, Mexico August 9-13, 2004. http://hdl.handle.net/10535/754

Beudels R, Hardi H. 1981. *Feasibility Study of the Rinjani Complex, Lombok.* UNDP/FAO National Park Development Project INS/78/061. Field Report No. 13. Bogor: FAO.

Cater C, Cater E. 2007. *Marine Ecotourism.* Oxford: CABI.

Calumpong H. 2000. *Community Based Coastal Resources Management in Apo Island.* Philippines: Silliman University.

Cochrane J. 2006. Indonesian national parks: Understanding leisure users. *Annals of Tourism Research* **33** (4): 979-997.

Gurung H.B. 2002. Ecotourism, sustainable development and environmental education: A case study of ACAP. In Tilbury D, Fien J, Schneuder D. (eds) *Education and Sustainability: Response to the Global Challenge.* IUCN Commission on Education and Communication CEE; 55-63.

Hampton M. 1998. Backpacker tourism and economic development. *Annals of Tourism Research* **25** (3): 639-660.

McKinnon J, Suwan Y. (2000). *Gunung Rinjani National Park Project PRA report: Participatory Rural Appraisal in Senaru and Sembalun Lawang.* Tourism Resource Consultants, Wellington.

NZAID. 2002. *Review of Gunung Rinjani National Park Project Lombok, Indonesia for the New Zealand Agency for International Development: Review Team Report*. NZAID, Wellington.

Schellhorn M. 2010. Development for whom? Social justice and the business of ecotourism. *Journal of Sustainable Tourism* **18** (1): 115-135.

Scheyvens R. 1999. Case study: Ecotourism and the empowerment of local communities. *Tourism Management* **20** (2): 245-249.

Scheyvens R. 2007. Ecotourism and gender issues. In Higham J. (ed.) *Critical Issues in Ecotourism: Understanding a Complex Tourism Phenomenon*. Oxford and Burlington, MA: Butterworth Heinmann; 185-213.

Timothy D. 2002. Tourism and community development issues. In Sharpley R. and Telfer D.J. (eds) *Tourism and Development: Concepts and Issues*. Clevedon: Channel View Publications; 149-164.

Tourism Resource Consultants. 2005. *Gunung Rinjani National Park: Rinjani Trek Ecotourism Programme*. End of transition phase report. Tourism Resource Consultants, Wellington.

Wilkinson PF, Pratiwi W. 1995. Gender and tourism in an Indonesian village. *Annals of Tourism Research* **22 (2):** 283–299.

Ancillary Student Material

Further reading

Cole S. 2007. *Tourism, Culture and Development: Hopes, Dreams and Realities in East Indonesia*. Clevedon: Channel View Publications. A detailed case study on host community involvement in tourism in Indonesia.

Dowling RK, Newsome D. 2006. *Geotourism*. Oxford: Butterworth-Heinemann. An introduction to the geotourism concept.

Scheyvens R. 2002. *Tourism for Development: Empowering Communities*. Harlow: Prentice Hall. An excellent critical perspective on community involvement in tourism

Sharpley R, Telfer D J. 2002. *Tourism and Development: Concepts and Issues*. Clevedon: Channel View Publications. An edited collection of chapters discussing the challenges of tourism development.

Related websites and audio-visual material

The following websites offer background information on Gunung Rinjani and the Rinjani Trek Ecotourism Programme. The key resources also include those listed in the reference section of the case study.

Rinjani Trek Ecotourism Program http://www.lombokrinjanitrek.org/ (Tourist trekking information and images)

Official Indonesia tourism ministry page for Mount Rinjani http://www.indonesia.travel/en/destination/256/mount-rinjani-national-park

Tourism for Tomorrow Awards http://www.tourismfortomorrow.com

Indonesian tourism statistics http://www.budpar.go.id

Youtube videos http://www.youtube.com/watch?v=gazQcWDVNrc

Self-test questions

Try to answer the following questions to test your knowledge and understanding. If you are not sure of the answers then please refer to the suggested references and further reading sources.

1   What are the threats to sustainable tourism in Rinjani?

2   What are some of the external factors that have challenged international tourism to Rinjani?

3   What methods has the RTMB used to ensure that local people are involved in decision making and the benefits of tourism?

4   Which groups find it more difficult to be involved in tourism opportunities?

5   Why should community involvement not been seen as a short-term process?

6   How has the RTMB coped with issues of seasonality in the trekking?

Key themes and theories

The key themes raised in the case study relate to the following areas:

- ◆ Opportunities for host communities in tourism
- ◆ Visitor management in protected areas
- ◆ Domestic versus international tourist needs
- ◆ Power structures in tourism
- ◆ Tourism awards

The key theories relate to:

- ◆ Empowerment of host communities
- ◆ Tourism development and the role of non-governmental organisations (NGOs)
- ◆ Preservation of culture and heritage
- ◆ Participatory approaches

If you need to source further information on any of the above themes and theories then these headings could be used as key words to search for materials and case studies.

 Scan here to get the hyperlinks for this chapter.

10

World Heritage Site Designation:

New Lanark World Heritage Site, Scotland

Anna Leask

Introduction

There are currently 936 designated World Heritage Sites (WHS) inscribed on the UNESCO World Heritage List (WHL), located in a total of 153 States Parties[1]. The designation process is a highly formalised one. Every year, State Parties have the opportunity to nominate up to two sites from within their national territory for inclusion on the list. The resources of each nominated site are then evaluated against 10 set criteria, of which the site should meet at least one. Successful sites are inscribed onto the WHL and the States Parties responsible for them must agree to follow the Operational Guidelines determined by UNESCO. This case study outlines the general process of WHS designation before going on to examine how it operates in the UK. The discussion then moves on to consider the specific case of New Lanark, an industrial conservation village in Scotland (see Figure 1). The case study focuses on how the site achieved WHS status and the implications of this designation for the on-going management of the site.

World Heritage Site designation process

The 'Convention concerning the Protection of the World's Cultural and Natural Heritage' (also known as the 'World Heritage Convention') was approved by UNESCO in 1972 and came into force in 1976. The purpose of the Convention is to "ensure the identification, protection, conservation, presentation and transmission to future generations of cultural and natural heritage of outstanding universal value" (UNESCO, 2008, p.2). The World Heritage Committee (WHC) coordinates the inscription process, encouraging nominations from States Parties that have signed up to the Convention.

---

1   States Parties are countries which adhere to the World Heritage Convention and that have agreed to identify and nominate sites on their national territory to be considered for inscription on the World Heritage List.

Each nomination is evaluated by experts from the International Council on Monuments and Sites (ICOMOS) for built sites or the International Union for the Conservation of Nature (IUCN) for natural sites, or both in the case of mixed sites. The experts' task is to determine whether or not the site does indeed demonstrate 'outstanding universal value'. The aim is to "encourage conservation of the resources within the designated site and surrounding buffer zones on a local level and also to foster a sense of collective global responsibility through international cooperation, exchange and support" (Leask, 2006, p.7).

Figure 1: New Lanark. Photo reproduced by kind permission of New Lanark Trust

Before a site can be formally nominated, it should be shown on the Tentative List of the States Party. This is an inventory of sites considered to be appropriate for inclusion on the WHL, often the result of intense lobbying within a States Party, and those that the States Party plans to nominate over the following years. Each States Party may nominate up to two sites per annum, provided that one is a natural site. Once agreed, the relevant site must prepare a Nomination Document that details the criteria for inscription, site boundaries, buffer zone and features of 'outstanding universal value' inherent to the site. Since 1996, sites must also at this stage submit a Management Plan, detailing how the integrity of the site is to be maintained. Once these documents are submitted, experts undertake an in-depth evaluation of the site, culminating in a recommendation being made to the WHC. The options include inscribing the site onto the WHL, deferring the decision pending further detail or discussion of documents or rejecting the nomination. The future of the WHL has recently been debated (Fyall and Rakic, 2006), particularly in view of the imbalances that have developed in terms of the different types of site represented on the List and their geographical distribution. Full details of the inscription process can be seen on the web pages of UNESCO (2009) and in Leask (2006).

The motivations for heritage sites to aspire to be inscribed on the WHL are varied and complex, as are the benefits to be derived from WHS status. Seeking access to the WHL may be to gain international recognition for the resource, to source conservation expertise and support, or to achieve the perceived economic benefits from the additional tourism activity such designation may bring. It has been argued that the motivations are "varied, debatable in their benefits and often politically intensified" (Leask, 2006, p.12). Meanwhile it has been found that the anticipated tourism benefits of inscription – an increasingly common ambition among States Parties – are not always as clear-cut as they might at first appear (Fyall and Rakic, 2006).

The implications of designation for a site depend upon a number of factors, including past and present conservation efforts at the site, the environment within which it is situated, and the planning and management policies that apply to it. Various authors, including Hall and Piggin (2001), van der Aa (2005) and Shackley (2005), have researched the potential implications of WHS designation either at the national, regional or site level. As with the motivations for seeking designation, its implications are varied and depend on a wide range of factors, including the state of the heritage resource at the time of inscription, local interpretations of how UNESCO's Operational Guidelines should be applied and varying levels of commitment among stakeholders.

World Heritage Site designation in the UK

The UK is considered to be well represented on the WHL, with 27 sites successfully nominated since the UK signed up to the Convention in 1984. The recently revised UK Tentative List contains 15 sites that have been listed as seeking nomination. As discussed by Leask and Fyall (2001), the UK has taken a strategic approach to their nominations by targeting categories of site that are under-represented on the World Heritage List. This, it is hoped, will increase the nominated sites' chances of successful inscription.

The Department for Culture, Media and Sport (DCMS) is the UK State Party, along with Historic Scotland, Cadw in Wales and the Northern Ireland Environment Agency. The Local Authority World Heritage Forum helps UK local authorities to protect, conserve and present the sites, working with ICOMOS UK to assist World Heritage Coordinators in developing and sharing best practice. A recent report compiled for DCMS investigated the costs and benefits to the UK of involvement in the WHS system. The report determined that WHS status brought no additional statutory protection for the resource in the UK, though it is a key material planning consideration in determining planning applications. Responsibility for protecting the sites lies with the appropriate regional and local authority. The report also established that both the costs of maintaining the existing sites and of nominating new sites have risen in recent years, meaning that prospective sites may miss out as funds are directed to those already designated by UNESCO.

New Lanark World Heritage Site

New Lanark is an industrial conservation village sited in the Clyde Valley in Scotland. It is surrounded by the Falls of Clyde Nature Reserve and is located one hour's drive from both Glasgow and Edinburgh. The site was designated as a WHS in 2001 under criteria ii, iv and vi (UNESCO, 2009). Founded in 1785 as a brand new industrial settlement by the Scottish entrepreneur David Dale, it became famous as a model village under the enlightened management of the pioneering social reformer, Robert Owen. He founded the world's first infant school in the village, and offered free medical care and a humane and caring environment for his workers. The cotton mills remained in production until 1968, after which a massive programme of conservation and restoration was required. The New Lanark Trust, an independent charity, was founded in 1974 to achieve this aim. Most of the housing within the village is now also managed by a subsidiary of the New Lanark Trust, in addition to a small number of owner-occupied properties. The current population stands at approximately 180.

Today the village has been almost completely restored as a living, working community (see Figure 2), and has won many prestigious awards as one of Europe's top conservation projects. It is also one of Scotland's largest visitor attractions, with approximately 350,000 visitors per annum, and has an award-winning visitor centre. The riverside setting and the Scottish Wildlife Trust's Falls of Clyde Reserve, which is adjacent to the village, add further dimensions to the tourism product. Further information on New Lanark is available on the New Lanark website, where a site map can also be found.

Figure 2: Aerial view of the New Lanark WHS. Photo reproduced by kind permission of New Lanark Trust

New Lanark World Heritage Site designation

Originally nominated for inclusion on the World Heritage List in 1986, the New Lanark submission was initially deferred for two reasons: firstly because a UNESCO review of the criteria for industrial sites was pending, and secondly because it had been suggested that an offshoot of New Lanark (New Harmony in the USA) might also be worthy of consideration either as a joint or competing bid. A major problem lay in interpreting the criteria for nomination of industrial sites. In particular, demonstrating the conservation and other management challenges faced by 'industrial sites' was considered to be rather more demanding than was the case for 'cultural sites', which appeared to have a clearer path to inscription. The decision was ultimately taken to nominate a group of industrial heritage sites in the UK at the same time, with Derwent Valley Mills and Saltaire also inscribed in 2001.

The strength of the New Lanark nomination is best demonstrated by its inclusion in the Tentative List produced by the DCMS (1999) in an attempt to target perceived gaps in WHL provision at that time. In so doing, the DCMS (1999, p.79-81) described New Lanark as a site which "combines a unique natural setting with an outstanding cultural heritage [that is] tangibly associated with the Utopian Socialist ideas of Robert Owen". According to the Site Director, Jim Arnold (1998, n.p.), "it is because of the strength of New Lanark as an exemplar of UNESCO Cultural Criterion (vi), the tangible association with ideas of universal significance, that New Lanark should be specifically proposed by the UK Government for listing as a World Heritage Site in the year 2000".

The site was finally inscribed on the WHL in 2001, with success following many years of political lobbying and the preparation of a high-quality Nomination Document and Management Plan (Historic Scotland, 2000; Historic Scotland, 2009; Historic Scotland, 2011; UNESCO, 2009). In terms of appropriate Management Plans and buffer zones, New Lanark was undoubtedly better prepared in its 2000 nomination than when it first nominated in 1986. Sufficient site boundaries appeared to be in place, essentially delimited by land owned by the Trust, to the extent that the case for New Lanark's inscription on the WHL was, in the opinion of New Lanark, irresistible. Throughout this period, the New Lanark Trust and its partner housing body, New Lanark Association Ltd, had constituted the core management function. The strength and success of these two bodies is demonstrated by the numerous awards achieved by New Lanark in recent years. From January 2009, the New Lanark Association has been dissolved and the properties transferred to the ownership and management of the subsidiary company New Lanark Homes, part of New Lanark Trust.

Visitors to New Lanark

As evidenced by the numbers below, New Lanark is a highly successful attraction in Scotland with 334,185 visitors recorded in 2009 alone.

Table 1: New Lanark visitor numbers

Visitor numbers (estimated) (VisitScotland, 2008; New Lanark, 2009)

1980	10,000
1994	400,000
1999	400,000
2005	362,850
2007	333,620

Percentage of visitors paying entry to the visitor centre (New Lanark, 2008)

1997	36.5%	2000	36.0%	2008	37%

Paid Visits (2004 & 2008) by month: percentages of year total (New Lanark, 2008)

	2004	2008
January	2%	2%
February	6%	4%
March	6%	8%
April	9%	8%
May	10%	12%
June	11%	10%
July	12%	12%
August	13%	12.5%
September	9%	9%
October	8%	7.5%
November	6%	5%
December	9%	11%

Origin of visitors (2000 & 2008)

	2000		2008
Local	10%	All Scotland	45%
Central Scotland	12%		
Rest of Scotland	15%		
England	22%	England & Wales	33%
Europe	9%		
USA/Canada	5%	Overseas	22%

First time and repeat visitors (2007)

Repeat	40%	First time	60%

Sources: VisitScotland (2009) and New Lanark (2008, 2009, 2010)

The New Lanark visitor experience

New Lanark's visitor experience is housed in three of the village's historic buildings: The Institute for the Formation of Character (shown in Figure 3), the adjoining Engine House and Mill Three (reached by a linking glass bridge). One of the key attractions is the Annie McLeod Experience, which provides the visitor with a 'dark ride', fixed-flow experience. Here the visitor is moved along in capsules hung from the ceiling, through an audio-visual explanation of the history and future of New Lanark. Available in many foreign languages, the story is told through the eyes of Annie McLeod, charting the life of a young mill worker in 1820.

Figure 3: The Institute for the Formation of Character. Photo reproduced by kind permission of New Lanark Trust

In addition to the above, Picking up the Threads & People and Cotton provides an example of a working 19th-century spinning mule and other textile machinery. There are also exhibitions relating to the lives of children in New Lanark, as well as people involved in cotton-manufacturing, ranging from black cotton-pickers to mill workers. Nearby, the Millworkers' House provides an example of a tenement house, enabling visitors to see what the living conditions were like in the past. Two recreated scenes, one set in the 1820s and the other in the 1930s, are on display. Visitors can also access the house of Robert Owen, where some of the rooms have been refurnished to recreate an atmosphere of this type of accommodation and show how it compared to that of the mill workers. Since 2001, visitors have also been able to experience a classroom environment from the 1820s, with costumes for children to try on and space for school group activities. An even more recent addition is the Roof Garden and Viewing Platform. Completed in 2008, this provides an all-year-round plant and floral attraction with sculptures and a mini-nature trail, as well as panoramic views of the entire village.

Although access to New Lanark is challenging, cars and buses are able to offload visitors at a car park in close proximity to the attraction, and from there visitors are able to walk down to the site. This also affords them views of the village in its wider setting. Public transport links are, however, quite limited. Local bus routes come into the village from Lanark, while Lanark train station is approximately 2 km away. The site contains a number of retail and catering outlets for visitors, as well as offering Youth Hostel accommodation, the New Lanark Mill Hotel, eight self-catering cottages known as the 'waterhouses'. There is a leisure suite with a swimming pool, gym and beauty room, which opened in 2008. For visitors particularly keen on the natural heritage, there exists the Falls of Clyde Wildlife Reserve (run by the Scottish Wildlife Trust) and the Clyde Walkway.

As with many sites and attractions, New Lanark operates an extensive programme of events and educational visits. In the case of the educational visit, student resource packs are available for use with many linking directly to the National Curriculum. The site offers one of the best educational visit packages available at any Scottish visitor attraction and is a Heritage Education Trust 'Sandford Award' winner. A Visitor Centre Passport Ticket (£8.50 standard adult entry in 2011) provides access to five areas of the site, including the main visitor centre in the Institute and Mill No.3, the Millworkers' House, the Village Store Exhibition, the roof garden and viewing platform, Robert Owen's School and Robert Owen's House. A further Mill Ticket was introduced in 2008, offering access to the Roof Garden and Viewing Platform, the Annie McLeod Experience and a textile machinery exhibition. Access to all other areas is free of charge. In 2011, the attraction entered into a seasonal joint-ticketing venture (operated between April and September) with the Falls of Clyde Reserve which is managed by the Scottish Wildlife Trust and is located within the WHS area. All types of tickets are purchased at the main visitor centre which is housed in the Institute building and visitors are able to see the exhibitions and the reserve in any order.

Management issues at New Lanark and implications of designation

New Lanark does not currently have an agreed Management Plan in place, although one is currently being drafted by the WHS Coordinator and is due to go out to for public consultation in early 2011 with a view to finalising the Plan by late 2011. A previous draft, written in 2003, identified a range of management issues experienced at the site. These included conservation, development pressures, access and visitor management, funding and resources, promotion and education, and monitoring and information management. The role of tourism is not specifically addressed in the plan, although many issues do relate to this activity in some way. The key tourism management issues identified by Leask and Fyall (2001), MacIntosh and Prentice (1999), Historic Scotland (2000) and the site management team are as follows:

Visitor management

As demonstrated by the visitor figures, seasonality does present some challenges. This is a common feature among Scottish visitor attractions and it results in periods of peak activity that can potentially affect the visitor experience in a negative manner, such as long queues for the dark ride and difficulty in accessing all areas of the site due to the volume of visitors. New product developments have been introduced, such as a special 'Christmas Experience' and other events held outside of the peak visitor season, with the aim of helping to counteract such effects.

Figures also show that New Lanark's visitors have widespread origins: surveys undertaken in 2007 showed that 45% of visitors came from Scotland, 33% from England and Wales, and 22% from overseas. Visitors do not always visit the whole site. Most begin by focusing on the central areas. Those who do not venture further either do not appreciate the full extent of the visitor experience that is available to them or have not allowed themselves sufficient time for their visit. Many visitors do not pay for access to the Visitor Centre itself but use the free-access areas only. This may be due to a lack of awareness of what the site and its constituent parts have to offer. Alternatively, it may simply be that there is quite a high proportion of regular repeat visitors (repeat visitors comprised approximately 40% of the total in 2007 and 38% in 2009). Repeat visitors may not be willing to pay to visit the exhibitions every time they come.

Access

Access to the New Lanark WHS is good if the visitor is using private car or coach. If they are using public transport, however, access is rather more challenging. Access to the various parts of the site is also good, with reasonably free movement of people around the central areas. Traffic management is an ongoing issue, as traffic congestion and the presence of too many cars negatively impacts on the visitor experience within the village itself. A car park has been constructed up above the village to encourage traffic away from the village centre and this has been reasonably successful. Of course, residents, independent businesses operating from within the village, visitors with special needs, hotel guests, youth hostellers and staff still require direct access to the central village area.

Site management

A lack of core funding is an ongoing issue for New Lanark. A particular problem is that the managers of the site must reapply annually to their main funding bodies (Historic Scotland and South Lanarkshire Council) for maintenance grants. Capital funding has been forthcoming over the years from a variety of sources, including the Heritage Lottery Fund and European Regional Development Fund via the Strathclyde European Partnership. An unusual added dimension to revenue generation at the site is that the New Lanark Trust generates hydro-electricity on site, using the original mill lade and a 1930s water turbine which remained in one of the mills. The site self-supplies power for the hotel and visitor centre buildings, and any surplus is sold to the National Grid.

One very important issue is with the balance of visitor, business and resident needs in successfully managing the site and the surrounding areas. The site has a wide variety of stakeholders, often with conflicting views and objectives. Many of the management issues at New Lanark have been addressed through new product development and management techniques, with a consistent programme of building redevelopment over recent years. The majority of the buildings have now been refurbished and the site appearance consistently upgraded.

Implications of World Heritage Site designation

One direct result of designation was the appointment of a WHS Coordinator to promote, develop and implement the Management Plan, working to pull all the associated stakeholders together with a common vision. This post, originally based at South Lanarkshire Council, ran from 2003-05 when the post fell vacant until Historic Scotland supported a replacement post in 2008. This post, now based within New Lanark and Historic Scotland, has brought new vitality to the task of writing and agreeing a Management Plan. The key role of the Coordinator is to liaise with stakeholders and other advisors such as the Local Authority World Heritage Forum.

The requirement to have a Management Plan in place is significant in providing an impetus for stakeholders to raise awareness of the key issues they have and in providing a framework for them to work together with a common aim. Regular monitoring of management policies and practices is a requirement of WHS designation and should benefit the overall site management by strengthening links between setting management objectives and management practices. The draft Management Plan currently issued for consultation sets out a number of long-term aims and associated short-to-medium term objectives for the management of New Lanark over the five-year period between 2011 and 2016. One of these aims recognises the need to "improve access to, and within, the World Heritage Site and promote its as a high-quality leisure and recreation destination for the local community and visitors alike" (Historic Scotland, 2011: 28). This is to be achieved through meeting specific objectives such as considering how the visit experience might be enhanced, examining how improvements to the public realm, signage, amenity and environment could be implemented, and considering how best to meet the traffic management and public access needs of the site, including transport connections, parking management and visitor orientation.

While not directly linking to funding, WHS status should, in principle, assist in supporting and strengthening funding bids. Currently there is little evidence of funding benefits through UNESCO World Heritage opportunities but the status does offer this route. Similarly, the status should also support sensitive development of the site and surrounding buffer zone, which should serve to protect the resource from inappropriate development.

It is difficult to state how many visitors are aware of the World Heritage status, but it is considered to be low. Responsibility for promoting the WHS lies with various players, including VisitScotland, VisitLanarkshire, South Lanarkshire Council and the site itself, although promotion is currently limited to the use of the logo by the site. Limited use is made of the WHS emblem on national signage to the site, council and tourist board promotional materials, and websites. There is no dedicated area on site that promotes the designation, through for example displays or the provision of literature. This lack of awareness, along with the subsequent lack of recognition of the contribution that this could potentially make to tourism activity both onsite and in the surrounding area, can only be described as unfortunate. The site could potentially be used as a flagship visitor attraction in the Lanarkshire area, drawing in the currently elusive international visitors.

Conclusions

It is clear that WHS designation has had several positive impacts at New Lanark, even though the limited use of the logo in promotional material and lack of awareness of the designation among visitors and residents appears to be a missed opportunity. Further engagement with opportunities afforded by UNESCO partnerships and programmes could also assist in targeting the coveted international visitor market to the site and surrounding area. The development of a Management Plan may provide opportunities for greater stakeholder engagement and bring wider economic and social benefit to the site and surrounding area.

WHS designation clearly offers a variety of positive and negative impacts to heritage resources. One key implication is the development of Nomination Documents and Management Plans, in addition to the resulting documents and set policies. The opportunities afforded by this process are significant in drawing stakeholders together with a common aim. As discussed by Fyall and Rakic (2006), it is likely that States Parties will continue to nominate sites in the pursuit of the various perceived and actual benefits of designation. Tourism is clearly beneficial to the sites but broader questions exist in relation to the extent to which the designation really does contribute to increased visitation and greater economic benefits. Further research on both an international and site-specific basis is required to predict the future of the World Heritage List.

References

Arnold J. 1998. Letter to Historic Scotland. New Lanark, Scotland.

DCMS. 1999. *World Heritage Sites: The Tentative List of The United Kingdom of Great Britain and Northern Ireland*. London: Department for Culture, Media and Sport.

Fyall A, Rakic T. 2006. The future market for World Heritage Sites. In Leask A, Fyall A. (eds) *Managing World Heritage Sites*. Oxford: Elsevier; 159-176

Hall CM, Piggin R. 2001. Tourism and World Heritage in OECD countries. *Tourism Recreation Research* **26** (1): 103-105.

Historic Scotland. 2000. *Nomination of New Lanark for Inclusion in the World Heritage List*. Edinburgh: Historic Scotland.

Historic Scotland. 2009. http://www.historic-scotland.gov.uk/index/heritage/worldheritage/world-heritage-sites-in-scotland/new-lanark.htm

Historic Scotland. 2011. New Lanark World Heritage Site: Draft Management Plan. http://www.historic-scotland.gov.uk/newlanarkmanagementplan.pdf

Leask A. 2006. World Heritage Site designation. In Leask A, Fyall A (eds) *Managing World Heritage Sites*. Oxford: Elsevier; 5-19.

Leask A, Fyall A. 2001. World Heritage Site designation: Future implications from a UK perspective. *Tourism Recreation Research* **26** (1): 55-63.

MacIntosh A, Prentice R. 1999. Affirming authenticity: Consuming cultural heritage. *Annals of Tourism Research* **26** (3): 589-612.

New Lanark. 2008. Material sourced from historical records and student packs.

New Lanark. 2009. www.newlanark.org

New Lanark. 2010. Email communication with New Lanark Director.

Shackley M. 2005. Managing the Cedars of Lebanon: Botanical gardens or living forests? In Harrison D, Hitchcock, M. (eds) *The Politics of World Heritage: Negotiating Tourism and Conservation*. Clevedon: Channel View; 137-145.

UNESCO. 2008. *Operational Guidelines for the Implementation of the World Heritage Convention*. UNESCO World Heritage Centre. Paris: France. http://whc.unesco.org/archive/opguide08-en.pdf

UNESCO. 2009. http://whc.unesco.org/en/list/

van der Aa B. 2005. *Preserving the Heritage of Humanity? Obtaining World Heritage Status and the Impacts of Listing*. Netherlands Organisation for Scientific Research, The Hague: Netherlands.

VisitScotland 2010. *Visitor Attraction Monitor 2009*. http://www.visitscotland.org/pdf/visitor-attraction-monitor-2009.pdf

Ancillary Student Material

Further reading

Beeho A, Prentice P. 1997. Conceptualizing the experiences of heritage tourists: a case study of New Lanark World Heritage Village. *Tourism Management* **18** (2): 75-87.

Feilden B, Jokilehto J. 1998. *Management Guidelines for World Cultural Heritage Sites,* 2nd Edition. Rome: ICCROM.

Harrison D, Hitchcock M. 2005. *The Politics of World Heritage: Negotiating Tourism and Conservation.* Clevedon: Channel View.

Historic Scotland. 2000. Nomination of New Lanark for Inclusion in the World Heritage List. http://www.historic-scotland.gov.uk/v1/index/shop/product_detail.htm?legacypath=/index/shop/product_detail.htm&productid=611

Leask A, Fyall A. 2007. Special Issue, Managing World Heritage Sites. *Journal of Heritage Tourism* **2** (3): 131-238.

Related websites and audio-visual material

The following websites offer background information on the New Lanark World Heritage Site status and the New Lanark site in general. In addition, there are a range of sources for further material on World Heritage Site designation. The key resources also include those listed in the reference section of the case study.

Historic Scotland: http://www.historic-scotland.gov.uk/index/heritage/world-heritage/world-heritage-sites-in-scotland/new-lanark.htm

UNESCO: http://whc.unesco.org/

UNESCO World Heritage website http://whc.unesco.org/en/list/429

Self-test questions

Try to answer the following questions in order to test your knowledge and understanding. If you are not sure of the answers, then please refer to the suggested references and further reading sources.

1   Who manages New Lanark World Heritage Site and what does this mean for the management approach taken onsite?

2   What is a UNESCO World Heritage Site and why did New Lanark apply for this designation?

3   Who are the key stakeholders involved in the management of New Lanark and how are they involved in the site planning and management?

Key themes and theories

The key themes raised in the case study relate to the following areas:

♦   World Heritage Site designation

♦   Site and visitor management

♦   Effective management of heritage visitor attractions

♦   World Heritage Site designation as a management tool

If you need to source further information on any of the above themes and theories, then these headings could be used as key words to search for materials and case studies.

     Scan here to get the hyperlinks for this chapter.

Index

A

Abbreviations

ACAP	Anapurna Conservation Area Project
AED	Arab Emirate Dirham
ASC	Aspen Skiing Company
B&B	Bed and breakfast
BBNP	Brecon Beacons National Park
CCO	Contemporary Cases Online
CH_4	Methane
CO_2	Carbon dioxide
CO_2-eq	Carbon dioxide equivalent
DCMS	Department for Culture, Media and Sports
DEFRA	Department for Environment, Food and Rural Affairs
DKV	Dubai Knowledge Village
DMAO	Dubai Media Affairs Office
DTCM	Department of Tourism and Commerce Marketing
ERDF	European Regional Development Fund
FIFA	Fédération Internationale de Football Association
GCC	Gulf Cooperation Council
GHG	Greenhouse gas
GRNP	Gunung Rinjani National Park
GRNPP	Gunung Rinjani National Park Project
ICE	Intercity Express
ICOMOS	International Council on Monuments and Sites
IUCN	International Union for the Conservation of Nature
MBA	Master of Bumps Academy
N_2O	Nitrogen oxide
NBGW	National Botanic Garden of Wales
NSAA	National Ski Areas Association
NZAID	New Zealand Aid Programme
NZODA	New Zealand Official Development Assistance
OECD	Organisation for Economic Cooperation and Development
PRA	Participatory Rural Appraisal
RCA	Rinjani Conservation Area
RIC	Rinjani Information Centre
RSPB	Royal Society for the Protection of Birds
RTC	Rinjani Trek Centre
RTEP	Rinjani Trek Ecotourism Programme
RTMB	Rinjani Trek Management Board
TUI	Touristik Union International
UAE	United Arab Emirates
UK	United Kingdom
UNESCO	United Nations Educational, Social and Cultural Organization
UNEP	United Nations Environment Program
UNWTO	United Nations World Tourism Organization
WAG	Welsh Assembly Government
WDA	Welsh Development Agency
WHC	World Heritage Committee
WHL	World Heritage List
WHS	World Heritage Site
WMO	World Meteorological Organisation
WPA	Work Projects Administration
WTB	Wales Tourism Board
WWOOF	World Wide Opportunities on Organic Farms